THE EMERGENCE OF THE NATION, 1783–1815

The EMERGENCE of the NATION

1783
1815

JOHN C. MILLER
Stanford University

David M. Potter, Carl N. Degler, Editors
American History Series

Scott, Foresman and Company
Glenview   London

To the memory of David Potter

Cover: Reception of President Washington at New York, 1789. *Picture: Library of Congress*

Library of Congress Catalog Card No. 74–167647
Copyright © 1972 by Scott, Foresman and Company, Glenview, Illinois 60025.
Philippines copyright 1972 by Scott, Foresman and Company.
All Rights Reserved. Printed in the United States of America.
Regional offices of Scott, Foresman and Company are located in Dallas, Oakland, N.J.,
Palto Alto, and Tucker, Ga.

FOREWORD

This book is the second title in a series of eight (to be offered alternatively in two large volumes) that will encompass the history of the United States from the first explorations and settlements to the present. Together the series will constitute in general coverage and time span the kind of work that students usually employ as a textbook for a college survey course in American history. Both this book and the series as a whole, however, are intended to be different from the material covered in the usual survey text.

Customarily, a textbook is largely filled with a chronological account of the "essential" facts of the past. Facts and chronology are, it is true, the building stones of historical knowledge, and familiarity with both is essential, but they do not provide the structure of the past by themselves. Rather, it is the framework of an era that the student must grasp if he is to retain and make sense out of the myriad facts that any book—text or other—throws in his path. By framework, however, we are not suggesting a skeleton or outline but the unity or essential thrust of the period—in short, its meaning.

Emphasis falls throughout upon explanation of the past. Why did events turn out as they did? What significance did these developments have for subsequent American history? What importance do they have for the present? How does the American experience compare with that of other countries in similar circumstances? How and why did American attitudes and values alter during the period in question?

The organization and some of the less important facts that are to be found in more conventional textbooks are absent from these pages. It is the conviction of the author and the editors of the series that understanding the relationship among events is more important than just memorizing customarily agreed-upon facts. Therefore, some facts have been omitted simply because they do not contribute to an understanding of the structure of the period.

This book has been written for American college students; that is, readers who have some acquaintance with the history of the United States. While the usual effort has been made to clarify and define obscure or unfamiliar terms and persons, a certain basic familiarity with the subject has been taken for granted. No student who has passed successfully through an American high school need worry about his ability to comprehend what appears within these covers, but it is hoped that his understanding of the direction and the causes behind the movements of American history will be enhanced by reading this book.

David M. Potter
Carl N. Degler

PREFACE

During the period 1783–1815, the United States became a country animated by a national spirit. Although the Union had been created by the Articles of Confederation and the federal Constitution, the American people as a whole lacked a transcendent sense of loyalty to the United States; priority in the scale of allegiance was often given to the individual states. It remained, therefore, to perfect the Union by adding the essential ingredient of nationalism. In 1786 it was questionable if the Union, subjected to powerful centrifugal forces, would survive; by 1815 the future of the Union and the continued growth of the national spirit which sustained it seemed assured.

The central theme of *The Emergence of the Nation* is the victory of nationalism over the economic, geographical, and ideological barriers that stood in its way. The magnitude of these obstacles gave to the proponents of nationalism a sense of urgency. To them, the creation of a pervasive atmosphere of intellectual conformity—a consensus regarding American ideals, institutions, and aspirations—seemed to be the best foundation on which to establish a strong Union. They were aided by the fact that during this period nationalism began to be identified with democracy—a process which culminated in Jacksonian Democracy. But democracy did not spring full-blown in the United States during or immediately after the American Revolution. Like nationalism, democracy was obliged to overcome established ways of thinking and to capture the control of institutions which had long served as bastions of aristocracy.

To effect this more perfect Union, the presence of an outside, hostile power was essential. For many Americans, Great Britain supplied this need. The American Union and the national feeling which invigorated it were inadvertently abetted by Great Britain. The former mother country, because of its mastery of the sea and its determination to crush Revolutionary and Napoleonic France, gave short shrift to the rights of neutrals. With the second largest merchant marine in the world and as the chief supplier of the European belligerents, the United States found its claims to the freedom of the seas flouted by both sides in the European conflict, especially by Great Britain, which was in a much stronger position than France to seize American ships and impress American seamen. While the defense of American rights at sea tended to unite the American people, the two principal efforts to implement those rights—the embargo of 1808–1809 and the War of 1812—proved to be profoundly divisive. Fortunately for the cause of American nationalism, the War of 1812 was short-lived and ended in a victory, which, although won, after the peace treaty had been signed, bolstered Americans' patriotic pride.

After 1815 Americans ceased to be divided by foreign affairs; to all intents and purposes, Europe slipped beneath their horizon. The colonial state of mind in which foreign attachments and antagonisms took precedence over national self-interest was completely exorcised. For the first time since the outbreak of the Wars of the French Revolution, the American people were free to give their undivided attention to the internal development of their country. But the removal of all danger of foreign aggression and of involvement in foreign wars permitted Americans to engage in a divisive sectional conflict. The Emergence of the Nation was followed by the emergence of the sections as implacably hostile entities within the American Union. The national feeling which had been centered upon the Union as a whole was deflected to particular sections. The failure of the revolutionary and post-revolutionary generations to remove completely the evil of slavery from the nation set the stage for the enactment of a great national tragedy.

John C. Miller

CONTENTS

MAPS AND GRAPHS

THE EMERGENCE OF THE NATION, 1783–1815

CHAPTER ONE

THE
TRIBULATIONS OF
A NEW REPUBLIC

*I*N 1783 MANY AMERICANS, Thomas Jefferson among them, spoke of the United States as an empire. Certainly the territorial expanse of the new Republic fully entitled it to that designation. As a result of the Treaty of Paris, which in 1783 brought an end to the War of Independence, the United States extended from the Atlantic to the Mississippi River, embracing an area larger than that of any European country except Russia. So extensive were the territorial concessions of the peace treaty that George Washington said he had not met a man who did not acknowledge that the terms far exceeded his expectations.

In acclaiming the United States as an empire, Americans added the proviso that it was an "empire of liberty." During the War of Independence, the leaders of the Revolution were sustained by their conviction that the Republic they were struggling to bring into being was destined to become "the hope of the human race" and the refuge for "the virtuous part of mankind." It would be the nation commissioned by Providence to show that liberty could be combined with order, justice, and high intellectual and artistic achievement. The American Revolution, the first colonial revolt in modern history, proclaimed principles of universal applicability: "America hails Europe, Asia, and Africa," an American said in 1783. "She proffers peace and plenty!" As the spokesmen of the revolutionary generation saw it, Americans were engaged not merely in creating a new society and a new kind of government for their own happiness but in erecting a model for mankind. In 1630 John Winthrop said that the Puritans had come to New England to build a "City on a Hill." From the beginning, America intended to be a country on a hill.

The Mission of the New Republic

American patriots believed that these hopes would be disappointed if the United States became the image of Europe. The Old World was regarded as the implacable enemy of the American promise. Great Britain, said Thomas Jefferson in his *Notes on Virginia* (1781), was almost too far gone in corruption, immorality, and luxury to admit of hope of redemption: "the sun of her glory is fast descending to the horizon. Her philosophy has crossed the Channel, her freedom the Atlantic." Apparently nothing was left for Englishmen to do but to migrate to the United States and partake of the rising glory of America. In Great Britain, however, Jefferson's vauntings were dismissed as "puerile insolence." "Such cant," observed the *Scots Magazine*, "is admirably calculated to charm the gaping throng of America, when first intoxicated with the idea of INDEPENDENCE."

The Goal of Unrestricted Trade. Even before its independence had been confirmed, the United States undertook to execute the mandate with which Providence had presumably invested it. In the commercial treaties drawn up for the Continental Congress in 1783–1784 by Thomas Jefferson, the United

Kerchief reflecting the pride Americans felt when the British ship *Macedonian* was captured by an American vessel. *Picture: The New–York Historical Society, New York City*

States challenged the principles of mercantilism upon which all the European empires were founded. In place of a world divided into exclusive trading areas, the United States proposed to create a world based upon free trade, equal commercial rights to all nations, and, hopefully, perpetual peace. In short, this new world order would be the antithesis of imperialism. American diplomats were instructed by the Continental Congress to write into all commercial treaties made with foreign powers the principle that countries at war should respect the rights of neutrals on the high seas and refrain from molesting the passengers or the cargoes of neutral vessels. From the beginning of its existence, the United States boldly proclaimed the principle that free ships make free goods. In one sense, this merely represented an effort to gain commercial advantages for neutrals engaged in activities which would aid a belligerent, but in another sense, it was an effort to limit the scope of war and to mitigate its consequences upon nonbelligerents.

The Goal of Social Reform. Likewise, the social reforms which accompanied the American Revolution were expected to make the United States a model for less advanced countries. In the southern states and in the four lower counties of New York, the Church of England had been disestablished, that is, deprived of its status and financial support as the officially approved state church. This action was a long stride toward realizing the ideal of complete separation of church and state. Massachusetts and Connecticut, however, retained in modified form their state-supported ecclesiastical establishments which had existed from the beginning of the Puritan settlement.

One of the dominant concerns of the eighteenth-century Enlightenment, of which the American Revolution was an expression, was to ameliorate the condition of mankind. After the Revolution, Americans made a significant contribution toward relieving the lot of less fortunate citizens. "In America," said Baron Kinkowstrom, a Swedish traveler, "every one still remembers the time when he was poor and needed help. The heart of the American has not shut out the cry of the needy." The new Republic abounded in private philanthropical societies for such diverse purposes as the relief of newly arrived immigrants, destitute widows and orphans, distressed seamen, and refugees from the revolt-torn island of Santo Domingo. Partly as a result of the work of these private relief agencies, poverty in the United States was much mitigated. Henry Fearon, an English traveler, reported that he saw in the United States only three beggars, one of whom accosted him on the steps of the House of Representatives in Washington.

In some states, the death penalty was prescribed for only one or two crimes—in contrast to Great Britain where over two hundred crimes were capital. Although imprisonment for debt was still common in the 1820's, it was gradually being abolished. Robert Morris, at one time the wealthiest man in the country, spent the years 1799–1801 in a debtors' prison. Beginning with the construction of the Philadelphia prison in 1790, the United States took the lead in prison reform. In 1830 when Alexis de Tocqueville, the French political

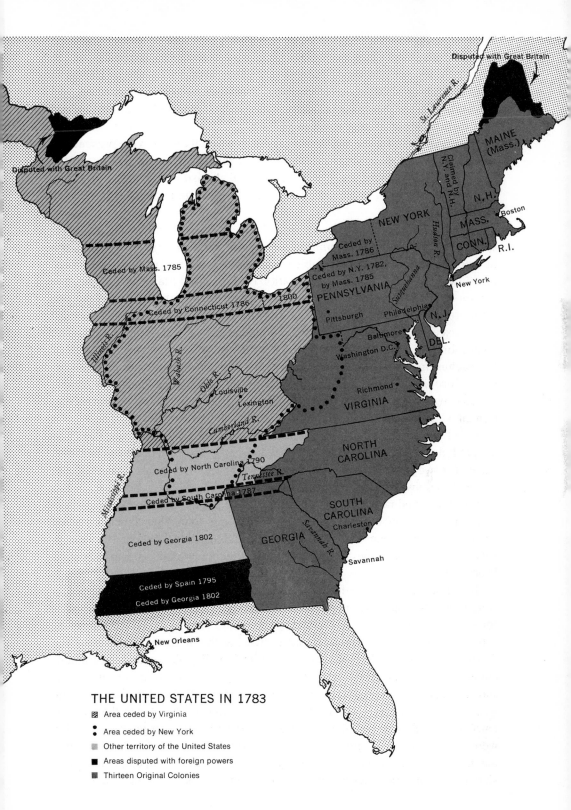

THE UNITED STATES IN 1783

- ▨ Area ceded by Virginia
- ⁞ Area ceded by New York
- ░ Other territory of the United States
- ■ Areas disputed with foreign powers
- ▦ Thirteen Original Colonies

Labels on map:

Disputed with Great Britain

Disputed with Great Britain

St. Lawrence R.

MAINE (Mass.)

Claimed by N.Y. and N.H.

N.H.

Boston

MASS.

CONN.

R.I.

NEW YORK

Ceded by Mass. 1786

Ceded by N.Y. 1782, by Mass. 1785

Hudson R.

New York

Ceded by Mass. 1785

Ceded by Connecticut 1786

1800

PENNSYLVANIA

Susquehanna R.

Pittsburgh

Philadelphia

N.J.

DEL.

Illinois R.

Wabash R.

Ohio R.

Louisville

Lexington

Baltimore

Washington D.C.

Richmond

VIRGINIA

Cumberland R.

Ceded by North Carolina 1790

Tennessee R.

NORTH CAROLINA

Mississippi R.

Ceded by South Carolina 1787

SOUTH CAROLINA

Charleston

Ceded by Georgia 1802

GEORGIA

Savannah R.

Ceded by Spain 1795

Ceded by Georgia 1802

Savannah

New Orleans

scientist, came to the United States, his purpose was to study American methods of rehabilitating criminals. Among the innovations introduced in the United States was solitary confinement. "The prisoner," said Dr. Benjamin Rush of Philadelphia, "is therefore abandoned to the gloomy society of his own reflections." This therapy, the doctor supposed, would produce contrition and reformation. More usually it led to insanity.

This solicitude for the welfare of criminals was not owing to the presence of a large criminal population. At this time, the United States ranked as one of the most law-abiding countries in the world. English visitors remarked upon the safety of New York as compared with the crime-infested streets of the British metropolis.

The Great Anomaly: Slavery in an Equalitarian Republic. In many respects, America seemed committed to an ideal of social progress and humanitarianism, but there was one notable exception: slavery remained a deep-rooted institution. In 1790, taking the population of the United States as a whole, one person in six was a slave. Slavery was concentrated in the South, where one third of the population was enslaved, but slavery was legal as late as 1781 in all states except Vermont, which was not admitted as a state until 1791. The institution was abolished by judicial interpretations of the state constitutions of Massachusetts and New Hampshire. Other states acted through statute law, usually providing for gradual emancipation. But in New York and New Jersey, where slaves were more numerous than in other northern states, the emancipation of slaves was not voted until 1799 and 1804 respectively. These laws provided for the emancipation only of the slaves born after the legislation was adopted, and before receiving their freedom, males were required to serve as slaves for twenty-eight years and females for twenty-five years. Theoretically, under these laws slavery might have increased for another generation, but in fact it diminished rapidly either because of voluntary emancipation by owners or because of sales outside the state. By 1830 less than 3000 slaves remained where there had been 40,000 in 1790. Yet eighteen blacks were still held in servitude in New Jersey when President Lincoln issued his Emancipation Proclamation.

But if some of the northern states proceeded only slowly to emancipate a comparatively small slave population, the southern states rejected all proposals for emancipation, and from Delaware southward slavery remained a primary economic and social institution and a growing threat to the stability of the American Union. True, in the southern states, the Revolution and the Enlightenment had intensified earlier doubts and misgivings regarding the justice of slavery, and its profitability was being increasingly called in question, but little was done to improve permanently the condition of the slaves themselves. During the 1780's, the manumission of slaves and their instruction in religion were encouraged in Virginia, but in 1800, partly as a result of a slave revolt, a harsh reaction set in. This reaction took the form of laws impeding manumission, prohibiting meetings by slaves, and making it impossible for them to learn to read and write. Even the churches were forbidden to teach blacks to read the Bible. The year 1819, when the University of Virginia was established, was also ironically marked by the enactment of a law prohibiting slaves and black freemen from meeting together in groups for educational purposes. A later statute decreed that any free Negro who left Virginia for the purpose of securing an education could not return.

The Articles of Confederation and the American Union

The reforms of the revolutionary era were brought about by private charitable societies or by the municipal or state governments, not by the new general government. This was not because of any greater zeal on the part of the states but simply because the general government did not yet have power to deal with the internal affairs of the Confederation. Its sphere was almost wholly confined to external affairs. But, even in the areas where it appeared to have supreme authority, the United States presented the spectacle of a government incapable of fulfilling the ends for which it had been instituted and which the public welfare required.

Originally a revolutionary body acting without legal authority or, indeed, legal restraint, the Continental Congress gained in legitimacy but declined in power when the Articles of Confederation, as a result of the belated ratification by Maryland, finally went into effect in 1781. Clearly, the Articles, which circumscribed the power of the Continental Congress, ended its great days— the days when it had created the Continental Army, issued the Declaration of Independence, printed paper money, negotiated treaties with foreign powers, and, in general, exercised supreme power for national purposes with at least the tacit consent of the people. But by 1783 the authority as well as the prestige of the Continental Congress were sadly diminished. In the spring of that year, threatened by mutinous soldiers of the Pennsylvania Line, it had left Philadelphia for the academic tranquillity of Princeton, New Jersey. At that time, colleges were havens of peace and quiet.

The Lack of National Organization. In actuality, the Articles of Confederation represented a retreat from the idea of national union which Patrick Henry had expressed when he declared himself to be an American first and a Virginian second. During the Revolution the shared aspirations and dangers of the struggle for freedom had generated nationalist impulses based upon the conviction that America was one united country. But the Articles reflected a return toward concern for the powers of the separate states. While the Articles purported to create a "perpetual union," this union was, as the Articles themselves stated, a "firm league of friendship" rather than a supreme government capable of acting decisively for national purposes. "Each state," the Articles declared, "retains its sovereignty, freedom and independence." The Continental Congress was given only those powers expressly delegated. All other powers were reserved to the states. The word *expressly* was intended to preclude any enlargement of the powers of the general government by the kind of broad interpretation later applied by Alexander Hamilton to the federal Constitution. Clearly, the objective of the framers of the Articles was to create a union of states, in some respects comparable to the present-day United Nations. The principle that the government derived from the American people as a united whole found no expression in the Articles of Confederation.

Essentially, this was a federal form of government, as federalism was defined in the eighteenth century. Compared with the Constitution, drawn up in 1787, the Articles heavily weighted the balance of power in favor of the states at the expense of the general government. Although the Continental Congress was empowered to borrow money and to issue bills of credit, i.e., paper money, the power to raise revenue and to impose taxes was vested exclusively in the states. Consequently, the states had supreme power in the Confederation.

As a result, the Continental Congress was wholly dependent upon the states. The framers perpetuated a practice which they had first known as British subjects when the Crown could requisition supplies and money from the colonial governments. Under the Articles of Confederation, the Continental Congress could make such requisitions from the states. Although this system had demonstrated its inadequacy during the colonial period, the framers of the Articles expected that the states would voluntarily support an independent government of their own choosing. In practice, however, the power to requisition proved to be little more than a power to beg.

From a nationalist point of view, the "radical vice" of the Confederation was that the laws of Congress applied only to the states, not to the people. "Instead of obeying the law," Alexander Hamilton, a spokesman of nationalism, observed, each "state examined it; and by its own peculiar interests. Thus thirteen bodies judged congress, and each took its own course." Nor did Congress have means of enforcing its laws by imposing fines or issuing injunctions: if a state refused to obey a requisition imposed by Congress, the only way Congress could compel compliance was by risking civil war. And with an army of about seven hundred men, the Continental Congress was no match for even the smallest state. "The idea of governing thirteen states and uniting their interest by mere resolves and recommendations, without any penalty annexed to a non-compliance," said Noah Webster, the dictionary-maker, "is a ridiculous farce, a burlesque of government, and a reproach to America."

The Obsessive Fear of Power. Because the Articles were framed at a time when Americans were engaged in a war for freedom, every precaution was taken against the encroachments of power. The main concern of the framers was with freedom and its preservation. The ultimate safeguard erected by the Articles of Confederation against tyranny was the rule of unanimity. There could be no change in the Articles without the unanimous consent of the states. Even in the adoption of laws, a simple majority could not act. The Articles required that the consent of nine states be secured to enact substantive legislation. Only adjournment of the Congress was to be determined by the vote of a bare majority. This requirement permitted minority rule, especially in view of the fact that attendance at the Congress was poor, and representatives of more than nine states were rarely present at any one time. One state could, and often did, negate the will of eight states.

Moreover, the one state which obstructed the will of the majority might be the smallest state in the union. For the Articles of Confederation embodied the principle of state equality. In the Continental Congress, each state had one vote. Delaware was the equal of Virginia. In 1777, taking advantage of the necessities created by the war, the small states had succeeded in compelling the large states to accept the principle of state equality. However, the large states had never been reconciled to this settlement. Their dissatisfaction with this feature of the system contributed in part to the eagerness later displayed by some of the large states to scrap the Articles.

The powers conferred on Congress in the conduct of foreign affairs appeared, at least on paper, to present a sharp contrast to its narrowly restricted powers in domestic affairs, and in this respect they served as a model for the framers of the federal Constitution. Congress had the sole right of appointing and receiving ministers. It could make treaties of commerce and amity, and it had the exclusive right of waging war and concluding peace. But the power to make decisions was meaningless without means to carry them into effect. Here, as elsewhere, Congress lacked the coercive authority which alone could give force to its directives. For example, while it could make commercial treaties, it had no way of enforcing them. It could not establish a customs house anywhere in the Republic. The states retained the privilege of imposing duties and of regulating their trade except in cases where those duties conflicted with treaties made by the general government. Congress could declare war, raise and commission armies, and direct their operations, but it could not levy money, clothing, or provisions or command the militia or otherwise conscript troops as the exigencies of war required. Finally, while Congress enjoyed the power of regulating the value of its own coinage and that of the states, it had no control over the emission of paper money by the states. In short, while the Articles restricted powers narrowly in some areas and conferred them generously in others, in no case did it give the strength necessary to make the powers functional.

Nor was the structure of the government as a whole calculated to give weight to its counsels or efficiency to its administration. In this government, all power was concentrated in the legislature: there was no attempt to apply the principle of the separation of powers upon which John Adams and other admirers of the British constitution laid such high value. There was no judiciary worthy of the name, and the executive branch consisted solely of the President of Congress, an honorific office the incumbent of which was sometimes compared with a maître d'hôtel. Executive duties were usually entrusted to congressional committees, the membership of which fluctuated with changes in the personnel of the state delegations.

Thirteen Sovereign Republics. Thus the revolution seemed to have culminated in the establishment of thirteen sovereign republics leagued together for certain specific purposes. In this system, the Continental Congress became hardly more than a diplomatic body to which the states sent ambassadors. Members of Congress were the representatives of state governments, not of constituencies of people. George Washington described the United States as a country consisting of "thirteen Sovereignties pulling against each other, and all tugging at the federal head." It was a government based upon the assumption that men could act in accord with the dictates of reason and self-interest; therefore, compulsion could be dispensed with. In that sense, it was an expression of the optimistic, rationalist philosophy of the Enlightenment. It exemplified Tom Paine's dictum that that government was best which governed least, and it achieved Thomas Jefferson's ideal of a government the citizens of which were hardly aware of its existence. Without tax collectors, law-enforcement officers, and judges empowered to lay down the law to recalcitrant citizens, the government of the United States seemed to rest no more heavily than a feather upon the citizens of the Republic.

The Problems of the New Government

Yet not everyone rejoiced in this particular version of freedom. For during the period of the Articles of Confederation, the United States was not quite the tax-free, unregimented Elysium it might appear to be to twentieth-century Americans. Because of its inability to collect taxes, the government was brought to the verge of insolvency. By weighting the balance of power in favor of the states, the Articles created a situation in which the continued existence of the general government and of the Union itself was jeopardized.

An Unmanageable Public Debt. American rejoicing over the ending of the war and the recognition of their independence was tempered by the realization that they were deeply in debt. Incurred by the Continental Congress and the states during the war, this debt represented the price of freedom. Although a large part of it had been repaid with depreciated paper money, the unpaid balance, about $80 million, constituted a heavy burden for the new Republic. Some citizens, appalled by the magnitude of the sum involved, urged that it be repudiated forthwith; then, they argued, Americans could settle down to enjoy the felicities of peace and independence. But Alexander Hamilton, James Madison, and Thomas Jefferson, among others, warned that if the public debt were not paid, the state governments and the Continental Congress would forfeit their credit. Then, unable to borrow, no matter how dire the emergency, the United States would face a bleak prospect indeed.

Divisive as were the issues raised by the debt and its repayment, there was general agreement upon one score: the foreign debt, including interest, had to be paid in order to preserve the credit of the Republic abroad. Totaling about $10 million, this debt was owed to the governments of France and Spain and to private bankers in the Netherlands, at that time the banking headquarters of Europe. This meant that if the debt were to be scaled down, it would be the domestic creditors, civilian and military alike, who would bear the brunt of repudiation. In 1783 the soldiers, many of whom had not been paid for several years, were given a small amount of cash, which Robert Morris, the Superintendent of Finance, raised by pledging his personal credit. They were then thanked for their services and told to go home peaceably. For the remainder of their back pay, they accepted paper certificates of dubious value and warrants which entitled them to claim tracts of public land. Instead of receiving half pay for life, as they demanded, the officers of the Continental Army were given a commutation equivalent to a pension for five years, payable in government securities. Within a few years, the majority of officers had sold these certificates at little more than one tenth of their face value.

Civilian creditors fared better. The interest owing them on their obligations was paid in new certificates called "indents." Even so, the price of state and Continental securities depreciated—in some instances to as low as ten cents on the dollar. Inevitably, therefore, they became objects of speculation rather than of investment. In 1784 a newspaper asked rhetorically: "Where is the man whose promissory note is not preferable to a state security?"

While the debt was owed partly by the general government and partly by the states—the Continental Congress owed approximately $40 million or about half the total—the power to raise revenue was wholly in the hands of the states. Having debts of their own, the states naturally tried to liquidate their own obligations, leaving the Continental Congress to find its own financial salvation by borrowing abroad. But foreign governments and investors were loath to lend money to a government whose financial prospects were as unpromising as those of the United States. In 1783 the French government announced that henceforth the United States was strictly on its own financially; not another sou would be forthcoming from the French treasury. Robert Morris continued to draw drafts upon the French government which it reluctantly honored, but this expedient did no more than postpone the day when Americans would be compelled to set their own house in order.

An Unmanageable Economic Depression. This task was made more difficult by the postwar depression which struck the United States. Instead of immediately inaugurating an era of plenty and prosperity, independence created serious economic dislocations. By leaving the British Empire, Americans forfeited their right to trade with the British West Indies, Canada, and other parts of the Empire. They also lost the subsidies and bounties granted by the British government to the colonial producers of rice, indigo, naval stores, and timber and the protection given American ships by the British navy.

Weakness in Negotiating with Other Governments. The British government did not feel obliged to come to the aid of the hard-pressed Republic. Instructed by the Continental Congress to negotiate a commercial treaty with Great Britain, John Adams danced attendance at the Court of St. James for over four years with nothing to show for his efforts. But even without a treaty, American trade tended, wherever possible, to revert to its prewar channels, which meant, of course, with Great Britain and its dependencies. The tobacco trade, for example, except for a brief interval when France agreed to take the bulk of the American crop, was monopolized by the same British firms which formerly preempted it. As a result, lamented Thomas Jefferson, despite independence, Virginia planters reverted to their prewar status as "a species of property annexed to certain British mercantile houses."

Exclusion from Foreign Markets. As a consequence of independence, America had looked forward to gaining access to foreign markets, particularly those of France and Spain, which had been closed to them as British subjects. But as the event soon proved, this avenue of commerce did not open to the anticipated degree. France showed little inclination, and Spain even less, to accommodate the United States by removing the mercantilist walls they had erected around their empires. Although the French government made some concessions to the United States in the West Indies and in France itself, commerce between the two countries did not live up to expectations, despite the efforts of Benjamin Franklin and Thomas Jefferson, two of the ablest men ever to represent the United States in Paris.

The Lack of Money. The economic problems of the Republic were compounded by the shortage of gold and silver resulting from the large sums expended upon imported manufactures in 1783–1785. After seven years of self-denial, Americans bought so many foreign goods, which had to be paid for in bills of exchange or specie, that precious metals were drained out of the country. Americans were left with virtually no hard currency with which to carry on trade. The United States had no national coinage. In 1785 the Treasury contained only eighty tons of copper, and most Americans continued to reckon in pounds and shillings long after the dollar had been established as the official monetary unit of exchange. As a result of these circumstances, American businessmen were obliged to try to make capitalism work without benefit of a stable circulating medium and without the means of replenishing the specie which had been drained away. True, these difficulties were not new to Americans, for much the same conditions had prevailed during the colonial period.

The Plight of Commerce. The postwar depression affected northern commerce far more adversely than it affected agriculture. Although the indigo and rice growers of South Carolina could take little comfort from the economic consequences of independence, the Chesapeake tobacco growers enjoyed brisk business and firm prices. Wheat and flour likewise found good markets abroad. "Every article of produce commands a good price," said Robert Morris in 1786, "and nothing remains on hand to perish for want of purchasers." In general, by 1786 the price of commodities and labor was higher than before the Revolution.

But in the seaports, conditions were far less propitious, particularly during the years 1783–1786. The consequences of the dislocations produced by independence were apparent on every hand. During the war the American merchant marine had suffered heavy losses which, because of the Republic's depleted financial resources, could not be readily replaced. Since American shipyards could no longer sell ships to British buyers for British registry, as they had before the Revolution, shipbuilding came to a virtual halt. Moreover, since American ports were open to British ships without discriminatory duties, British shipmasters took over a large part of American commerce.

Of all the states, Massachusetts found her plight most serious. From 1786 to 1790, no new ships were constructed for the New England cod fishery, and in Marblehead alone thirty-three vessels remained tied up at the wharves. The Nantucket whale fishermen, cut off from foreign markets, contemplated declaring their island an independent country or emigrating to France or Nova Scotia. Important markets in the West Indies were closed to New England ships, and no New England rum could be sold in Canada. The Bay State seemed to have gained its independence at the price of its prosperity: "she will have the glory," a disconsolate Yankee observed in 1784, "of being a sovereign, independent, poor state."

The Demand for Paper Money. Economic distress produced a demand for the states to resume issuing paper money, a practice abandoned late in the war when this kind of money had depreciated almost to the point of worthlessness. The proponents of paper money were not simply debtor farmers who hoped to pay their debts cheaply with depreciated currency. Many businessmen and large landowners adversely affected by the money stringency wished to see paper currency made legal tender. On the other hand, those who owed money abroad—debts which could be paid only with hard money—and those who feared that paper money would again produce an uncontrollable inflation put their faith in specie.

But the most strenuous opposition to paper money, unredeemable in specie, came from the members of the mercantile community who were beginning to use bank notes in their business transactions. The first bank to open its doors in the United States was the Bank of North America, established in Philadelphia in 1781 by Robert Morris; banks also were chartered during the 1780's in Boston and New York. These banks issued notes which were backed by reserves of specie and which circulated as money. Within the small but important areas served by these banks, progress was being made toward meeting the need for a stable circulating medium.

Because of the peculiar structure of the revolutionary state governments, it was comparatively easy for paper-money factions to gain control of the state governments. While the state constitutions gave lip service to the theory of the separation of powers and checks and balances, in practice most of these constitutions opened the way to political domination by the legislative branch. The same fear of a strong executive which reduced the President of the Continental Congress to a mere figurehead also tended to minimize the powers of the executives of the state governments. With the exception of New York and Massachusetts, the state governors were deliberately made subordinate to the legislature. As for the state judges, they were generally appointed by and were responsible to the state legislatures. Rarely did they attempt to claim the right of judicial review of state legislation.

As a result, when the advocates of paper money gained complete control of the state legislatures, they were in a position to enact their entire program into law. Besides the issuance of paper money, this program called for stay laws, which imposed a moratorium on the collection of debts, and tender acts, which permitted debtors to "tender" land or commodities which creditors were obliged to accept at specified values.

Against this so-called debtors' legislation, creditors raised the cry that they were being arbitrarily deprived of their property. Having recently concluded a war to safeguard the rights of property, they feared that they would be the principal victims of a second American revolution waged by "desperate debtors" against the property rights of affluent citizens.

Conservatives identified paper money, stay laws, and tender acts with democracy, a word not in common use in the eighteenth century. Historically, democracy meant the direct, personal, and uninhibited rule of the majority of the free citizens assembled in the agora or city square—the form of government that prevailed in some of the Greek city-states. In Greece, democracy had proved incompatible with stable government and freedom itself had not survived the demagoguery and social conflicts to which it gave rise. In the United States, democratic government was contrasted with representative government, much to the disadvantage of the former. American conservatives had no intention of allowing the tragedy of Greek freedom to be reenacted in the United States. Yet, early in the history of the Republic, it became a question whether even representative government could resist radical change when demanded by a numerical majority acting in the name of the common people.

Between 1784 and 1787, seven states resorted to paper money and various forms of debtor-relief legislation. In a few other states, paper-money factions, after gaining control of the lower house of the legislature, were held in check by the senate. In Rhode Island, the worst offender against the rights of creditors, when the judges tried to interpose their authority to check the overweening power of the legislature, they were called before the bar of the assembly and made to answer for their actions. The power of judges to declare acts of the legislature invalid when such acts were found inconsistent with the state constitution, proved to be of no avail in halting the course of the state legislatures. Instead of a government of limited powers, which many framers of state constitutions had intended to establish, Americans had succeeded, it appeared, in erecting governments in which the majorities in the state legislatures were supreme.

This experience taught conservatives the importance of safeguarding the priority of the fundamental law as it was embodied in the state constitutions by an effective system based upon the separation of powers and checks and balances. But despairing of effecting these changes in the state governments, they increasingly attempted to gain for the general government the power to protect property against encroachments by the states.

Attempts to Strengthen the General Government

As matters stood, this reliance upon the general government seemed a forlorn hope. No matter how critical the emergency, the Continental Congress could do little to change the course of events. Instead, it seemed likely to be overwhelmed by the steady drift toward the fragmentation of power in the Republic. Washington described Congress as "a half-starved, limping Government, that appears to be always moving upon crutches, and tottering at every step."

Proposals of Power to Lay an Impost. Before this enervated government collapsed entirely, some patriots tried to set it on its feet and infuse it with new vigor. In 1782 Robert Morris, the superintendent of finance, urged Congress to demand of the states that it be given full power to lay taxes, including tariffs, land taxes, excise, and poll taxes. Morris also recommended that the national debt be funded—that is, that revenue be allocated on a regular, fixed basis to discharge the government's long-standing obligations. Although Congress balked at Morris' entire package, it asked the states to give it authority to lay tariff duties, the so-called impost, and to provide Congress with supplementary revenue. Even with the revenue requested, Congress could do no more than pay its debts when they fell due.

Twelve states acceded to this request, although some of these states annexed qualifications to their grant. But at this point, the rule of unanimity defeated the plans of the Congress. In December 1782 the Rhode Island legislature rejected the impost. Thereupon other states rescinded their consent.

For this action, Rhode Islanders professed to believe that a grateful posterity would regard them as "the saviors of the liberties of America." But liberty—conceived of in this instance as states' rights—was not the Rhode Islanders' sole concern. If the impost went into effect, Rhode Island would be compelled to relinquish the privilege of taxing out-of-state consumers who imported their European merchandise through Rhode Island ports.

Congress promptly proposed another impost tailored to meet the ostensible objections of Rhode Island. But it appeared that years would pass before the thirteen independent jurisdictions could agree upon any measure. In the meantime, the financial problems of Congress were multiplying almost as rapidly as the compound interest was accumulating. Robert Morris resigned his post as superintendent of finance, and Congress, fearful of entrusting power to a single individual, turned over the control of the country's finances to a board consisting of members of Congress.

The Failure of Requisitions. Since Congress had to pay its bills with specie, it requisitioned large amounts of gold and silver from the states. But the states were almost wholly bereft of hard money. In the early 1780's, for example, South Carolinians paid their tax in indigo, and the state government was grateful to receive it. Even if the states had been charitably disposed toward the general government, they could hardly have bailed it out of its financial predicament. Most of them were fully occupied in trying to keep themselves afloat.

In any event, little specie reached the coffers of the Continental Congress. When that body struck the rock of national resources, no more than a trickle came forth. From 1782 to 1787, four states paid no specie whatever; seven states paid about half of the sum requisitioned; and only two states, Pennsylvania and New York, contributed all that was required of them. In 1785 the government's total revenue did not exceed $200,000, compared with expenses of over $2 million, and most of this money was contributed by two or three states. In 1782 when Tom Paine urged Congress to create the post of Historiographer of the United States and to commission him as historiographer to write a history of the American Revolution, he was told that no funds were available. Having received no monetary reward for his services to the Revolution, Paine was disgusted by what he regarded as the ingratitude and parsimony of Congress. This kind of treatment, he declared, would banish genius to foreign countries. Paine set the example by going to France in 1787.

State Assumptions of the Continental Debt. Most alarming of all to the advocates of a central government capable of administering the affairs of a united people, some of the more prosperous states, Pennsylvania among them, began to assume the debts owing by the Continental Congress to the citizens of those states. While the general government was thereby relieved of some importunate creditors, it also meant that this important body of well-to-do citizens, now compelled to look to the states rather than to the general government for the payment of interest and principal upon their certificates, would almost certainly seek to strengthen the state governments rather than the Continental Congress. Thus the transfer of the national debt accentuated the disproportionate share of power already possessed by the states and seemed to prepare the way for the eventual assumption of all power by those sovereign jurisdictions.

Rays of Hope for the Republic

Recovery from Economic Depression. By 1786 the worst of the depression was over. Although the fishing industry failed to improve, commerce revived as American shipmasters opened new markets in India, China, the Hawaiian Islands, and the Pacific Northwest. In 1790 Captain Robert Gray, in command of the *Columbia,* discovered the river which bears his ship's name. But the Americans had no monopoly in this area. The British were in the Pacific

Northwest even before Gray, and in 1792 Captain George Vancouver explored Puget Sound.

Of even greater importance was the increase in trade with Europe and the consequent improvement in the Republic's balance-of-payments position. But none of this returning prosperity provided funds for the Continental Congress. Unless a sizable transfusion of capital was immediately forthcoming from the states, Alexander Hamilton predicted in 1786 that America faced the "awful dissolution" of the Confederation. In this crisis, despairing of aid from the states, the Continental Congress looked westward to the region north of the Ohio and east of the Mississippi rivers. Here, alone, the outlook gave hope of financial succor.

Public Lands as a National Asset. Although Congress' authority over the states was limited, it possessed extensive powers over the western lands which constituted the national domain. The framers of the Articles of Confederation had not intended that Congress should be the custodian of the unsettled territory west of the Alleghenies. But in 1784 Virginia ceded to the general government its claim to the region north of the Ohio, and most of the other states with western land claims followed suit. In consequence, the Continental Congress became the custodian of a domain larger than the settled area of the original thirteen states.

With such vast potential wealth at the disposal of the general government, it appeared that Congress, if given sufficient time, could pay the national debt simply by selling land. For this purpose, Congress began as early as 1784 to facilitate the sale of land by providing for surveys and easy credit. Indeed, with settlers already beginning to cross the Alleghenies after the end of the war in 1783, Congress was obliged to act lest its best lands be preempted by squatters.

When Congress accepted Virginia's cession of claims in the Northwest, it also accepted the stipulation that the states carved from this territory should be admitted to the Union on terms of equality with the original states. Accordingly, in 1784 Congress adopted an ordinance drawn up by Thomas Jefferson providing for the eventual self-government of the national domain. As Jefferson planned it, the region was to be divided into fourteen prospective states, the settlers were to enjoy manhood suffrage, and statehood could be attained after the population reached twenty thousand. Jefferson's plan was notable for its repudiation of all suggestion of colonialism: it granted self-government to the inhabitants virtually from the beginning of settlement. Jefferson's original draft excluded slavery from the territory after 1800 but because of southern opposition, this provision was omitted. In fact, Jefferson's plan, although adopted, was never put into operation.

A System of Land Survey and Sale. In order to get revenue into the hands of Congress, however, it was necessary not only to provide a form of government but, even more urgently, to devise a system for surveying and distributing the land. In 1785, therefore, Congress adopted an ordinance providing that the land for sale be divided into rectangular townships measuring six by six miles and that each of the resulting thirty-six sections be sold at a minimum price of one dollar an acre. In payment for these lands, Congress agreed to accept its own depreciated certificates at their face value.

A land office was opened, but so few purchasers appeared with cash or certificates that Congress turned perforce to land companies which offered to buy blocs of millions of acres. In 1787, primarily to facilitate the transfer of large areas of the public domain north of the Ohio to these land companies, Congress drew up the Northwest Ordinance. In this ordinance, Congress decreed that the region should ultimately be divided into not less than three nor more than five states. Prior to statehood, the new areas would be organized as territories. After the termination of this territorial stage, the Northwest Ordinance promised that the people of a territory would ultimately enjoy full equality with the citizens of the original states. During the territorial period, they were to be governed by an elected legislature and an appointed governor and council. They had the right to appoint a nonvoting delegate to Congress. When a territory acquired a population of sixty thousand, it became eligible for admission to the Union as a state—subject, however, to the consent of the existing states through their vote in Congress.

With a view to accelerating the settlement of the public domain (after all, the land companies were in the business of selling land) Congress assured newcomers of certain rights: acquisition of land in fee simple, trial by jury, and the writ of habeas corpus, the first instance of a bill of rights promulgated by the general government. Equally important, slavery was not permitted. This prohibition was possible because southern congressmen, having had second thoughts on the matter, came to the conclusion that if slavery were permitted, the tobacco-producing states would have a dangerous competitor in the territories and states north of the Ohio.

Although the Continental Congress succeeded with the aid of the Northwest Ordinance in selling large tracts of land to land companies in exchange for depreciated certificates, which brought the price to as low as ten cents an acre, the land companies themselves failed to sell enough land to settlers to meet their obligations to the government. As a result, they went bankrupt long before they completed the payments to which they had committed themselves. It simply went to prove that the Continental Congress was land poor. The states as well as the general government had millions of acres which they were trying to sell to settlers and speculators. Transportation was woefully inadequate, and the Indians were hostile. Clearly, if Congress expected to pay the national debt from the proceeds of the sale of its land, it needed creditors with the patience of Job.

But even if the creditors had been willing to wait, the government could not go on indefinitely without funds. Before 1787 it was clear that sales of land alone could not solve the financial crisis. If the general government were to be saved, it must be saved by a grant of powers far beyond anything that had been included in the Articles.

Foreign Affairs at an Impasse

Nonfulfillment of the Peace Treaty with Great Britain. By 1786 in foreign as well as in domestic affairs the position of the United States seemed to be steadily deteriorating. The Continental Congress appeared wholly unable to defend American interests against the adverse policies of other countries—an exhibition of impotence which further diminished popular support for the general government. The treaty of peace between Great Britain and the United States proved to be a fertile source of controversy and ill will between the two countries. In the treaty, Britain had ceded to the United States the area north of the Ohio and south of the Great Lakes and had promised to surrender seven forts which were strategic for the control of the northwestern region. Britain had also agreed to return to American owners the slaves who had taken refuge behind British lines during the War of Independence. But as time passed, British officials became unwilling to abandon the Northwest Posts which were vital to the control of the fur trade and the Indians who inhabited the region. British humanitarians began to regret a promise to reenslave blacks who had put their trust in British assurances of emancipation and who had settled in Nova Scotia and in Sierra Leone, an African colony founded by the British to provide a homeland for the ex-slaves. The British found a justification for their decision not to honor the objectionable terms of the treaty in the fact that Americans had defaulted on some of the obligations to which they had committed themselves in the peace treaty. The Americans had promised to interpose no obstacles to the collection of the prewar debts which United States citizens owed to British merchants and other creditors. It was also stipulated in the treaty that the Continental Congress was to recommend to the states that compensation should be paid to Loyalists for the losses they had sustained when their property had been confiscated during the war. Although this recommendation was duly made by the Congress, the states, as was their sovereign right, declined to act upon it. Nor did the states promptly and unequivocally remove all obstacles to the collection of British debts. As a result, the United States was accused by the British of violating the treaty and, moreover, of having committed the breach of faith before the British themselves had refused compliance.

With each side refusing to obey certain provisions and blaming the other for its refusal to comply, Anglo-American relations degenerated into an acrimonious, sterile, and protracted dispute over which side was guilty of the first violation. As evidence of its displeasure with the United States and its expectation that the Republic would soon collapse—an event which few British statesmen would have regretted—His Brittanic Majesty's government sent no minister to the United States until 1791. John Adams, the United States minister to Britain, said that he might have been more profitably employed hoeing turnips on his farm at Braintree, Massachusetts.

Spain in Control of the Mississippi. Relations with Spain, the other European power with territory contiguous to the United States, were likewise strained by disputes over trade and territory. Spain, one of the last of the great powers to recognize the independence of the republic, feared that the westward expansion of the United States would not stop at the border between the two countries. To protect the Spanish possessions, the government of His Catholic Majesty closed the Mississippi to American traffic where the river flowed through Spanish territory and demanded that the United States stay out of the region south of the Ohio which was to be reserved in perpetuity for the exclusive use of the Indians. Spain refused to admit the United States claims that its territory extended south to the thirtieth parallel, thereby encompassing most of the present states of Alabama and Mississippi. Finally, as the ally of the Creeks, Choctaws, and other southern Indian tribes, Spain supplied them with arms and ammunition with which the tribesmen harried the American frontier.

Spain was the only European power which paid the United States the compliment of holding it in any kind of awe. From other great powers, except France, the United States was fortunate to receive any token of respect. But Spain's apprehensions were occasioned not so much by what the government of the United States might do as by what American frontiersmen might take it upon themselves to do. To the Madrid government, an invasion of Spanish territory by land-hungry American pioneers seemed a distinct possibility. For this reason in 1785 the Spanish government proposed through its minister, Don Diego de Gardoqui, a treaty by which Spain would open Spanish ports to American ships and certain commodities to American trade in exchange for an agreement by the United States to renounce for thirty years its claim to the navigation of the Mississippi where it flowed through Spanish territory.

This proposal revealed a depth of subtlety not usually evidenced in Spain's dealings with the American Republic. For Gardoqui's offer had the effect of dividing the union into opposing northern and southern blocs. The northern commercial states, having little interest in the navigation of the Mississippi but a very substantial interest in a commercial treaty with Spain, welcomed the Spaniard's overtures. On the other hand, the southern states, regarding the navigation of the Mississippi as essential to the growth and prosperity of the West and a commercial treaty as inconsequential, opposed the Spanish proposal. Since at this time the West was largely a projection of the South—Virginia and North Carolina colonized Kentucky and Tennessee—the South acted as the spokesman of western interests in the Continental Congress.

As a result of this sectional disagreement, the efforts of John Jay, the American secretary of foreign affairs, to open formal negotiations with Gardoqui proved abortive. The southern states were able to block the proposed treaty because the Articles required the approval of nine states for important legislation, and the North could not muster the required number. But the South found itself outnumbered in the vote, and only the nine-state rule prevented what southern leaders regarded as a betrayal of the South and the West by the North. From this revealing experience Southerners learned the importance of not permitting a mere majority to determine the foreign policy of the United States. This lesson was soon afterwards embodied in the provision of the United States Constitution which requires a two-thirds majority for the ratification of treaties.

But the immediate effect of the deadlock in Congress was the failure of the United States either to open Spanish ports to American ships or to secure the navigation of the Mississippi. Judged by its immediate results, the failure of American diplomacy was complete. Although Spain continued to fear American frontiersmen, it preferred to deal with them directly rather than through the United States government.

Cowed by the Corsairs. It was in the Mediterranean, however, that the United States suffered its most painful international humiliation because of its inability to protect its ocean-borne commerce. After the last ship of the Continental Navy was sold in 1785, the United States had no naval force to protect American commerce. Since the merchant ships of the United States no longer enjoyed British protection, they became easy prey for the corsairs who operated out of the ports of North Africa. American ships were seized and their crews condemned to slavery and held for ransom. Although the United States succeeded in making a treaty with Morocco in 1787, it was not able to ransom the surviving seamen held by Algiers until 1792.

Inability to Make Commercial Treaties. All the great powers rejected the commercial treaties which the United States proffered after 1784 with the brave hope of inaugurating a new order based upon freedom of trade and the rights of neutrals. Only Sweden and Prussia actually signed treaties which incorporated the principles laid down in Jefferson's plan of 1784. Even friendly nations raised the embarrassing question of how the Continental Congress proposed to enforce the treaties which it offered. British officials blandly suggested that it might be preferable for them to make separate commercial treaties with each of the thirteen states.

To strengthen its hand in dealing with foreign powers, especially Great Britain, the Continental Congress asked the states in 1784 to give it additional controls over commerce, especially the right to regulate interstate commerce and to prohibit imports from foreign countries. But here, again, the rule of unanimity prevented any effective action. In general, the commercial states which imported merchandise from abroad opposed a grant of power to Congress which would impair their sovereign right of regulating trade as they chose. The states themselves laid duties upon British ships and merchandise entering their ports. These duties produced much needed revenue for the state treasuries and gave legislators the comfortable feeling that they were taking reprisals upon Great Britain. On the other hand, import duties were exceedingly unpopular in the states which bought their foreign manufactures through the commercial states. New Jersey, for example, was so resentful of paying "tribute" to New York that it opened its ports freely to British ships and goods and threatened to retaliate upon New Yorkers. As a result, the Union was thrown into dissension without causing serious inconvenience to the British.

Attempts to Reform the Government

The Annapolis Convention. In 1786 with the states on the verge of internal commercial warfare, James Madison, through his friend John Tyler, proposed to the Virginia legislature that the states be invited to appoint delegates to a convention for the purpose of devising a uniform system of commercial regulations for the Union. As a meeting place, Madison suggested Annapolis, Maryland. By making the convention appear to be the work of the Virginia and Maryland planters sympathetic toward the plight of northern merchants, Madison hoped to assuage the sectional antagonisms that had reached such alarming proportions as a result of Spain's proposals for a commercial treaty.

Although Virginia and five other states sent delegates to the Annapolis Convention, none of the New England states did. Only twelve delegates appeared at Annapolis in September 1786—too few to do anything about commerce or, indeed, any other matter of national concern.

The Call for a Broader Convention. The delegates might have announced their failure and gone home to let events take their course. But the bolder spirits, led by Alexander Hamilton, audaciously tried to snatch victory from defeat by making the Annapolis Convention a stepping-stone to a constitutional convention. Under the sway of Hamilton and Madison, the delegates called for another convention empowered to consider commerce and to propose such changes "as shall appear . . . necessary to render the Constitution of the Federal Government adequate to the exigencies of the Union." Ostensibly, the agenda of the proposed meeting was to be confined to revising the Articles of Confederation along the lines already recommended to the states. But Hamilton and Madison were already maturing plans that envisaged the replacement, not the reform, of the Articles of Confederation and the existing government of the United States.

The idea of a convention of the states to create a more cohesive union by revising the Articles of Confederation had been suggested as early as 1781. While the Articles made no provision for such a convention, they did not expressly forbid it. Tom Paine, one of the most national-minded of the revolutionary patriots—as a native of England, he was devoid of state loyalties—claimed the honor of having been the first to raise his voice in favor of a convention. But even the mention of such a design sent a shock wave of alarm through the Confederation, for the Articles were regarded as a bulwark against arbitrary rule, the ultimate safeguard of states' rights, and the embodiment of the ideals of the American Revolution.

The Stimulation of Cultural Nationalism. The failure of all efforts to strengthen the general government through the regular channel of amending the

Articles of Confederation reinforced the conviction held by many of the revolutionary leaders that the root of the Republic's difficulties lay in the lack of national feeling on the part of the American people. As they saw it, the remedy consisted in making the schools, the press, the pulpit, and the work of artists and writers serve the cause of nationalism. Every means of communication, in short, must be used to make Americans aware of their national identity, their uniqueness, their political and moral superiority to all other peoples, and their responsibilities as the champions of republicanism. Above all, Americans must be made to feel "an inviolable attachment to their own country."

In the opinion of these nationalists, the War of Independence had ended before the American people had been fully animated with the kind of patriotism that transcended local attachments and prejudices. The American Revolution, it appeared, was unfinished, inasmuch as it had fallen short of creating a sense of American nationhood. What remained to be done, therefore, was to effect a cultural and ideological revolution along nationalist lines. Political independence was merely the first stage of the revolution: the second, and equally important, stage was the transformation of the American mind.

Cultural nationalists acted upon the belief that unless Americans were made to feel as one people, the republican experiment might fail and they felt a special responsibility to mankind to prevent such an occurrence. As Jefferson said in 1811, "The eyes of the virtuous all over the earth are turned with anxiety on us, as the only repositories of the Sacred Fire of liberty." Failure in America might well prove that mankind everywhere was incapable of self-government.

The most ardent proponents of cultural nationalism were Thomas Jefferson; Dr. Benjamin Rush, the Philadelphia physician-educator-reformer; and Noah Webster, the dictionary-maker. These men acted upon the belief that the best method of indoctrinating the people with nationalism was to begin with the children and that the schoolroom as well as the family ought to provide instruction in patriotism and good citizenship.

In 1782 with the publication of a blue-backed speller, later to become famous, Noah Webster began his long career as an apostle of Americanism. Webster had perceived that uniformity of spelling would foster uniformity of pronunciation and that uniformity of speech was important in cultivating a sense of unity among the American people. In the preface to his speller, Webster took a position calculated to promote the sale of his own book, which by 1829 had sold twenty million copies, as well as to advance the cause of cultural nationalism. For the children of the United States to use foreign textbooks would, he declared, "be to stamp the wrinkles of decrepid age upon the bloom of youth and to plant the seeds of decay in a vigorous constitution."

Webster and other proponents of nationalism regarded Europe as an enemy. True independence seemed to require that Americans break completely with the ideas and institutions of the Old World as well as its "vices and corruptions." Webster, Jefferson, and Rush solemnly warned their countrymen against the baneful effects of an education or prolonged residence in Europe. In their philosophy there was no place for the eighteenth-century ideal of a citizen of the world. They became the advocates of an isolationism which went far beyond a mere political withdrawal from the affairs of Europe.

Jefferson, Rush, and Webster advised Americans to cultivate their own national character by speaking an American language, reading American books, and thinking American thoughts. Noah Webster said that no child ought to escape a course in American history: "He should lisp the praise of liberty, and of these illustrious heroes and statesmen who have wrought a revolution in her favor." He recommended a judicious rewriting of the history of the American Revolution in which the American leaders would assume the stature of demigods. In his *Reader,* the first edition of which appeared in 1785, Webster included selections from American history written in this key.

The objective of these nationalists was to create "a race of Americans" who would think alike, act alike, and ask no more of their country than to be able to serve it. Diversity, at least in the realm of ideas, seemed to them to be an obstacle to the kind of intellectual solidarity they believed essential to the success of the republican experiment. Only a nation of republicans, it was agreed, could ensure the success of republican government. Viewed in this light, conformity to the accepted American ideal became a supreme virtue.

It followed that any deviation from the republican creed became un-Americanism. Yet none of these nationalists advocated compulsion as a means of attaining the desired consensus. They thought that uniformity of belief was the responsibility of the schools rather than of the magistrates. To Jefferson, Rush, and Webster, the superiority of republicanism was so clear and unmistakable that they did not doubt that all right-thinking citizens would perceive this great truth, particularly if it were pointed out to them at an early age by a schoolmaster. Thus, conformity was not merely compatible with freedom; freedom itself led to conformity.

On the other hand, because of the malleability of the human mind, these republicans felt that it was necessary to exercise special vigilance over the political opinions of teachers. An ill-disposed, "monarchical" pedagogue could corrupt an entire schoolroom. In Jefferson's bill for education in Virginia, drawn up during the War of Independence, he required that every teacher "give assurances of fidelity to the commonwealth," in other words, take a loyalty oath. Despite his devotion to "the illimitable freedom of the human mind," Jefferson later established at the University of Virginia canons of political orthodoxy to which he expected professors of political science to adhere.

These efforts to inculcate a sense of the uniqueness and special mission of the United States helped provide an essential ingredient to American nationalism and later expansionism. Insofar as Americans could be brought to feel that they were conducting a great experiment in republican government and were acting under a mandate from Providence, the bonds of union would be secure.

But in 1786 it was plain that the sense of national mission had not yet erased state and sectional jealousies nor uprooted the deeply imbedded distrust of centralized government. To attain a fully developed pride of country which was indispensable to the creation of a more perfect union, Americans needed to feel a shared pressure or danger from outside similar to that which had been supplied by Great Britain during the War of Independence. Fortunately for the cause of American nationalism, Great Britain continued to provide this pressure during the period of the Articles of Confederation. With British troops still on American soil in the Northwest Posts, with the British government disdaining a commercial treaty with the United States, and with British merchants and manufacturers still engaged, as southern planters believed, in exploiting American producers and consumers, Great Britain continued to appear to many Americans as an implacable enemy. The old cry of British tyranny still sounded in the United States, warning Americans that their union was not complete and their freedom not secure until Great Britain had been taught to respect the rights, the independence, and the territorial integrity of the Republic.

The Crisis of the Union

Despite this unexpected aid from Great Britain, time and the tide of events would not wait for cultural nationalism to condition the American mind for a more perfect union. In 1786–1787 the country was caught up in a crisis which, in the opinion of many patriotic Americans, made immediate and decisive action necessary even though the work of the cultural nationalists was still far from complete.

In part, the crisis was financial in origin. Payment of interest on the Dutch loan was scheduled to fall due in the spring of 1787. The Dutch bankers let it be known that if the United States defaulted, no further loans would be forthcoming, which meant in effect that the United States government would slip into bankruptcy. The Continental Congress had no funds upon which it could draw in this emergency. The government's credit was saved due to the last-minute efforts of Thomas Jefferson and John Adams, who succeeded in persuading the Dutch bankers to make another loan to the Republic. This loan was used to pay the interest on the previous loans. But borrowing to pay bills as they fell due, although providing temporary relief, increased the amount of the debt. Moreover, the day of reckoning was fast approaching; payment on the principal of the French debt was scheduled to begin in 1788. Clearly, something more than financial improvisation was required of American statesmen.

Worse still, as financial pressure upon the Continental Congress mounted, its hopes of revenue from the states grew dimmer. By 1786 every state save one had ratified the second impost proposed by the Continental Congress three years previously. The situation was exactly similar to that of 1782 when Rhode Island was the sole holdout. In 1786, however, New York played the role of spoiler. The farmers of New York opposed giving the Continental Congress the power to lay an impost because tariff duties allowed the state to avoid the taxation of agricultural land. In 1786 at the instigation of Governor George Clinton, the champion of the plain people of the state, the New York legislature rejected the impost. Under the rule of unanimity, there was nothing to do but to pronounce the impost dead and to inter it along with the other changes proposed by the Continental Congress.

The Paralysis of Government. The request by the Congress in 1784 for additional commercial powers seemed likely to go the way of the impost. By 1786 eleven states had approved the plan, but the outlook in the two remaining states was bleak. Thus, after five years of effort, not a single one of the Congress' recommendations for change in the Articles of Confederation had gone into effect. In each instance, the will of a small minority had prevailed. Americans, it seemed clear, were living under a government which could not reform itself. And as the crisis deepened, the general government seemed to become progressively more impotent.

Americans had lived for years with financial crises: being unable to meet their public financial obligations was certainly nothing new in their experience. Late in 1786, however, they were confronted by a wholly new problem: the breakdown of government authority.

Turmoil in Massachusetts. This unexpected event occurred in a state which most Americans regarded as least likely to experience disorder. The government of Massachusetts, organized under the constitution of 1780, had been acclaimed by conservatives everywhere as a model of the system of checks and balances and the principle of the separation of powers. Moreover, the state practiced the kind of fiscal responsibility advocated by James Madison. After 1783 it issued no paper money, enacted no tender acts, gave debtors no holidays, and imposed taxes payable in specie to liquidate the state debt. And in 1786, despite the fact that its debt was larger than any other state, Massachusetts took upon itself the added burden of paying the interest on continental certificates, i.e., bonds, owned by its citizens. The state was run by the creditors and they ran it in their own interest.

This fiscal policy bore heavily upon the common people of the state. In order to pay the public debt, most of which was held by affluent citizens, taxes had to be raised beyond the ability of many taxpayers to pay. About 40 per cent of the state's revenue was derived from a poll tax which, by requiring rich and poor alike to pay the same amount, discriminated against the poor. Since specie was almost unavailable, the problems of the taxpayer were made more acute. And since Massachusetts, in contrast to most of the other states, had an effective system of tax-collecting, defaulters found themselves haled into court where the machinery of the law, with rare efficiency, separated them from their property.

Private debts were collected with equal rigor. If the proceeds realized from the sale of the property of a defaulting debtor failed to meet the full amount of his obligation, he was liable, at the discretion of his creditor, to be imprisoned. Staying out of jail became a major problem. The interest rate on mortgages ran at 25–40 per cent, and the tax bill alone of some farmers exceeded the family's cash income. In 1786 a tax bill amounting to $1,500,000 was presented to the people of Massachusetts. It was estimated that this sum equalled one third of the value of all the real estate in the state. Confronted by a tax bite of such magnitude, even much vaunted New England thrift could hardly make both ends meet.

Conditions were worst in western Massachusetts, where marginal farmers abounded. Many of these farmers were veterans of the War of Independence. Postwar Massachusetts did not qualify as a land fit for heroes, particularly after the heroes had served their purpose. The more militant of these farmers began to take the law into their own hands. They closed courts by force, terrorized creditors, and summoned conventions which issued demands for paper money, tender acts, and the whole paraphernalia of debtor-relief legislation.

Daniel Shays, a former army officer, helped to convert the uprising of the western farmers into a full-scale insurrection. In January 1787 over a thousand farmers prepared to attack the United States armory at Springfield, Massachusetts. Since the Continental Congress had no troops to spare, the government of Massachusetts was compelled to rely entirely upon its own resources. An army was hastily mobilized and sent to quell the rebellion. It proved to be a surprisingly easy assignment. After a brief cannonade in which four insurgents were killed, the rebels took to their heels. Some of them, including Shays himself, did not stop until they had reached safety in New York.

Despite its tame ending, Shays' Rebellion had a decisive effect upon the call for a constitutional convention. The preservation of law and order suddenly became of prime importance. Nationalists capitalized fully upon this newfound concern. What had happened in Massachusetts, they warned, could occur in any of the states, particularly those which had resisted demands for debtor-relief legislation. James Wilson of Pennsylvania said that in 1787 "the flames of internal insurrection were ready to burst out in every quarter. . . . From one end to the other of the continent, we walked on ashes, concealing fire beneath our feet."

Congress Sanctions the Convention. Some of the heat of this conflagration in New England was felt by the Continental Congress. Earlier, the Congress had been decidedly lukewarm toward the call sounded by the Annapolis Convention. But in February 1787 Congress finally gave its sanction to the convention. Some of the states had already appointed delegates. With Congress' approval the rest of the states, except Rhode Island, elected, through their legislatures, delegates to a meeting scheduled to be held in Philadelphia in May 1787. Great Britain's refusal to execute the terms of the treaty of peace which it found unacceptable, the spectre of "mob rule" and armed revolt which

Shays' Rebellion raised, and the mounting financial troubles of the general government—all helped precipitate a fateful test of the strength of American nationalism.

SUGGESTED READING

The United States in its international setting is discussed in such books as Robert R. Palmer, *The Age of the Democratic Revolution: A Political History of Europe and America, 1760–1800*, 2 vols., (1950); Eric J. Hobsbawm, *The Age of Revolution, 1789–1848** (1962); Felix Gilbert, *To the Farewell Address: Ideas of Early American Foreign Policy* (1961); Richard W. Van Alstyne, *The Rising American Empire** (1960); Hans Kohn, *American Nationalism** (1961); William P. Murphy, *The Triumph of Nationalism* (1967); and Gordon S. Wood, *The Creation of the American Republic; 1776–1787* (1969).

The best survey of the economy of the United States during the period 1783–1815 is Curtis P. Nettels, *The Emergence of a National Economy, 1775–1815* (1962). Merrill Jensen in *The New Nation: A History of the United States During the Confederation, 1781–1789* (1950) has effectively challenged the thesis put forward by John Fiske in *The Critical Period of American History* (1888) that the period of the Articles of Confederation was one of uninterrupted economic decline. However, Jensen may have gone too far in discounting the hardships experienced by Americans, especially the merchants and town workers, during the early years of the Confederation. George R. Taylor's "American Economic Growth Before 1840," *Journal of Economic History*, XXIV (1964) is an important piece of research. Bray Hammond, *Banks and Politics in America from the Revolution to the Civil War** (1957) is indispensable. Samuel Eliot Morison, *The Maritime History of Massachusetts, 1783–1860** (1921) is a delight to read; it should not be missed by any student of American history.

Important books on the subject of slavery are Winthrop Jordan, *White Over Black** (1968); Robert McColley, *Slavery and Jeffersonian Virginia* (1964); Herbert S. Klein, *Slavery in the Americas: A Comparative Study of Cuba and Virginia* (1967); Arthur Zilversmit, *The First Emancipation: The Abolition of Slavery in the North* (1967); Edgar J. McManus, *A History of Negro Slavery in New York* (1966); and Eric Williams, *Capitalism and Slavery* (1966).

Shays' Rebellion is treated by Robert J. Taylor, *Western Massachusetts in the Revolution* (1954); Marion L. Starkey, *A Little Rebellion* (1955); and *Richard B. Morris*, "Insurrection in Massachusetts" in Daniel Aaron, ed., *America in Crisis* (1952). The effect of this and the other events of the period of the Confederation upon political thinking is brought out by John R. Howe, Jr., *The Changing Political Thought of John Adams* (1966).

For the history of the Continental Congress see Edmund C. Burnett, *The Continental Congress** (1941), which stands out above all other accounts. Irving Brant, *James*

---

* *Available in a paperback edition*

Madison: The Nationalist, 1780–1787 (1948) and John C. Miller, *Alexander Hamilton: Portrait in Paradox** (1959) treat the efforts to strengthen the Articles of Confederation. Allan Nevins, *The American States During and After the Revolution* (1924) describes in detail state politics during the period. Elisha P. Douglass, *Rebels and Democrats: The Struggle for Equal Political Rights and Majority Rule During the American Revolution** (1955) holds the view that an internal revolution occurred as a consequence of the revolt against Great Britain. In *Middle-Class Democracy and the Revolution in Massachusetts, 1691–1780** (1969) Robert E. Brown argues that democracy was firmly established even before the advent of the Revolution.

Among the state histories dealing with the period of the Articles of Confederation are Thomas C. Cochran, *New York in the Confederation* (1932); Robert J. Taylor, ed., *Massachusetts, Colony to Commonwealth: Documents on the Formation of Its Constitution, 1775–1780** (1961); David Hawke, *In the Midst of a Revolution* (1961); Jackson Turner Main, *The Social Structure of Revolutionary America** (1961) and *The Upper House in Revolutionary America* (1967).

E. J. Ferguson, *The Power of the Purse: A History of American Public Finance, 1775–1790** (1961) describes the financial troubles which beset the states and the general government. Commerce during the early period of the Republic is discussed by Ernest S. Dodge, *New England and the South Seas* (1965).

A Russian's View of Life in the Early Republic / Pictorial Essay

Paul Svinin came to America from Russia as secretary to the Russian consul general, Andrey Dashkov. His writings and the watercolor sketches of American scenes that he made during the two years he spent in the United States provide us with an interesting picture of life in the early Republic. Although he was only in his twenties, Svinin had traveled widely and was well educated. He had both artistic and literary abilities, both of which he used while in Philadelphia to educate Americans about Russia. He contributed both articles and illustrations about Russia to periodicals. After his return to Russia, he wrote a series of articles and a book, *A Picturesque Voyage in North America*, giving his impressions of life in the United States.

Svinin was particularly interested in the mechanical devices that Americans were inventing, due, as he says, to a shortage of manpower. The steamboat

fascinated him. He gives an enthusiastic description of the amenities offered aboard the steamboat *Paragon*. He also describes other labor–saving devices that he saw in use in factories. His interest in practical matters is reflected in his belief that bridges were the branch of architecture in which Americans were most advanced. He was so impressed with bridges that he wrote, "some of them are truly worthy of the glorious age of the Roman Empire." Aside from bridges, he considered architecture in the United States to be at a low level.

Svinin felt that the United States and Russia had much in common. One of these common factors, he thought, was religious toleration. He discusses several of the religious groups in America and describes a visit to a Negro Methodist church in Philadelphia and a Methodist camp meeting. He compares the emotional outcries of the Methodists unfavorably with the harmony of the

All the pictures used in this pictorial essay are Svinin's own watercolors. At the left is a picture of one of Fulton's steamboats, probably the *Paragon*. The picture shows some of the shipboard activities that Svinin wrote about. Above is a picture of the covered bridge over the Schuylkill River in Philadelphia, one of the bridges that impressed Svinin during his stay. *Pictures: The Metropolitan Museum of Art*

Below is Svinin's watercolor of a Negro Methodist meeting. After attending such a meeting, Svinin wrote that only a beneficent spirit could have saved him from being crushed in the excited crowd. On the right is a baptism by immersion in an Anabaptist ceremony. *Pictures: The Metropolitan Museum of Art*

music in the Greek Orthodox Church. However, he commends the charitable spirit of the Quakers, although he holds them responsible for the solemnity he found in Philadelphia on Sundays—"One does not see a single smile—it is as though the city were in mourning."

Svinin's watercolors include several scenes of life in Philadelphia, which he found to be the most beautiful, as well as the largest, city in the United States. However, he discovered from personal experience that its climate in the summer was abominable. He comments favorably on the cleanliness of Philadelphia's houses and streets, which make up for the monotony of the architecture. One of the exceptions to his low opinion of American architecture was Benjamin Latrobe's Bank of the United States, which Svinin thought to be the most beautiful building in the country.

Svinin wrote enthusiastically about the wonders of nature to be seen in the young country. He describes Niagara Falls in superlatives. He apparently made more than one visit to the Falls and drew several pictures of it. He also did watercolors of other natural phenomena, including the Natural Bridge in Virginia, of which he wrote, "What an object for the naturalist! What a field for the conjectures of the philosopher!"

He found the progress of the young Republic in the fine arts amazing. In an article published in Russia, he describes the state of painting, architecture, and sculpture. He found that portrait painting was so popular that even "the most wretched paint–slinger receives no less than twenty dollars for a bust portrait."

At the right is a picture of Indian heads "drawn from nature" that Svinin did while in America. He attended a performance of Indian dances given by the Osage Indians on their way to Washington. Svinin compared the customs of the Indians to those of the Caucasian mountaineers. Below he shows a winter scene in Philadelphia with the Bank of the United States in the background. Opposite is one of the several pictures Svinin drew of Niagara Falls. *Pictures: The Metropolitan Museum of Art*

Svinin's book and his portfolio of watercolors on America disappeared from notice in the nineteenth century. Both were rediscovered almost simultaneously in the 1920's by two men. R. T. H. Halsey acquired the watercolors from an American Red Cross worker who had purchased them while working in Russia during World War I. At about the same time, Dr. Avrahm Yarmolinsky found the book while in Russia acquiring books to strengthen the New York Public Library's Slavonic Department. Eventually the two men met. One of the results of that acquaintanceship was *Picturesque United States of America: A Memoir on Paul Svinin*, published by Dr. Yarmolinsky in 1930.

CHAPTER TWO

THE CREATION OF A MORE PERFECT UNION

THE MEN WHO ASSEMBLED in Philadelphia in May 1787 were compared by contemporaries with the Assembly of Notables then meeting in Paris. But the American notables came to terminate a revolution and to consolidate its gains, whereas the French Notables, although they were unaware of it, had come to start a revolution.

Certainly the members of the Constitutional Convention were entitled to the designations of notables. In general the states vied with each other in sending their most eminent citizens to Philadelphia. John Adams and Thomas Jefferson were not present because they were serving the United States in London and Paris respectively, and Patrick Henry declined to attend because, he said, he "smelled a rat." George Washington presided over the meeting as president; Benjamin Franklin was a delegate from Pennsylvania; and James Madison assumed from the start the role of philosopher and guide to the convention. Among the delegates were signers of the Declaration of Independence, past and present members of the Continental Congress, state governors, judges, lawyers, and planters. Without exception, the delegates came from the long settled eastern part of the country. The West, as a section, had no representatives. Nor were any yeomen farmers present; the agricultural interest being represented mainly by the southern planters.

The Decision to Make the Government National

Patrick Henry's rat, by which he meant a consolidated government, immediately revealed itself. Despite the directives of the Continental Congress and several states that the delegates confine their work to drafting amendments to the Articles, it soon became evident that the most influential members of the convention did not consider themselves bound by any restrictions whatever. On May 30, almost before the delegates had warmed their seats, Edmund Randolph, the governor of Virginia, proposed a plan of government drawn up by James Madison. The Madison-Randolph or Virginia Plan proposed a radically new approach to the problem of creating a more cohesive union and a stronger central government.

The Virginia Plan. Randolph told the delegates that the only hope of preserving the Union lay in virtually annihilating the power of the states and in giving the national government—he freely used the word *national,* seldom heard during the period of the Articles of Confederation—power to tax, legislate for, and if necessary coerce the people of the United States. The national government, as envisaged by the Virginia Plan, was to be divided into three distinct branches, and the legislature was to be divided into a house and senate. A powerful executive was to replace the President of Congress, and a hierarchy of federal courts was to provide for the first time direct enforcement of the laws of the union. By a system of checks and balances, each branch was to be kept within the bounds assigned it by the Constitution.

The Constitutional Convention of 1787. *Picture: Independence National Historical Park Collection, Philadelphia*

Finally, to ensure that the authority of the national government should permeate the Union, the Virginia Plan empowered the national legislature to negate any state law which in its opinion was contrary to the national interest. This provision would give the national government supreme and unrestricted powers and, as Randolph admitted, would leave the states with hardly a shred of the sovereign power they had enjoyed under the Articles of Confederation.

While the delegates agreed that the country was ailing, the Virginia Plan struck many of them as stronger medicine than the patient would tolerate. On the other hand, Alexander Hamilton thought that the Virginia Plan did not go far enough toward concentrating power in the general government. Hamilton, who was a West Indian by birth and therefore lacked strong state attachments, favored melting down all the states to form a consolidated union to be animated by an all-powerful central government. Hamilton dismissed the Virginia Plan as "the same pork" as the Articles of Confederation with a little change of the sauce. He made clear that his dish was an approximation of the British constitution with a president and senate elected for life. But, as several delegates were quick to point out, this was building castles in the air, whereas the task of the convention was to erect a government upon the solid bedrock of reality. Above all, the convention had to be guided by what was practicable, and the principal criterion of practicability was what the American people, acting in separate state units, would approve.

The most explosive idea Randolph introduced was his suggestion that state equality be abolished by instituting proportional representation in both houses of Congress, which would mean that the large states, by virtue of their population, would dominate the government. By this provision, Madison hoped to redress the wrong done the large states in 1777 when state equality was written into the Articles of Confederation. Here Madison struck the small states in their most sensitive spot. For they conceived of the state as the primary unit and felt that their existence depended upon the principle of one state, one vote. Deprived of equality, they feared that they would lose their influence in the general government and that the large states would preempt the national revenue and enact tariff and tonnage laws to the disadvantage of the small, noncommercial states. Some spokesmen of the small states even professed to fear that they would ultimately be absorbed by their larger neighbors.

The New Jersey Plan. Speaking on behalf of the small states, William Paterson of New Jersey put forward the New Jersey or Small State Plan as a substitute for the Virginia Plan. Essentially, Paterson proposed a revision of the Articles of Confederation and thereby put himself in accord with the expectations of the American people and with the directive of the Continental Congress. Even though drastically limited in the changes which it proposed, the New Jersey Plan would have given Congress the impost and control over commerce and would have established a system of federal courts.

So inflamed were the passions raised by the issue of state equality versus proportional representation that for several weeks the convention seemed on the verge of dissolution. The American people knew nothing of this crisis. The convention met in the utmost secrecy, and the delegates were forbidden to inform any outsider of what was transpiring inside the Pennsylvania State House where the convention met.

The Connecticut Compromise. The impasse was finally resolved by the appointment of a committee consisting of one member from each state. On July 5, 1787, this committee reported the Great or Connecticut Compromise, sponsored by Roger Sherman of Connecticut, in which state equality was perpetuated in the Senate while proportional representation prevailed in the House of Representatives. This compromise was accepted by the convention by the margin of five states to four, Virginia voting in the negative. Only after the House had been given the exclusive right to originate money bills which could, however, be amended by the Senate were the large states reconciled to the Connecticut Compromise.

By admitting state equality in the Senate, the Constitution gave the states a foothold within the very citadel of the general government. Nevertheless, one of the features of the Confederation most objectionable to nationalists was eliminated: no longer did an entire delegation cast one vote for the state as a unit. Instead, senators voted as individuals rather than as ambassadors whose duty was to register the will of sovereign states. Moreover, since congressmen's salaries were to be paid by the federal government, they were made financially independent of the states.

The Issues of Slavery and Sectionalism

The real gainers by the Connecticut Compromise were not the small states. They were never in danger of being absorbed by the large states. The South and later the West were the real beneficiaries, although not the advocates, of this arrangement. In American history, states' rights have been the mask assumed by sectionalism, and as a minority section the ante bellum South found that equality in the Senate was its shield and buckler against northern oppression. This was especially true since the southern states contained, on the average, smaller white populations than the northern states. In 1860, for example, the state of New York, with a population of four million, was represented by two senators, whereas the fifteen slaveholding states, with a population of eight million free people, sent thirty senators to Washington.

An attempt to create a more cohesive union was bound to occasion a dispute over slavery. Even though slavery was not yet the "peculiar institution" of the South, it was already beginning to make trouble between the two sections. Under the Articles of Confederation when requisitions were laid by the Continental Congress, the sum was determined by the population of the state. The question had arisen in the Continental Congress whether slaves were to be counted along with whites. Southerners insisted that slaves were not

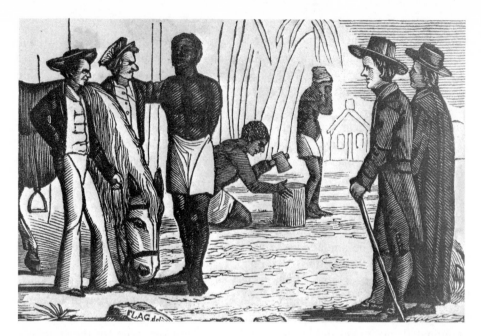

This picture, called "Exchanging a Citizen for a Horse," shows clearly that slaves were treated as property, not as people. Because of this treatment, Southerners argued that the slaves should not be counted in the population for purposes of taxation. *Picture: Library of Congress*

persons but property. As such, they ought not to be counted any more than should sheep, cattle, and horses. To which Benjamin Franklin drily remarked that there was an important difference between sheep and slaves: "Sheep," he said, "will never make any insurrections."

The Three-fifths and Fugitive Slave Clauses. Here the practice of the Continental Congress under the Articles of Confederation proved useful. In apportioning requisitions, the old Congress had counted three fifths of the slaves. Since the new Constitution provided that representation in the House of Representatives and votes in the electoral college were to be determined by population, southerners insisted upon incorporating the three-fifths rule into the new frame of government as a basis for counting population. Therefore, over weak northern opposition, southerners wrote this clause into the Constitution. It was not the result of a compromise: the North received no *quid pro quo* except that three fifths of the slaves would also be counted for the purposes of direct taxation. Gouverneur Morris of Pennsylvania, who opposed the three-fifths clause, said that because of southern intransigence on this issue he was "reduced to the dilemma of doing justice to the Southern states or to human nature, and must therefore do it to the former."

The three-fifths clause proved to be the greatest concession made by either section to secure the adoption of the Constitution. In 1790 as a result of it, Virginia, with a smaller free population than Massachusetts, sent five more representatives to Congress and therefore possessed five more votes in the electoral college than did the Bay State. Without benefit of the three-fifths clause, Thomas Jefferson would not have been elected President of the United States in 1800. Finally, the three-fifths clause gave slavery a privileged and virtually indestructible position in the federal government. The Constitution makes clear that property could consist of human beings.

The framers of the Constitution were obviously embarrassed by the existence of slavery in a society which purported to be a model for mankind. Most of them sincerely hoped that slavery would die of its own accord. Only one speech in praise of slavery was made in the Constitutional Convention. The members could not bring themselves to use the word *slave* or even *bondservant*. Instead the slaves were covered by the euphemistic phrase "persons held to Service or Labor" which in 1787 included white indentured servants as well as black slaves. To placate the slaveowners, the Constitution provided that fugitives should be "delivered up on Claim of the Party to whom such Service or Labor may be due." Although the framers obviously intended that the rendition of fugitive slaves should be primarily a state responsibility, this clause of the Constitution became the basis for a Fugitive Slave Act in 1793 which obligated the federal government to aid in returning runaways to their masters.

The circumlocution with which the delegates approached the subject of slavery indicated both their aversion to the institution and their awareness of the disruptive potential of the slavery question. The convention realized that it could not take an unequivocal position either for or against slavery *per se* without imposing an intolerable strain upon the fragile bonds of union.

Economic Aspects of Sectionalism. Once the issue between the large and small states had been settled, the sectional division reflected in the three-fifths clause provided the focal point for conflicts of interest within the convention. The main struggle was between the commercial and shipping northern states and the agricultural, staple-producing, exporting states of the South. At first, victory clearly inclined to the South. Northerners demanded that Congress be permitted by a mere majority vote to lay a tax upon exports and to enact a tariff and navigation system, by which was meant discriminatory tonnage rates designed to benefit American shipping. By acting as a unit, the southern states, with the aid of some of the agricultural northern states, were able to block this demand and to insert into the Constitution not only an outright prohibition of taxes on exports but also a requirement that navigation laws be enacted by a two-thirds majority of Congress.

The African Slave Trade. But after this success, the South failed to maintain the united front to which it owed its influence. When the convention came to consider the African slave trade, fundamental differences among the southern states were brought to light. Virginia, having a surplus of slaves, competed with Africa in supplying the plantations of South Carolina and Georgia. As domestic producers of slaves and, in some instances, as idealists, the Virginians were determined to protect their market against foreign competition and to remove the blot of the African trade from the United States. Accordingly, they favored giving Congress power to stop this trade at any time after the establishment of the new government. The South Carolinians and Georgians, on the other hand, opposed giving Congress any power whatever over the trade. Charles Pinckney of South Carolina delivered an encomium upon slavery and the slave trade, and he served notice upon the convention that his state would not accept any frame of government which gave the general government power to prevent the free importation of blacks from Africa. The delegations from Georgia and South Carolina backed up this speech by threatening to walk out of the convention.

As was its settled practice, the convention appointed a committee to find a way out of the impasse. Such a way opened when South Carolina and Georgia, resentful of Virginia's treachery, decided to enter into a bargain with certain northern delegates whereby these two slave-hungry states agreed to vote in favor of empowering Congress to enact navigation acts by a simple majority in exchange for a vote by the northern commercial states in favor of a provision which would forbid any federal interference with the slave trade until 1808. It was now the Virginians' turn to cry treachery, but the bargain was consummated in spite of the objections of the Old Dominion.

By thus delaying for twenty years the national prohibition of the African slave trade, the proponents of the trade hoped to stock southern plantations with blacks from the slave barracoons of Africa. In actuality, however, there was opposition to the trade not only on moral grounds but also because slave purchases drained the money supply. For these reasons, the trade was prohibited by all the states except Georgia and South Carolina, and in the latter state it was open only between 1804–1808. Yet during this period of grace for American slave traders, fifty thousand or more human beings suffered the ordeal of the middle passage and a lifetime of slavery in order to make possible the more perfect union of white Americans.

The Broad Agreement on the Constitution

While many compromises went into the making of the Constitution, the drafting of a frame of government in 1787 was made possible only by the existence of a broad agreement upon fundamentals and the determination of the delegates to establish an efficient central government capable of upholding the credit, dignity, and rights of the United States.

The Federal System. Instead of creating a unitary government along the lines sketched by the Virginia Plan, in which the states would hardly have been more than administrative agents of the central authority, the Constitution effected a division of sovereignty between the states and the general government. Each exercised sovereignty within a sphere defined by the Constitution. Some functions, especially those regarded as common to the entire country, were assigned to the general government; other functions were placed exclusively in the hands of the states; and a third area was shared by the two jurisdictions concurrently. Because the states and the general government coexist within the same territory, the United States has diverse systems of law, an entire galaxy of taxing powers, and dual police and armed forces. Both the state and federal governments operate directly upon the people. In the United States, each citizen is subject to two governments.

Although the Constitution did not establish the "high toned" central government envisaged by the Virginia Plan, it contained several clauses which, as Alexander Hamilton perceived, might later be used to achieve a vast extension of federal powers. These were the commerce clause, the necessary and proper clause, and the general welfare clause. Although some of these phrases were derived from the Articles of Confederation, in the context of the document of 1787, they assumed new and far-reaching implications. They helped make possible the broad interpretation of national powers. In short, unlike the Articles, the Constitution created a government capable of meeting changing circumstances by invoking flexible powers which the courts, Congress, and the President found implied or inherent in the language of the instrument.

A Government with Power. Under the Articles of Confederation, it had been difficult to carry on interstate business or, indeed, business of any kind. The Constitution remedied this defect by making possible a single, integrated monetary system, which, however, was long delayed; by prohibiting the states from laying tariff and tonnage duties without the consent of   Congress; by directing that all federal duties, imposts, and excises be uniform throughout the United States; by requiring that "the citizens of each state shall be entitled to all the privileges and immunities of Citizens in the several states"; and by giving the federal government exclusive power to regulate interstate trade and to prescribe a common standard of weights and measures.

Thus, as regards the relative positions of the general government and the states, the Constitution brought about a change almost as revolutionary as that of 1776. From a position of humiliating impotence, the general government acquired powers by which it gradually became dominant. Instead of being dependent upon the states for its very existence, the general government, under the Constitution, became independent of the states, leaving the latter no means short of nullification and secession for regaining their lost preeminence. As events proved, although it took a long time before the implications of federal power were fully realized, the Constitution made the sphere of federal power potentially much greater than the sphere allotted to the states. The general government was given unlimited powers of taxation, although the United States Supreme Court later decided that an income tax was unconstitutional; the states were prohibited from making paper money legal tender or impairing the obligation of contracts, a reaction against the paper money and debtor-relief laws enacted by the states; and the national government was enabled to enforce its decrees through a federal system of courts. No longer were the states to enjoy the position of intermediaries between the general government and the people. Finally, the state governments were effectively isolated from each other by the provision that "no state shall, without the consent of Congress . . . enter into any general agreement or compact with another state." The tables, it appeared, were to be turned completely: the federal government became the guarantor of a republican form of government in the states.

Within the definition accepted in 1787, this kind of government was not federal. The Constitutional Convention had in fact created a new synthesis. While the frame of government it devised was in some respects federal, since it made the states autonomous in some matters, in other and equally important respects it was national and made the central government autonomous in other areas. Nevertheless, the supporters of the new Constitution took the name *Federalist,* leaving to its opponents the invidious, but wholly unwarranted, name of Antifederalists. Thus the advocates of the Constitution won the first battle in the campaign for ratification: they routed their opponents upon the field of semantics.

The Governmental Mechanism. As for the central government itself, it was characterized by a system of checks and balances between its three branches. The executive, legislature, and judiciary were each provided with the constitutional means of defending their own powers against the encroachments of the other branches. Hamilton thought that this system of "power as a rival of power" would be so effective that it would be "next to impossible that impolitic or wicked measures should pass the great scrutiny." Yet the framers did not intend to divide the government into rigid, compartmentalized, autonomous branches. The doctrine of the separation of powers was certainly given application, but each branch shared in functions that were not strictly within its province. The President could exercise legislative as well as executive powers, for instance, by issuing administrative orders. Congress could perform executive functions, such as approving appointments, and the federal courts, by construing the meaning of statutes, could exercise a legislative role. This role has sometimes been extended so broadly as to incur charges of usurpation of legislative powers.

Was the Constitution Democratic?

All this was accomplished without impairment to the democratic gains of the American Revolution. Indeed, in several areas, the federal Constitution appeared more democratic than the state constitutions. Unlike the states, the federal government required no property qualifications for holding office, and it implemented the principle of religious freedom by dispensing altogether with religious tests. The federal Constitution did not disbar Jews, Roman Catholics, or even nonbelievers from any public office, although some state constitutions did. The federal Constitution was a great experiment in religious as well as political liberalism.

Unless liberty was identified with states' rights, the American people were not the losers by this shift of power from the states to the general government. In fact by the adoption of the Constitution, the people stood to gain a large measure of control over the central government, a privilege they had certainly not enjoyed under the Articles of Confederation. They were now promised the right to elect directly members of the House of Representatives. In some states, and ultimately in all, they gained the right to elect presidential electors.

On the other hand, the framers clearly did not intend to establish the kind of government in which the popular will prevailed at all times without let or hindrance. The immediate concern of most of the members of the convention was to protect the "opulent minority" from expropriation by democratic majorities. The government of the United States, in consequence, is not based upon the principle that the majority have the right to govern arbitrarily, nor does it contemplate a government in which the people govern in the usual sense of that word. The people merely decide who shall govern and, broadly speaking, to what ends. Although the people are declared to be sovereign, there are things which even a majority cannot do. The Constitution itself, for example, cannot be amended except with the approval of three fourths of the states. The Constitution, which is the supreme law of the land, created a system which comes closer to being a government of laws rather than of men than any other country has been able to devise.

The Break with the Confederation. The framers of the federal Constitution proposed not only to effect a revolution in the relations between the states and the general government. They also recognized that it was necessary to make a sharp break with the law of the land in order to carry their plan into execution. The Articles of Confederation, which in 1787 were still in force, required that any changes in the fundamental law be approved by all thirteen state legislatures. Every previous effort to amend the Articles had been frustrated by this rule of unanimity. It was a foregone conclusion that if the proposed Constitution were subjected to the same rule it would suffer the fate of the impost. Rhode Island, the erring sister of the Confederation, had not even recognized the existence of the Constitutional Convention. In New York Governor Clinton, whose forces had defeated the effort to strengthen the commercial powers of Congress, was known to be hostile to the Constitution.

Faced with the certainty of having its work blocked by one or more of the state governments, the Constitutional Convention decided to break the rule of unanimity. It decreed that the proposed frame of government was to be submitted not to state legislatures but to popularly elected conventions and that it should go into effect after nine states, not thirteen, had ratified it.

These changes were more democratic than the procedures ordained by the Articles of Confederation. By appealing directly to the people to sanction its handiwork, the Constitutional Convention applied the doctrine of the sovereignty of the people to the process of constitution-making. Consequently, the Constitution of the United States, if adopted, could be regarded as the creation of "We, the People" of the United States, even though they acted severally by states rather than collectively as one people.

The Constitution Viewed Pragmatically. None of the framers was prepared to pronounce the result of the labors of the Philadelphia convention as the best of all possible constitutions. Most of the delegates agreed with James Madison's observation that it was the best constitution that could be wrung from the jarring sectional, state, and personal interests. Nevertheless, the Constitution bore the signatures of thirty-nine members. At various times during the proceedings, fifty-five men attended the convention, but of this number sixteen had left Philadelphia before the convention completed its work. Of these sixteen, four disapproved of the finished Constitution. Of even greater concern to the framers was the fact that despite Benjamin Franklin's plea for unanimity, three of the delegates still in attendance—Elbridge Gerry of Massachusetts, and George Mason and Edmund Randolph of Virginia—refused to sign the Constitution.

The Controversy Around the Constitution

Obviously, the framers of the Constitution could not afford to neglect any circumstance which might favor ratification. For the American people were being called upon to embrace ideas which seemed to be at variance with some of the basic teachings of the colonial and revolutionary experience. Americans had learned to fear centralized government, to cherish local liberty, and to believe that that government was best which governed least. In 1787–1788 they were asked to recast their thinking and to look upon an energetic central government as the guardian of their property and of republican government itself.

The traditional distrust of power, derived from the colonial and revolutionary periods, was widespread in 1787–1788. This feeling was given expression by the Antifederalists, the most articulate of whom were Richard Henry Lee, George Mason, and Patrick Henry of Virginia; Luther Martin of Maryland; and Governor George Clinton of New York. These men held the view later enunciated by Lord Acton, the nineteenth-century British historian, that while all power corrupts, absolute power corrupts absolutely. From their viewpoint, the United States was too large, its economy too diverse, and its mode of life too varied from one region to another for it to be ruled as a whole by any government except an absolute and despotic one. If the United States fell under the sway of a centralized government, they feared that the "overbearing insolence of office," the lust for power, and the arrogance of wealth would lead to the subversion of all liberty. Liberty and strong, coercive government, they pessimistically believed, could not be reconciled.

The Antifederalists. Suspicious of government and of the officials who administered it, the Antifederalist spokesmen lacked any compensating faith in the wisdom of the people and in the people's ability to prevent the encroachments of power. In effect, they insisted that the prevention of any effective exercise of power on a national scale was the only reliable guarantee of liberty. Their solution to the dilemma of power was to protect the minority by making it impossible for the majority to rule. In the name of liberty, they were prepared to negate the idea of popular government not, it is true, as regards the states but certainly as regards the general government. In their view, the only true security for liberty was a weak central government constitutionally debarred from interfering in the internal affairs of the states.

In this respect the Antifederalists were far removed from the mainstream of twentieth-century liberalism, although their democratic sympathies were not dissimilar from those of present-day liberalism. On the other hand, the Federalists were conservative in their opposition to paper money, debtor-relief, and other populistic measures and in their determination to protect property interests from the assaults of majority rule. The Antifederalists felt such an acute distrust of power that it led them to adopt the even more undemocratic position of attempting to prevent the establishment of a central government capable of effective action by any controlling group, whether democratic or not.

Was There a Conservative Plot? There was an element of kinship between Antifederalism and twentieth-century Progressivism which later caught the attention of historians, especially Charles A. Beard, who in 1913, at the height of the Progressive Movement, depicted the framing and adoption of the Constitution as a victory of conservatism and property rights over democracy and human rights. Beard sympathized with the Antifederalists because they, like the Progressives of his generation, feared the power of concentrated wealth and the political influence it commanded. Although some of the Antifederalist leaders were themselves men of wealth, they attacked the proposed Constitution as the culmination of a long-standing plot to destroy republican government and to establish an aristocracy and perhaps even a monarchy in the United States. As they pictured it, the advocates of the Constitution were "partisans of arbitrary power" who moved toward their objective by means of "dark, secret and profound intrigues."

Obviously, the Antifederalist leaders were aware that nothing was more calculated to prejudice the American people against the proposed frame of government than the charge that it was an aristocratic plot. Even though the Antifederalists did not succeed in 1787–1788 in convincing a majority of the electorate that this was true, their propaganda later had a profound effect upon a whole generation of American historians.

The Question of a Bill of Rights. The Antifederalists' fears were given substance by the failure to include in the Constitution a Bill of Rights. Although most of the state constitutions included an enumeration of the inviolable rights of the citizen, the framers gave scant consideration to the proposal that a bill of rights be incorporated in the Constitution. The majority of the framers inclined to the view that such guarantees were not necessary in a government which was stated to have no powers except those which were enumerated. A government which possessed only the powers which were explicitly given to it was fundamentally different from the state governments, which possessed all powers that were not explicitly denied. To the Antifederalists, however, the want of such guarantees was decisive: any government not specifically restrained from invading the liberties of the press and of speech, the liberty of conscience, the right of trial by jury, and other basic freedoms would inevitably encroach upon them.

By seizing upon this omission from the Constitution, the Antifederalists were able to portray themselves as the champions of freedom. Yet most of the amendments they proposed aimed not at placing the civil liberties of the individual beyond the reach of government control but at reducing the powers of the central government and enhancing those of the state governments. Despite appearances, the rock-ribbed Antifederalists were, in fact, the true conservatives of this period. In resisting the forces of change, they made it clear that they wished to perpetuate a system which denied power to the central government but not necessarily to create a system which vested power in the people.

Local Fears and Jealousies. Equally decisive in determining attitudes toward the proposed Constitution were the apprehensions of various local groups that their interests might be adversely affected. For this reason the same economic groups in different states took different positions towards the Constitution. For many Westerners, the fact that the East favored the adoption of the Constitution was enough to condemn it. Nor could the question of slavery be excluded from the debate over the Constitution. Patrick Henry warned that a northern commander at the head of a northern army might decree the abolition of slavery. "May Congress not say," he asked rhetorically, "that every black man must fight?" It seemed even more probable to Southerners that if federal courts were created, British creditors would use them to collect obligations owed by southern debtors. Finally, the clause giving Congress control over foreign and interstate commerce posed the danger that northern merchants and manufacturers would monopolize southern commerce.

The Federalist. The spokesmen for the new Constitution made their most cogent statement in its defense in the *Federalist,* a series of essays by James Madison, Alexander Hamilton, and John Jay. Indeed, the *Federalist* ranks as a classic treatise upon government. The purpose of the authors, however, was not to win the applause of posterity but to secure the ratification of the Constitution without which the *Federalist* might have been left to accumulate dust on the shelf as a purely theoretical piece of political literature.

The central theme of the *Federalist* was that the United States, despite its size and diversity, could enjoy the benefits of a strong, energetic central government which would not infringe upon the liberties of the people or subvert the constitutional rights of the states and that peace, order, and respect for the rights of minorities were compatible with majority rule. In place of the blind rejection of any real political power on a national scale, which the Antifederalists considered to be the only viable way to protect popular liberty, the authors of the *Federalist* took the position that power must be given government commensurate with the responsibilities entrusted to it and that stability and energy in government are necessary to the maintenance of freedom. Power, they observed, did not always corrupt; sometimes it created in its possessors a sense of responsibility and dedication to the public good. Ambition took many forms, among them the desire to stand well in history. The love of fame, in short, was a spur which often gave constructive direction to the impulses for power.

The *Federalist,* although identified with conservative attitudes, actually revealed more confidence in the people than did the Antifederalist spokesmen. Although both sides deplored "popular licentiousness," "the folly and wickedness of mankind," and the susceptibility of the people to demagoguery, the *Federalist* took the position that if properly controlled by a system of checks and balances, a large measure of democracy might be admitted into the system. The Constitution, the authors argued, provided all necessary security against "democratic excesses." It ensured that the second, sober thought, "the deliberate sense of the community" rather than the transitory impulses and delusions of the people would prevail. The *Federalist* found added security in the public spirit generated by republican institutions. As Hamilton said, "there is a portion of virtue and honor among mankind" which made the people at least intend to further the public good, a statement that deserves more emphasis than the apocryphal story that he called the American people "a great beast."

The Constitution did not adopt principles of direct democracy; it provided for a system in which neither the President, the members of the Senate, nor the federal judiciary were to be elected by the voters. Only the House of Representatives was to be so elected. But in a broader sense, the *Federalist* acknowledged that all legitimate authority must come ultimately from the people. The principle of popular sovereignty, although not of direct and uncontrollable popular rule, was the fundamental principle of the United States Constitution, as the authors of the *Federalist* saw it.

Among the guarantees of liberty cited by the *Federalist* was the fact that the states would serve as a check upon any abuse of power by the federal government. As the *Federalist* pointed out, the powers delegated to the federal government were few and specific whereas the powers reserved to the states were "numerous and indefinite." From this fact Madison concluded that the state governments constituted a greater danger to liberty in the United States than did the federal government.

Antifederalists Versus Federalists. Antifederalism appealed especially to farmers, particularly the less prosperous ones who lived outside the intellectual and economic radius of the seaport towns and who were therefore least affected by the dislocation experienced by commerce; to politicians whose expectations of preferment were bound up with the perpetuation of the power of the state governments; and to the large number of citizens, of both high and low estate, who could not divest themselves of their fears of a strong central government.

Against the Antifederalists was arrayed the weight of talents, property, education, and wealth. The aristocracy of the country was far more united in supporting the federal Constitution than in supporting the Declaration of Independence. But the aristocracy alone could not have carried the Constitution; there were not enough well-to-do Americans to accomplish that feat. But, as Madison said, the seacoast seemed everywhere in favor of the Constitution. In the seaports the sailors, dockworkers, and artisans supported the Constitution as enthusiastically as did the merchants, lawyers, and professional men in general.

Without the aid of the southern planters, however, the Constitution would assuredly have gone down to defeat. Essentially, the strength of the Federalists was based upon an alliance of northern merchants and southern planters. In its intention, at least, the Federalist party represented a coalition of powerful economic groups in both the North and the South.

Potential Divisions Among the Federalists. Yet, from the beginning, there existed within this coalition the seeds of dissension. Northerners, for example, owned the bulk of the outstanding securities issued during the Revolutionary War by the state and general governments. In many instances, northern businessmen and the more substantial farmers, having disposable cash—unlike the southern planters who were land- and slave-poor—bought these securities from the original holders, mostly soldiers and farmers, at a fraction of their face value.

The Constitution pledged the new government to pay the debts, although not necessarily in full, contracted by the Continental Congress. It could be readily foreseen, therefore, that if the Constitution were adopted, Continental securities would increase in value. Accordingly, the proposed Constitution touched off a wave of speculation in securities by Europeans as well as Americans. Because a large number of the Federalists who sat in the Constitutional Convention and in state ratifying conventions owned such securities, they had a direct pecuniary interest in the outcome. As a result, the Antifederalists—and later historians—could allege that the Constitution was the work of mercenary speculators who voted themselves a financial windfall. As the Antifederalists pictured it, it was the American people who, along with the Constitution, were framed at Philadelphia.

Charles Beard's Interpretation. Even assuming that security ownership determined attitudes toward the proposed Constitution, it does not follow, as Charles Beard supposed, that the owners of state and continental certificates constituted a true "consolidated economic interest" united in supporting the Constitution. For security holders, like other individuals, were caught in the economic and financial crosscurrents generated by the plan drawn up at

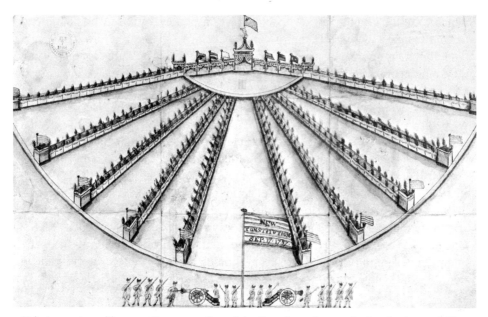

This banquet pavilion was the scene of a celebration, three days early, by six thousand New Yorkers who were certain that their state would ratify the Constitution. *Picture: The New-York Historical Society, New York City*

Philadelphia. In the three states which had assumed payment of interest upon the continental securities held by their citizens, many security owners feared that any change in the existing relationship between the states and the general government might deprive them of their income from the securities. Nothing was said in the Constitution about the assumption of state debts, although it is true that Hamilton, Madison, and Jefferson had advocated such a step as early as 1783. Nor did the proponents of the Constitution hold out such a prospect as an inducement for ratification. Precisely because the Constitution offered nothing concrete to the state creditors, it tended to divide rather than to unite holders of state and continental securities.

Moreover, the supporters of the Constitution had many other and broader benefits to think about besides a rise in the price of governmental securities. While they no doubt hoped to be the beneficiaries of this anticipated increase, such expectations were hardly more than incidental to the other economic, financial, and political increments to which they looked forward. These included a central government capable of regulating, protecting, and expanding the commerce of the United States; providing an adequate circulating medium; safeguarding property against the depredations of state legislatures; suppressing domestic violence; implementing the terms of the treaty of peace; and making a commercial treaty with Great Britain. Compared with these desiderata, a rise in the value of governmental securities was accounted no more than a welcome fringe benefit. Moreover, many of the financial advantages accruing to security holders from the adoption of the Constitution could not be foreseen in 1787–1788, since they were generated by Hamilton's fiscal program of 1790, which took the country by surprise and astonished even those who had hoped to gain from an increase in the price of securities.

Economic interests, which, in Charles Beard's view, were the prime determinants of human actions, often impel individuals in opposite directions: self-interest is not always an unequivocal guide. Large land-speculators, in particular, were acutely aware of these crosscurrents. On the one hand, they wished to keep the price of government bonds (certificates) low because such securities could be exchanged at face value for public land. Cheap securities therefore meant cheap land. On the other hand, they needed the protection against the Indians and the removal of the British from the Northwest Posts that only a strong central government could effectuate. Patrick Henry, who was a heavy speculator in the operations of the Yazoo Land Company and was committed to large purchases of land payable in certificates, opposed the Constitution. Yet the rise in the price of those securities resulting from the adoption of Hamilton's funding-assumption plan made Henry a far richer man than he could have hoped to become from his land speculations alone.

Ratification

Electing the Ratifying Conventions. Despite the momentous issues raised by the Philadelphia convention's plan of government, only a small proportion of the qualified voters went to the polls to elect the members of the state ratifying conventions. This seeming indifference was owing in part to the indecision and even bewilderment felt by a large number of citizens when they were presented with the Constitution. In consequence, they retreated into a kind of wait-and-see neutralism. The difficulty of getting to the polls, particularly in rural areas, discouraged a large turnout, and there were no political parties to organize and arouse the electorate. In any event, a small minority, consisting of about 5 per cent of the adult, white, male population determined the outcome.

Some Early Victories. With deceptive ease, the Constitution breezed through the first five ratifying conventions. From December 1787 to February 1788, the Constitution was ratified in quick succession by Delaware—the first state to act—Pennsylvania, New Jersey, Georgia, and Connecticut. Three of these states—Delaware, New Jersey, and Georgia—ratified unanimously.

Clearly, the small agricultural states, appeased by the adoption of the Connecticut Compromise and eager to abolish the privileges of the commercial states, fervently embraced the Constitution. In view of the fact that Philadelphia was the only large population center in any of the first five states to ratify, it was apparent that farmers, when they took the trouble to vote, favored adoption.

The Opposition Comes into Action. These happy auguries were not borne out when the Constitution reached New Hampshire and Massachusetts. The New Hampshire ratifying convention was so loaded with Antifederalists that supporters of the Constitution could escape defeat only by agreeing to an adjournment until June 1788. In Massachusetts a "black cloud" of Antifederalist delegates swept in from the former Shaysites region, making a majority of the members Antifederalists. Nevertheless, the opponents of the Constitution lamented that lawyers, judges, clergymen, and educated men in general were against them "and for that reason," they complained, "they appear able to make the worse appear the better cause." But they did, nevertheless, have the support of Elbridge Gerry, one of the three members who had refused to sign the Constitution, Sam Adams, the revolutionary leader, and Governor John Hancock.

John Hancock held the key to the outcome of the struggle over ratification in Massachusetts. An astute politician who never lost an election, Hancock remained absent from his chair as president of the convention, alleging ill health. An ambitious man, he wanted to be on the winning side and to extract the maximum political gain from his support. He soon found that the Federalists could offer more than could the Antifederalists. Behind the scenes a bargain was struck: in exchange for his endorsement of the Constitution—certain to shatter the ranks of the Antifederalists—Hancock was assured of the Federalists' support for the presidency of the United States if Virginia did not accede. If Virginia ratified, he was to have the consolation prize of the vice-presidency. This prospect wonderfully restored Hancock's health.

Even with Hancock's support, the Federalists had to agree to recommend nine amendments of the kind soon after incorporated in the Bill of Rights. The final vote was 187 to 168, a narrow squeeze but much better than anything the Federalists might reasonably have expected at the beginning of the convention.

The Crisis of Ratification in New York. After surmounting relatively easy hurdles in Maryland and South Carolina, the Constitution reached New York where Governor Clinton and his Antifederalist supporters awaited its arrival, supremely confident that they could stop it. And, indeed, the results of the election to the New York convention seemed fully to warrant that expectation. Since all property qualifications upon voting had been removed especially for this election, the result could be regarded as an expression of public opinion. Except for New York City, an Antifederalist slate was returned. The delegates were impervious to Alexander Hamilton's oratorical efforts. The Constitution appeared headed for certain defeat until late in June 1788 when news reached Poughkeepsie that the ninth state, New Hampshire, had ratified. The Constitution thereupon went into effect as the supreme law of the land: if New York did not ratify, it excluded itself from the union.

Even so, in exchange for the unconditional ratification of the Constitution, the Federalists had to agree to support a call for a second constitutional convention where, presumably, the Constitution would be rewritten to satisfy the Antifederalists' objections.

The New Roof. Virginia's convention, which met concurrently with New York's, subjected the Constitution to a more searching criticism than it had hitherto encountered. The Virginia Antifederalists, who in the beginning enjoyed a clear majority, were led by George Mason, Patrick Henry, and Edmund Randolph. The Federalist forces looked to James Madison for leadership. But Edmund Randolph, by going over to the Federalists, really decided the issue. After that event, the Antifederalists could not hold their ground. Still, the Constitution was ratified by the narrow margin of 89 to 79 without, however, any mention of a second constitutional convention.

Only in North Carolina was the Constitution actually defeated in 1787–1788. Rhode Island disdained even to call a convention. Even so, eleven states gathered under the new roof. Albeit peacefully, a second American revolution—in many respects, the consummation of the first revolution—had been effected. Washington hailed this achievement as "a new phenomenon in the political and moral world; and an astonishing victory gained by enlightened reason over brute force." By assembling wise men rather than armies, Americans had demonstrated that a free people, acting with moderation, can abolish and institute governments peacefully.

SUGGESTED READING

Among the most important books dealing with the Constitution are Max Farrand, *The Framing of the Constitution of the United States** (1913); Andrew C. McLaughlin, *The Confederation and the Constitution, 1783–1789** (1905); Stanley Elkins and Eric McKitrick, *The Founding Fathers: Young Men of the Revolution* (1962); Charles Warren, *The Making of the Constitution* (1928); Benjamin F. Wright, *Consensus and Continuity, 1776–1787** (1958); Carl Van Doren, *The Great Rehearsal** (1948); Stuart Gerry Brown, *The First Republicans: Political Philosophy and Public Policy in the Party of Jefferson and Madison* (1954); Nathan Schachner, *The Founding Fathers* (1954); K. C. Wheare, *Federal Government** (1953); William Crosskey, *Politics and the Constitution,* 2 vols., (1953).

Biographies of individuals who participated in the Constitutional Convention are Broadus Mitchell, *Alexander Hamilton: Youth to Maturity, 1755–1788* (1957); J. C. Miller, *Alexander Hamilton: Portrait in Paradox** (1959); Irving Brant, *James Madison: The Nationalist, 1780–1787* (1948) and *James Madison: Father of the Constitution, 1787–1800* (1950); Charles P. Smith, *James Wilson: Founding Father, 1742–1798* (1956); Clinton Rossiter, *Alexander Hamilton and the Constitution* (1964) and *1787: The Grand Convention** (1966).

Charles Beard set forth his thesis in *An Economic Interpretation of the Constitution of the United States** (1913). Merrill Jensen expanded the Beard thesis in *The New Nation: A History of the United States During the Confederation, 1781–1789** (1950). The Beard thesis has been challenged by Robert E. Brown, *Charles Beard and the Constitution* (1956); Forrest McDonald, *We the People: The Economic Origins of the*

*Available in a paperback edition

Constitution (1958) and *E Pluribus Unum: The Formation of the American Republic, 1776–1790** (1965). A modified restatement of the Beard thesis may be found in Jackson T. Main, *The Antifederalists: Critics of the Constitution, 1781–1788** (1961).

The ratification of the Constitution may be best studied in S. B. Harding, *The Contest over Ratification of the Federal Constitution in the State of Massachusetts* (1896); Frank G. Bates, *Rhode Island and the Formation of the Union* (1898); C. E. Miner, *Ratification of the Federal Constitution by the State of New York* (1921); Robert L. Brunhouse, *The Counter-Revolution In Pennsylvania, 1776–1790* (1942); Robert Allen Rutland, *Ordeal of the Constitution* (1965).

For the Bill of Rights see Robert Allen Rutland, *The Birth of the Bill of Rights** (1962); Leonard W. Levy, *Legacy of Suppression: Freedom of Speech and Press in Early American History* (1960) and *Origins of the Fifth Amendment* (1968). For the *Federalist* see Gottfried Dietze, *The Federalist: A Classic on Federalism and Free Government** (1960).

There is a large and growing literature about the Antifederalists. See Forrest McDonald, "The Antifederalists, 1781–1789," *Wisconsin Magazine of History,* XLVI (1963); Jackson Turner Main, *The Antifederalists* (1961); Cecelia M. Kenyon, ed., *The Antifederalists** (1965); Alpheus Mason, *The States Rights Debate: Antifederalism in America** (1964); Morton Borden, ed., *The Antifederalist Papers* (1965); John D. Lewis, ed., *Anti-Federalists Versus Federalists* (1967).

CHAPTER THREE

THE FEDERALISTS AND THE CEMENT OF THE UNION

T HE RATIFICATION BY New York and Virginia removed the last obstacle to making the federal Constitution the law of the land. In general, the Antifederalists accepted the outcome without rancor; after all, the contest had been over a form of republican government, not over republican government itself. The promise of amendments and possibly a second constitutional convention removed some of the sting of the defeat. Most of the Antifederalist leaders pledged themselves to work for the success of the Constitution without, however, abating their resistance to its centralizing tendencies. Yet this concession did not gain them much strength, and they proved surprisingly weak in the elections held in 1788, the first in the history of the federal government. A large Federalist majority was returned in both houses of Congress; only Virginia returned two Antifederalist senators. John Hancock received none of the prizes. George Washington was unanimously elected President; John Adams became Vice-President. Thus the sectional duality of the new government was recognized: a southern President was paired with a northern Vice-President.

Launching the New Government

Because of the slowness of transportation—it required a month to travel overland from Charleston, South Carolina, to New York—Congress did not assemble until early in April 1789, and President Washington was not inaugurated until April 30, six weeks later than the Constitution prescribed. North Carolina and Rhode Island were not represented. North Carolina did not ratify until later in 1789, and Rhode Island held out until 1791.

The First Acts of the New Congress. Congress atoned for this delay by the dispatch with which it moved to give form and substance to the framework of government delineated by the Constitution. The work of the First Congress of the United States, which sat from 1789 to 1791, was scarcely less important than that of the Constitutional Convention itself. For the Constitution, a comparatively short document of about 4000 words, did not create a government; it merely indicated in broad outline how it was to be organized and by what rules it was to be conducted. It was the task of the First Congress to make the new government a going concern.

To that end, Congress provided for the financial needs of the federal government by imposing a tariff upon imports. It established three executive departments, the departments of state, war, and the treasury; set up the federal judiciary; enacted the first navigation laws for the encouragement of the United States merchant marine; and proposed the Bill of Rights to the states. The second session of the First Congress, 1790–1791, enacted laws governing patents and copyrights, provided for the naturalization of aliens, ordered a decennial census, created a mint and the decimal system of coinage, and established the Bank of the United States. Likewise, during this period many of the precedents which have become familiar parts of the government of the United States were established.

The Question of a Treaty with the British. In 1787–1788 it had been generally supposed that one of the first acts of the new government would be to take reprisals upon Great Britain for its refusal to evacuate the Northwest Posts and to make a commercial treaty with the United States. Indeed, this prospect had provided a compelling reason for summoning the Constitutional Convention and adopting the Constitution. Madison, in particular, was eager to bring Great Britain to terms by means of high duties upon British merchandise and extra tonnage charges upon British ships entering United States ports. He did not doubt that when the British were confronted with such trade barriers, they would quickly see the error of their ways. The fact that his policy would benefit France only enhanced Madison's satisfaction. Like Jefferson, he believed that the United States owed a debt to France which could be repaid only by diverting American trade from Great Britain to the ports of France and its dependencies.

But Great Britain, having served to unite Americans by stimulating concerted opposition to its policies, now became a divisive force in the United States. Although Madison did not succeed in uniting the South in support of retaliatory legislation—he did not attempt to disguise the fact that southern exports would be compelled to bear the financial brunt of a commercial war with Great Britain—his most trenchant critics were the New England merchants and shipowners, the very people upon whom he proposed to confer, at least temporarily, a near-monopoly of the southern market. These businessmen were beginning to taste the sweets of returning prosperity and were unwilling to jeopardize their economic well-being by challenging Great Britain to economic combat. Hamilton objected on the ground that curtailing imports from Great Britain would reduce the payment of duties, which were the government's largest potential source of revenue, and would cripple the federal government in its infancy. Nor did he approve of the idea of forcing American trade into channels beneficial to France. Gratitude, he said, ought to play no part in the government's foreign policy particularly if, as in the present instance, it threatened to injure the United States.

Although Madison's bill discriminating against British ships and merchandise passed the House of Representatives, it was defeated in the Senate. In consequence, Great Britain was accorded the same privileges in United States ports which France, the most favored nation, received.

The Beginnings of Sectional Antagonism. This issue marked the beginning of the breach between Madison and Hamilton, the erstwhile collaborators in the *Federalist,* and the dissolution of the sectional coalition which had carried the Constitution to victory. In September 1789 Hamilton was appointed secretary of the treasury. Madison in Congress and Hamilton in the executive department were soon to become the leaders of opposing sectional interests. As Madison himself had predicted in the Constitutional Convention, sectionalism, rather than a struggle for power between large and small states, would prove to be the bane of the American Union.

Even the tariff of 1789, primarily to provide revenue but also to protect a few selected items, brought to light significant differences between the North and South. Some southern spokesmen complained that the tariff discriminated against the agricultural South which consumed more imported merchandise than did the North where domestic manufactures were relatively advanced. The role of the South in the new government, it was observed, was to provide revenue to be spent in building up northern manufactures and shipping.

The Bill of Rights. Of all the matters that came before the first Congress, James Madison attached particular urgency to the formulation of a Bill of Rights. Madison himself was committed by campaign pledges to work for amendments to the Constitution, and he had become convinced that they alone could appease the Antifederalist opposition. Moreover, although he was not disposed to put his faith in paper guarantees of liberty, he believed that the principles of free government enunciated with proper solemnity might gradually acquire "the character of fundamental maxims" and thereby "counteract the impulses of interest and passion." But in drawing up a list of amendments for approval by Congress and adoption by the states, Madison selected only those suggested by the state ratifying conventions which had to do with the protection of civil liberties.

During the summer of 1789, twelve amendments were adopted by Congress and submitted to the states. Two of the proposed amendments failed to win the approval of three fourths of the states. Of the ten amendments adopted, the first eight properly constitute the Bill of Rights; the ninth and tenth amendments were intended to preclude the possibility that the enumerated powers granted the federal government would be construed against the reserved rights of the states.

The Crystallization of Rivalry: Hamilton Versus Jefferson

Hamilton's Program for Assuming State Debts. While Antifederalist opposition was disarmed by the adoption of the Bill of Rights, sectionalism showed no signs of diminishing. On the contrary, the depth and intensity of the sectional conflict was not revealed until January 1790, when Secretary of the Treasury Hamilton, in response to a request made by Congress, submitted his Report on Public Credit. Hamilton's assignment was to devise ways and means of restoring the credit of the United States government. His report called for a far more comprehensive and drastic program than Congress had bargained for. The secretary of the treasury recommended not only that the foreign debt of about $12 million be paid in full but that the outstanding certificates of the federal government including accrued interest as well as principal be redeemed virtually at par to a total of $40 million. But he topped this audacity by proposing that the federal government assume the debts contracted by the states during the War of Independence. Finally, he urged that the old certificates be exchanged for new obligations and that a fixed schedule for accumulating funds to pay off the interest and principal be adopted, thereby assuring creditors of the government that it intended to honor its obligations to the full.

As Hamilton planned it, the federal government, by assuming the state debts, would win the allegiance of the creditor class. It would then preempt all available sources of revenue, leaving the cupboard bare for the states. In short, the situation would be the exact reverse of that which had prevailed under the Articles of Confederation.

A thoroughgoing nationalist, Hamilton sought to use fiscal policy not merely to reestablish the credit of the government but to accomplish far-reaching political and economic ends. By the assumption of state debts, for example, he intended to concentrate the financial power of the country in the federal government. Hamilton hoped that this plan would attach the state creditors to the federal government. The states would then lose the support of their affluent citizens and, in consequence, cease to exercise their taxing powers and quietly wither away.

Moreover, Hamilton was a firm believer in private enterprise, and his report was intended to foster the development of capitalism in the United States. Recognizing that one of the most crucial deficiencies of the capitalist system in the United States was the shortage of capital, Hamilton proposed to give government securities the attributes of capital by endowing them with a cash surrender value and transferability. In this way, the governmental debt could serve as the basis of a stable money supply and compensate for the scarcity of precious metals.

The fact that state and national certificates of indebtedness were already in the hands of a comparatively few affluent citizens seemed to Hamilton to be a favorable circumstance. When these securities were redeemed at face value, the ensuing gain would be concentrated and could be put to more constructive use than if it were widely dispersed through the population. Hopefully, it would be devoted to investment and development of new industries rather than for the purchase of consumer goods. Thus by proper management, the national debt would become a national blessing by providing cement to the union and by serving as a unifying force in the national economy.

Madison in Opposition. To Hamilton's dismay, James Madison, upon whom the secretary of the treasury had counted for support, took the lead in opposing the Report on Public Credit. Although he did not take exception to funding the debt and paying the domestic creditors their due, Madison called attention to the plight of the original holders of government securities who had sold them for a fraction of their face value. He argued that justice should be done by permitting them to share in the profit that would accrue exclusively to the current holders if Hamilton's plan were adopted. Madison also demanded justice for the states which, like Virginia, had largely settled their war debts and thus would have to help to pay the debts of other states after having already taken care of their own. While Hamilton was flexible upon the assumption of state debts, he refused to yield upon the question of paying the holders of government securities the full amount due without regard to the price they had paid to previous holders for those securities. He pointed out that the Continental Congress had promised foreign purchasers of its certificates that full title could be transferred. Therefore, he argued, to honor the claims of the original holders would cast a fatal blight upon the government's credit.

Madison's efforts in behalf of the original holders was rejected by Congress, but the legislature was immobilized by the conflict between the partisans of the Treasury and the large group of congressmen who followed Madison's lead. Uncertainty and delay vastly increased the incidence of speculation in the public debt, the very evil Madison sought to curb. For as a result of the deadlock in Congress, many speculators who had run up the price of state securities in their eagerness to make the most of the expected financial windfall began to unload their holdings lest Hamilton's report be rejected by Congress.

A Temporary Compromise. The situation appeared so critical that Secretary of State Thomas Jefferson, recently arrived from France where he had witnessed the opening scenes of the French Revolution, began to fear for the existence of the Union. Therefore when Hamilton approached him with a plea to save the Union, Jefferson acted promptly. A bargain was struck between Jefferson, Madison, and Hamilton whereby the assumption of state debts was sweetened for Virginia and other states whose debts were small by an outright grant from the federal Treasury. In exchange for Hamilton's support in locating the future capital of the United States on the Potomac, the Virginians agreed to procure the necessary votes to see funding-assumption bills through Congress with the full proceeds going to the current holders. Accordingly, in July and August 1790 Hamilton's report was adopted with some modifications, and Congress passed an act directing that after ten years temporary residence in Philadelphia, the national capital should be moved to the Potomac.

At first, Jefferson professed satisfaction with this arrangement. He had secured the transfer of the national capital to the Potomac, where in rural surroundings it could presumably attend to the needs of farmers better than if it were located in a big city. But he quickly found that he had raised a storm in the Old Dominion. In December 1790 at the instigation of Patrick Henry, the legislators asserted that the country had been delivered over to a "moneyed interest," that agriculture had been sacrificed to the commercial interests of the Union, and that the assumption of state debts was unconstitutional. But the law stood in spite of Virginia's protests. Hamilton had carried his main points, and the country was launched upon the full tide of an experiment in centralized government and capitalistic enterprise.

Hamilton's Bank of the United States. Despite evidence of a widening sectional split, Hamilton was not dissuaded from prosecuting his grand design of making the United States a great power. As a means to that end, he sought to strengthen the sinews of capitalism in the United States by establishing a central bank from which both the government and private citizens would profit. In December 1790, accordingly, he laid before Congress his Report on a National Bank. Here he proposed the creation of a quasi-governmental bank to be called the Bank of the United States. It was capitalized for $10 million and represented a pooling of governmental and private resources. The Bank of the United States was to serve aṣ a depository for governmental funds and to facilitate their transfer; it would also make loans to the government and to private individuals and issue bank notes which would serve as a circulating medium.

The crucial point which made the bank question intermittently controversial for the next two decades was that although chartered and sponsored by the federal government and privileged to handle federal funds, the Bank was to be privately owned and operated for the profit of its owners with only five government-appointed directors on its twenty-five man board. Furthermore, the Bank could present all bank notes issued by the state-chartered banks which, in the course of business, came into its possession to those banks and demand that the bank notes be redeemed in specie. This function gave it control over the issuance of bank notes throughout the country.

Two Theories of Government. Although the Bank bill passed Congress, its constitutionality was challenged by James Madison. Shaken by Madison's arguments, President Washington called for opinions from the members of his Cabinet. In his reply, Jefferson advocated strict construction of the Constitution. The Federal government, he asserted, could exercise only those powers which were enumerated in the Constitution, and the necessary and proper clause allowed only those means that were indispensable for executing these enumerated powers. In short, *necessary* meant *essential.* In the case of the proposed Bank of the United States, he insisted that it was not necessary to fulfill any of the enumerated powers of the Constitution and was therefore unconstitutional.

When Hamilton read Jefferson's state paper, he concluded that the Virginian was trying to interpret the Constitution in a way that would turn the clock back to the period of the Articles of Confederation. Hamilton's view of the Constitution, unlike his views of democracy, looked forward to the twentieth century. In defending the constitutionality of the Bank of the United States, he contended that like all governments, the United States government enjoyed implied powers, that is, powers that authorized it to employ all functions necessary and proper to the implementation of its enumerated powers. In short, necessary meant appropriate. At no time did Hamilton say that the federal government possessed the power to do as it pleased. Throughout his controversy with Jefferson and Madison, he admitted that the Constitution had created a government of enumerated powers. He insisted, however, that the Bank of the United States was a constitutional means of executing the enumerated powers which had been granted the federal government for collecting taxes, regulating trade, and providing for the common defense. In time, both the Supreme Court and the Jeffersonian Republicans came to agree with Hamilton.

Not without misgivings, President Washington signed the bill establishing the Bank of the United States. When its stock was put up for sale in the summer of 1791, speculators pushed the price of the shares far above par. Speculation in stocks and government certificates was becoming commonplace, and the country had its first stock-market crash in 1792. Jefferson accused Hamilton of having introduced the virus of speculation into the American bloodstream, but, in actuality, Hamilton had merely given Americans the wherewithal to indulge the strong speculative bent which had distinguished even the earliest settlers when they had surveyed the "inexhaustible" riches of the country.

The Bank of the United States proved its worth both to the government and the business community. But control of the institution was vested in the North, and its facilities were largely reserved for the merchants of the northern cities. The Bank's notes did not circulate outside the cities, and loans were rarely made to farmers. For these reasons, while the country as a whole profited from the stability and greater volume of trade which the Bank made possible, it was open to criticism as an instrument by which a few privileged individuals controlled the American economy.

The Hamiltonian Philosophy

Hamilton had no intention of strengthening sectionalism. He was a nationalist without either state or sectional loyalties. Yet the existing economic and financial state of the Union—the concentration in the North of fluid capital, manufactures, and shipping—made it inevitable that the implementation of his program would aggravate the sectional imbalance.

Hamilton took little satisfaction with this aspect of his achievement. He was distressed, for example, that such a comparatively small amount of stock in the Bank of the United States was bought by southerners. A firm believer in the force of economic interest upon individuals and sections, he recognized that the planters and farmers of the South had to be given a stake in the new economic and financial order which, so far, had lavished its bounties upon northern businessmen, investors, and speculators.

The Harmonizing of Sectional Interests. As Hamilton planned it, therefore, the capstone of his grand design was to be the integration of the Union by the dovetailing of the economies of North and South. He believed that wise political management could convert the economic differences between the two sections from a source of conflict into cement for the Union. This adhesive was material self-interest which, Hamilton supposed, offered the most secure foundation upon which any nation could be built.

Hamilton's Report on Manufactures. The unification of the country by

John Trumbull's "Painting of Alexander Hamilton" captures Hamilton's self-assurance and aggressive stance in public affairs. *Picture: Art Commission of New York*

making the sections complement each other economically was the central theme of the Report on Manufactures, which Hamilton submitted to Congress in January 1792. The secretary of the treasury began with the premise that the United States must diversify its economy or resign itself to remaining a second-rate power dependent upon overseas markets for the sale of its surplus agricultural products. He assumed that in the course of time Europe would consume less and less American foodstuffs and raw materials. To avert a situation in which the United States would find itself producing more than it could sell abroad, Hamilton urged Congress to foster the growth of "the precious embryo" of manufacturing by a system of bounties, premiums, and a protective tariff. Once manufacturing was firmly established in the United States, he believed that the national market, envisaged by the framers of the Constitution, would become a reality. Instead of being tied economically to Europe, the sections would be bound to each other. Northern factories would consume southern raw products; northern urban centers would provide a market for the vast quantities of food produced by American farms; and farmers and planters throughout the Union would buy the goods turned out by American factories. Thus, said Hamilton, Americans would prove the truth of the theorem that "mutual wants constitute one of the strongest links of political connection." Hamilton's vision was of one nation, economically indivisible.

He believed that the private capital necessary for starting these enterprises would come from bank stocks, loans by banks, foreign credits, and government securities, now selling at par and in the hands of the affluent. In promoting manufactures, these solid citizens would presumably find that their own and the nation's interest were in happy conjunction. As for the labor force required by factories, the secretary of the treasury advocated the use of women and children and, above all, laborsaving machinery.

In his Report on Manufactures, Hamilton argued that government aid to manufactures was authorized by the general welfare clause of the Constitution. Jefferson emphatically disagreed. In his opinion, the "heresies" advanced by Hamilton in this report went beyond anything previously suggested. The authority to establish the Bank, after all, was considered by Hamilton as being derived from an enumerated power of Congress, but the fostering of manufactures was not related to an enumerated power nor did Hamilton claim that it was. Under the conviction that a crisis was at hand, the secretary of state told President Washington that the way Congress acted upon Hamilton's Report on Manufactures would determine "whether we live in a limited or an unlimited government."

Jefferson Opposes Hamilton

But Jefferson failed to communicate his apprehensions to the President. Washington was an ardent advocate of domestic manufactures. When he was inaugurated in 1789, he wore a suit of American-made cloth, and when he toured New England in 1790, he did not fail to inspect every factory that lay along his route. Even Jefferson, as secretary of state, tried to bring foreign workmen to the United States, although such emigration was discouraged by British law. In 1803 he suggested that the federal government subsidize DuPont's gunpowder factory on the Brandywine.

Yet, judged by its immediate effects, Hamilton's Report on Manufactures hardly warranted the excitement it occasioned in official circles. Congress did little more than establish a bounty system for encouraging the fisheries. What rendered Hamilton's Report on Manufactures abortive—at least until Henry

THE PROVIDENTIAL DETECTION

Clay later breathed life into it and christened it the American System—was not the constitutional objections raised by Jefferson but the outbreak of the wars of the French Revolution. Contrary to Hamilton's prediction that the European market for American agricultural exports would shrink calamitously, European demand expanded steadily under the impact of war-induced manpower shortages. As a result, Americans sold more and bought more abroad than ever before. Not until the embargo of 1808–1809 did manufacturing begin to assume the proportions Hamilton had envisaged two decades previously.

The differences of opinion between Jefferson and Hamilton were not confined to a decorous exchange of state papers. In 1792 Washington's Cabinet was rent by an open conflict between the secretary of state and the secretary of

These two cartoons illustrate the personal attacks characteristic of newspapers of both parties. On the left, Jefferson is pictured as about to sacrifice the Constitution on the Altar of Gallic Despotism. On the right is a Republican attack on William Cobbett, editor of *Porcupine's Gazette* and a staunch supporter of President Adams. *Pictures: Left, From the collections of the Library Company of Philadelphia; Right, The Historical Society of Pennsylvania*

the treasury. The quarrel was brought to a head by the journalistic activities of Philip Freneau, the "Poet of the Revolution," who had become a newspaper editor. By offering Freneau a clerkship in the State Department, Jefferson and Madison persuaded him to come to Philadelphia in 1791 to establish a "truly Republican" newspaper, by which they meant an anti-Hamilton sheet, to counteract the influence of the pro-Hamilton *Gazette of the United States.* Freneau accepted the offer of a clerkship and established the *National Gazette,* a daily newspaper which specialized in pillorying the secretary of the treasury. Readers of the *National Gazette* were told that Hamilton was a monarchist, a practitioner of corruption, and an enemy of the rights of man. On the other hand, Jefferson was portrayed as an honest republican who loved the people and sought only the public good.

Stung beyond endurance by Freneau's barbs, Hamilton, under a nom de plume, attacked Jefferson in the newspapers for putting a hired character assassin on the public payroll. Both Jefferson and Hamilton threatened to resign, but President Washington succeeded in persuading them to remain at their posts. Nevertheless, Jefferson continued to let his friends know that he considered Hamilton a monarchist and that all his acts were directed toward the subversion of the Republic. Since these acts had been approved by President Washington, the secretary of state was setting himself in opposition to the administration of which he was a member. Jefferson justified this conduct on the ground that he had a higher duty to the cause of republicanism. This sense of duty carried him even to the length of helping to draw up resolutions presented to Congress early in 1793 by William Branch Giles, a Virginia congressman, calling for Hamilton's removal from the Treasury Department on the ground that he was guilty of mishandling government funds.

From these quarrels at the center of the government, there began to emerge two political parties—the Federalists and the Republicans, the latter being former Federalists who were joined by some of the former Antifederalists. Each group had its own set of policies, newspapers, rudimentary party machinery, and popular following. Henceforth, Federalists were Hamiltonians. Until 1792 James Madison remained the leader of the anti-Hamiltonian forces in Congress, but Hamilton's newspaper attacks upon Jefferson served to bring forward the secretary of state as the main rallying point of the opposition.

Throughout this period, Jefferson's conviction that the Republic was endangered by a monarchical conspiracy furnished him with a compelling reason for engaging in political activity rather than pursuing the more congenial paths of philosophy, science, and architecture. Although he absolved Washington from any part in this supposed plot, he firmly believed, and continued to believe to the day of his death, that John Adams was a monarchist at heart. But the deadliest of this malign species was, by Jefferson's system of classification, Alexander Hamilton. Here was a man, he exclaimed, who would not rest content until he had introduced into the United States that "class of human lions, tygers and mammoths called kings."

While Jefferson's sincerity is not open to doubt, it is clear that antimonarchism offered great tactical advantages by providing Republicans with a rallying cry far more appealing to the public mind than allegations of corruption or of attempting to centralize power in the federal government. In fact, Jefferson and his friends owed a considerable measure of their political success to their ability to convince a large number of Americans that there was a clear and present danger of monarchy in the United States. When Jefferson and his adherent called themselves Republicans, they meant to dissociate themselves from the monarchists, otherwise known as Federalists.

In actuality, what Jefferson took for monarchism was Hamilton's way of promoting centralized government and furthering capitalistic enterprise. Theoretically, Hamilton believed that electing a President and senate for life would give greater stability to the government than electing them for a term of years. He was especially concerned about the "tumults" provoked by elections. On the other hand, in theory, Jefferson thought that the United States would be better off if, like China, it renounced the use of the sea. But neither Hamilton nor Jefferson made theory his guide. Both succeeded in accommodating themselves to the realities of American life and confining themselves to seeking the possible rather than in hankering vainly after the ideal. Hamilton tried to make the federal government function as effectively as possible within the limitations imposed by the Constitution, though it is true that he construed those limitations loosely. Jefferson did not devote his energies to the annihilation of American commerce, although during his presidency he was accused of trying to do that very thing.

Even so, Hamilton and Jefferson held radically different views of what constituted the good life for the American people, of what ideals they ought to live by, and of what great national objectives were to be sought above all others.

The Jeffersonian Philosophy. Faith in the people, the first article of Jefferson's political creed, was inseparable from his conception of the nature of the universe. His political philosophy presupposed the existence of a cosmos ruled by law and the existence of a benevolent Creator who had endowed mankind with reason and social instincts, including altruism and a deep sense of justice which could be defined in terms of a universally recognized natural law. In the United States, Jefferson assumed that there was little need of compulsion or even of government: the people's behavior would be governed by their innate moral sense. After providing a basic education and preserving order, government ought to leave men free to follow their instinctual sense of right and wrong. This sense, he supposed, was far more reliable than directives regarding thought or conduct laid down by any government.

To Jefferson, the United States was always "this heavenly country" destined to serve as a model for mankind if it only remained true to the principles upon which it had been founded and to the agricultural way of life which Providence seemed to have ordained for its inhabitants. Jefferson regarded farming one's own land—ownership was quite as important as contact with the land itself—as the most wholesome, morally uplifting, and productive occupation in which an individual could engage. For Jefferson, the pursuit of happiness ended on a farm. "Those who labor in the earth are the chosen people of God, if ever he had a chosen people," he said, for they alone lived in harmony with the divine scheme of things. Naturally, therefore, he envisaged progress in terms of a forward movement along the lines upon which Americans had already embarked: more farms, more household manufactures, a wider diffusion of the ownership of land, more education, more equality, more moral refinement, and more happiness.

Jefferson loved the land that made possible the comfort, security, and happiness Americans enjoyed. Yet comparatively few of his countrymen of his own or succeeding generations shared Jefferson's reverence for the land and his gratitude for the blessings with which Nature had so lavishly endowed the United States. For many Americans, the wealth that could be extracted from the land took priority over the satisfaction of living in harmonious adjustment to Nature. And so the forests were ruthlessly despoiled, the mineral wealth extracted with little regard to the needs of future generations, and agricultural land exploited for cash crops. By its very bounty, Nature seemed to have

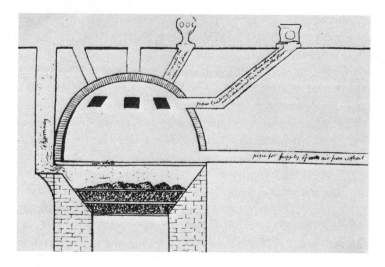

Jefferson's interests were not restricted to public affairs and agriculture. He was also an architect and an inventor. One of his inventions, the central-heating plant, is shown here. *Picture: Library of Congress*

ensured that Jefferson's message would be ignored, at least until the inexhaustible resources of the country began to be seriously depleted.

To Hamilton, on the other hand, farming was merely a way of making a living, no more meritorious than any other honest way. He saw no evidence that the Almighty had placed His seal of approval upon farming. Nor, in his opinion, were farmers particularly virtuous and law-abiding: during the period of the Articles of Confederation, they had proved themselves to be the chief troublemakers in the Confederation. Although he did not pretend to read the will of Heaven, Hamilton was sure of one thing: the United States already had a surfeit of farmers. What the country needed, as he saw it, was more factory workers, more machinery, more ships, more output of goods, more businessmen. Instead of individual happiness, Hamilton thought in terms of national happiness, which he equated with wealth, power, and economic diversity. Moreover, he considered duties to be quite as important as rights. It was the duty, for example, of every individual to labor in order that his country might be great.

The Impact of the French Revolution

Divisive as were the broils and contentions between Republicans and Federalists over domestic policy, the events of the French Revolution and the questions of foreign policy to which it gave rise stirred Americans' passions far more deeply and eventually produced a far sharper division of public opinion. In 1789, the year of President Washington's inauguration, the deputies elected to the French Estates-General defied the king and formed themselves into a National Assembly, pledging not to separate until they had provided a constitution for France. Soon after, a Paris mob stormed the Bastille, the symbol of arbitrary power. At first, the American people viewed these events as a projection of their own struggle for freedom. When Lafayette sent the key of the Bastille to President Washington, the gift was accepted as a symbol of the kinship between the two revolutions. During the years 1789–1792, Americans seemed to have found a new source of union in their enthusiasm for the cause of the French revolutionaries.

The Need for a Treaty with Great Britain. In its early years, the French Revolution showed only sporadic evidence of its later, violent phase; hence Americans were not yet seriously divided in their sympathies. At this time, therefore, relations with Great Britain were far more crucial to the new republic than those with France. American diplomacy was mainly directed toward securing from Great Britain a commercial treaty and the cession of the Northwest Posts, the unfinished business inherited from the Continental Congress.

Hamilton and Jefferson were far from agreement upon the best way of attaining these objectives. The secretary of the treasury believed that the wisest policy lay in conciliating the former mother country, whereas the secretary of state was of the opinion that only economic reprisals offered any hope of putting the British in a reasonable frame of mind.

These irreconcilable differences in attitude toward Great Britain were given special importance by President Washington's practice, adopted early in his first administration, of asking the heads of departments for written opinions upon all important questions of foreign and domestic policy without regard to their special areas of expertise. He freely consulted the secretary of the treasury upon subjects relating to foreign affairs, and he attached much importance to the opinions of the secretary of state upon fiscal matters. From this method emerged the Cabinet, an institution unknown to the Constitution.

With the President's approval, despite Secretary of State Jefferson's protests, Hamilton participated in the conduct of the country's foreign relations. He conferred with Major Beckwith, the unofficial British representative in Philadelphia, with Ternant, the French minister, and with George Hammond, who in 1791 became the first British minister accredited to the United States. Although Hamilton told these diplomats he could conclude nothing, he apparently felt free to propose anything. Without the President's knowledge, the secretary of the treasury proposed to Major Beckwith that Great Britain and the United States enter into an alliance. At the same time, he warned the Major against too intimate relations with Jefferson, whom he described as a moonstruck lover of all things French including the French alliance.

The "Reign of Terror" and Its Divisive Effect in America. The September Massacres of 1792, the deposition and execution of Louis XVI and Marie Antoinette, and the Reign of Terror, in which a large number of royalists and moderates were brought to the guillotine—all made many Americans begin to doubt that they were witnessing a replay of the American Revolution with an all-French cast. Within the administration and throughout the country as a whole, the French Revolution became a major cause of dissension. Although Jefferson recoiled from the crimes committed in France in the name of liberty, he regarded them as necessary to the survival of the revolution, which was beleaguered by foreign enemies bent upon restoring the monarchy. For this reason, he condoned Robespierre and the Reign of Terror. Not until the advent of Bonaparte did Jefferson lose his faith that liberty, equality, and fraternity would ultimately prevail in France. Indeed, as he saw it in the 1790's, they had to prevail or else the cause of republicanism would suffer a mortal blow, the effects of which might even reach the United States. If the French Revolution failed, Jefferson confidently expected that Hamilton and his fellow monarchists would make a bold push to crown an American king.

France and Great Britain at War. Since 1778 the United States had been an ally of France, committed to come to the aid of the French West Indies in case France were involved in a defensive war and requested such aid. Americans therefore could not remain disinterested spectators of events in Europe. Consequently, in February 1793 when the French Republic declared war upon Great Britain and when the French government appointed Citizen Edmond Genêt as the first minister of the French Republic to the United States, the Washington administration was confronted by its first real crisis in foreign affairs. Although technically the United States was not obliged to render aid to France—the French Republic had declared war upon Great Britain—there was no telling what demands the French government would make upon its ally. It was certain that at least the French would require the implementation of the Franco-American commercial treaty of 1778 by which the United States agreed to open its ports to French warships and privateers and their prizes while denying similar privileges to British warships and privateers. Thus the commercial treaty would in fact align the United States with France in its naval war in the Atlantic.

The Problems of Neutrality. Washington, Jefferson, and Hamilton agreed that the United States must remain neutral in the European conflict. The urgency of a declaration of the government's intentions was underscored by the arrival of Citizen Genêt in Charleston, South Carolina, in March 1793. Genêt demanded to be received as minister of the French Republic, and, he made clear, he was not content with mere passive neutrality on the part of the United States. Washington and Hamilton believed that since Congress was not in session, the President ought to issue a proclamation of neutrality, but Jefferson demurred on the ground that the Chief Executive lacked constitutional authority to commit the country either to war or to peace. Jefferson's objections were overruled. In April 1793 the President issued a proclamation which, at least until Congress met, laid down rules governing the conduct of American citizens and of the government itself. Out of deference to Jefferson's scruples, however, the word neutrality was omitted from the declaration.

Genêt Seeks American Involvement. Hamilton wished the government to

Citizen Edmond Genêt attempted to involve the United States in the war between France and Great Britain. *Picture: Culver Pictures*

refuse to receive Genêt; he argued that the French Republic had not yet demonstrated that it was the legal government of France. But here the secretary of the treasury was countered by Jefferson who took the position that the Franco-American alliance was an alliance of peoples, not of governments. President Washington sided with the secretary of state, and the decision was made to receive Genêt. By this action, the United States became the first government in the world to recognize the French Republic. It was an act of defiance directed against monarchical Europe.

The United States had declared its neutrality. The question now arose whether Citizen Genêt would permit it to remain neutral. In South Carolina, Genêt acted as though the United States were a French satellite. He equipped, manned, and commissioned privateers to prey upon British shipping off the coast of the United States, and he tried to raise armies of Americans to attack Canada and Spanish Louisiana. Americans seemed far more inclined to help France than to preserve neutrality. Genêt's overland journey from Charleston to Philadelphia resembled a triumphal progress. Wherever he went, he was met by cheering crowds, the waving of the tricolor and the American flag, and the discharging of cannon. Democratic or Constitutional Societies—described by the Federalists as "the impure offspring of Genêt"—sprang up in his wake, and Republicans began to call themselves Democratic-Republicans. Intoxicated by popular acclaim, Genêt began to think of himself as an apostle of liberty sent to redeem the American people from Federalist tyranny.

Partisanship on Foreign Policy. In this unrestrained enthusiasm for the French Revolution, Federalists saw a threat to their own ascendancy and to the republican institutions of the United States. For many Republicans had been conditioned by the repeated warnings of a monarchical plot to believe that the battle for liberty, equality, and fraternity had to be fought in the United States as well as in France. The enemy on the home front was aristocracy, particularly as it manifested itself in the role of the Federalist party. Celebrations of French military victories were often marked by the roasting of an ox, labeled "Aristocracy" for the delectation of the patriots. The next step, some timorous Federalists feared, would be the erection of an American guillotine.

Although President Washington received Genêt with a cold formality that chilled to the marrow most people who experienced it, the ebullient young Frenchman was not disconcerted. In any event, the warmth of his reception by Jefferson more than atoned for the President's hauteur. Yet the French minister refused to heed the secretary of state's warnings that neutrality was the law of the land. Instead, he threatened to appeal to Congress from the rulings of "old man Washington." And ignoring Jefferson's pleas, he converted the captured British merchantman *Little Sarah* into a privateer, renamed it *Le Petit Democrat,* and ordered it to put to sea from Philadelphia. While President Washington was absent at Mount Vernon, *Le Petit Democrat* made good its escape and began to prey upon British shipping off the Delaware.

Genêt Tries to Make the United States a Base of Military Operations. Despite the declaration by the United States government in 1793 that its jurisdiction extended three miles from its shoreline (the span of a cannonball), French privateers disregarded all limitations upon their freedom of action. British merchantmen were attacked wherever they were found. Even on land, the territorial integrity of the United States was violated. In Boston, the French consul, at the head of an armed body of French sailors, seized a ship from the custody of a United States marshal.

Genêt's flagrant violations of American neutrality threatened to involve the United States in war with Great Britain. Even Jefferson quickly became disenchanted with Genêt. He discovered that the Frenchman—"hot headed, all imagination, no judgment, passionate and even indecent toward the President"—threatened to bring ruin upon the Republican party. Accordingly, when the British government demanded that the United States enforce its neutrality, the Washington administration took prompt action. The recall of Genêt was required. The French government was happy to oblige: Genêt, a Girondist, was slated for the guillotine by Robespierre. Genêt saved himself by taking asylum in the United States, marrying the daughter of Governor Clinton of New York, and settling down to the placid life of a country gentleman.

While Genêt succeeded in resolving his problems with a romantic and financially advantageous marriage, the United States was not equally fortunate in disposing of the problems created by the wars of the French Revolution. It soon became clear that Genêt's removal merely provided a temporary palliative to the difficulties abroad in which the American people found themselves increasingly involved. In 1793 the United States entered upon a twenty-year struggle to protect, as a neutral, its ocean-borne commerce against belligerents determined to throttle all neutral commerce which might aid their adversaries. In consequence, the United States, the world's largest neutral carrier, was ultimately forced to choose between renouncing the freedom of the seas or fighting to uphold the principles it had proclaimed during the American Revolution.

SUGGESTED READING

The problems of organizing the new government are treated by Leonard D. White, *The Federalists: A Study in Administrative History* (1948); James Hart, *The American Presidency in Action* (1948); Joseph Charles, *The Origins of the American Party System** (1956); Edward Channing, *A History of the United States* (1905–1925); John S. Bassett, *The Federalist System, 1789–1801* (1906); J. C. Miller, *The Federalist Era, 1789–1800** (1960); Walton Hamilton and Douglass Adair, *The Power to Govern* (1937).

Hamilton can best be studied through Jacob E. Cooke, ed., *Alexander Hamilton: A Profile** (1967) and through the biographies written by Broadus Mitchell, Nathan Schachner, and J. C. Miller.

Among the best studies of Jefferson's philosophy are Adrienne Koch, *Jefferson and Madison** (1950) and *The Philosophy of Thomas Jefferson** (1943). Dumas Malone's multivolume biography of Jefferson discusses the period of his struggle with Hamilton in *Jefferson and the Rights of Man** (1951). Daniel J. Boorstin, *The Lost World of Thomas Jefferson** (1960) is important. See also Merrill Peterson, *Thomas Jefferson and the New Nation* (1970). Julian P. Boyd describes Hamilton's interference with State Department matters in *Number Seven, Alexander Hamilton's Secret Attempts to Control American Foreign Policy* (1964). For a discussion of Philip Freneau see Jacob Axelrod, *Philip Freneau* (1967). Paul Goodman has edited a collection of monographs, *The Federalists vs. The Jeffersonian Republicans* (1967). For further information on James Madison see Adrienne Koch, *Madison's Advice to My Country* (1966). The charges of monarchism are disposed of by Louise B. Dunbar, *A Study of 'Monarchical Tendencies' in the United States from 1776 to 1801* (1923).

For Citizen Genêt and the French Alliance see Charles D. Hazen, *Contemporary American Opinion of the French Revolution* (1897); Charles S. Hyneman, *The First American Neutrality* (1934); Charles M. Thomas, *American Neutrality in 1793: A Study in Cabinet Government* (1931); Alexander De Conde, *Entangling Alliance: Politics and Diplomacy under George Washington* (1958). Frederick Jackson Turner edited the *Correspondence of the French Ministers to the United States, 1791–1797* (1904). See also Eugene P. Link, *The Democratic-Republican Societies, 1790–1809* (1942); Marshall Smelser, "The Federalist Period as an Age of Passion," *American Quarterly*, X (1958); John A. Carroll and Mary W. Ashworth, *George Washington: First in Peace* (1957).

*Available in a paperback edition

CHAPTER FOUR

THE WANING OF FEDERALIST STRENGTH

The Diplomatic Crisis with Britain, 1793–1794

G ENÊT'S ANTICS AND The Reign of Terror in France benefited the
Federalists who posed as the defenders of American rights against an
aggressive foreign power and an equally foreign ideology. In December
1793 Jefferson resigned as secretary of state, leaving that office to be filled by
Edmund Randolph. But the Federalists' season of rejoicing was short lived: in
1793–1794 they were obliged to defend American rights against Great Britain's
aggression.

British Provocations. Late in 1793 the British government decided to try to
starve France into submission. Neutral rights were not permitted to stand in the
way of this objective. Acting under the authority of an order in council, the
British navy seized, without warning, American ships carrying cargoes of
foodstuffs between France and the French West Indies. Over three hundred
merchantmen were bagged before Americans fairly knew what it was all about.

Moreover, despite American protests, the British made a practice of
sending parties aboard American merchant vessels on the high seas to search
for and remove British subjects who had joined the American merchant
marine. Under the doctrine of inalienable allegiance, British subjects included
every person born a subject of the sovereign of Great Britain regardless of
whether the United States had granted him citizenship. Inevitably, because of
the similarity of language, mistakes were made, and Americans were forcibly
removed from American ships and pressed into His Majesty's service.

On land, as well as on sea, the British displayed what Secretary of State
Jefferson regarded as the arrogance of power. Early in 1794, believing that war
between the United States and Great Britain was inevitable, Lord Dorchester,
the governor general of Canada, tried to enlist the Indians of the Northwest on
the British side. In preparation for the impending rupture, the British built a
new fort on the Maumee River south of the Canadian line in what is now Ohio.

Under the impact of these events, the Republicans, already strongly biased
against Great Britain, demanded the sequestration of debts owed by Americans
to British subjects and reprisals against British commerce. Madison revived his
plan of imposing discriminatory duties upon British ships and merchandise.
The measure passed the House of Representatives, and an economic struggle
with Great Britain seemed certain.

Efforts to Make Peace. Even though the British government withdrew the
order in council which declared foodstuffs contraband, the Federalists were
hard pressed to prevent the adoption of measures by Congress which they
believed were certain to produce war between the two countries. Yet in April
1794 President Washington and Secretary Hamilton succeeded in seizing the
initiative from Madison and Congress by making a last-minute effort to
preserve peace. Chief Justice John Jay of the United States Supreme Court was

View of Boston and the south Boston bridge. *Picture: The Newberry Library*

A British boarding party attempts to remove a sailor from an American ship. *Picture: The Bettman Archive*

appointed minister plenipotentiary to Great Britain. Jay's instructions were drawn up by Alexander Hamilton, who no longer bothered to conceal the fact that he took all the affairs of the federal government as his province. Jay was instructed to secure the cession of the Northwest Posts, a commercial treaty admitting United States ships into the British West Indies, indemnification for losses sustained by American shipowners in the West Indies, and a guarantee that American neutral rights would be respected.

The Increased Strength of the Federal Government. While Jay was in London, several events occurred which strengthened his hand in his dealings with British ministers far more than he could have strengthened it by threatening reprisals. In August 1794 "Mad Anthony" Wayne won a victory over the Indians at the Battle of Fallen Timbers near what is now Toledo, Ohio. As a result, the tribesmen lost much of their value as a British counter in the diplomatic game being played in London. Moreover, in 1795 by the Treaty of Greenville, the vanquished Indians relinquished title to a large part of the Middle West north of the Ohio River, including the site of Chicago, and placed themselves under the exclusive protection of the United States. The way was now open to American settlers to take possession of some of the richest agricultural land in North America.

While Wayne was chastising the Indians, the federal government was engaged in suppressing an uprising of western farmers. The wheat growers of western Pennsylvania had no outlet for their surplus grain except by converting it into whiskey. These farmers resented the excise of 1791, which imposed a tax upon distilleries. In collecting the tax, federal agents paid scant regard to the sanctity of the home where the still was sometimes housed; their assessments were often arbitrary and, in the opinion of the farmers, grossly unfair. In 1794 after sporadic instances of resistance, an open revolt flared up over a large part of western Pennsylvania. Revenue officers were mobbed, the United States mails were attacked, and a small body of regular troops was forced to surrender to the insurgents.

The Washington administration responded to this flouting of the authority of the federal government with a display of force which stunned the whiskey rebels. Eight years after Shays' Rebellion, when the general government had been unable to raise a single soldier to protect federal property, over ten thousand men were placed under arms and sent to western Pennsylvania. The army was led by President Washington himself. Secretary of the Treasury Hamilton, ever eager for military glory, took care not to miss the show. But it proved to be a very tame affair. The rebels melted away, and only a handful were apprehended. Of these, two were tried for treason, found guilty, and sentenced to death; but Washington pardoned them both.

At the same time, the Barbary pirates suddenly resumed their seizures of American ships in the Mediterranean, an event which the Republicans attributed to British machinations. In response to these acts of war, Congress ordered the construction of six, later reduced to four, frigates. Thus ten years after it had been consigned to oblivion, the United States Navy was resurrected. Of all the enemies of the United States, it took the Barbary pirates to work the miracle. But the crisis blew over before the frigates were completed. In 1795 the United States purchased a treaty with Algiers by an outlay of gifts and the promise of an annual subsidy. Not until 1801 did the "swarthy Moor"—specifically, the Tripolitans—feel the force of the naval power they had summoned from the deep.

Whisky rebels in Western Pennsylvania jeer at a revenue officer who has been tarred and feathered. *Picture: The Bettman Archive*

Jay's Negotiations. The cordiality with which John Jay was received in London reflected this evidence of the increased strength of the United States government. William Pitt, the prime minister, and Lord Grenville, the foreign secretary, were eager to settle the dispute with the United States, and even King George spoke graciously to Jay. Not to be outdone in civility, Jay praised George III's "justice and benevolence," remarkable words coming from a former leader of the rebellion against that monarch. But Jay prided himself upon having discarded all the awkward "ancient Prejudices" that stood in the way of a settlement with Great Britain. To see him frolicking with lords and ladies, it was difficult to believe that he had ever been proscribed as an enemy of Great Britain.

In his negotiations with Lord Grenville, Jay acted upon the belief that "the quarrel between Britain and America was a family quarrel, and that it is time it should be made up." He did not threaten the British with economic or military reprisals, nor did he broach the possibility that the United States might join the Armed Neutrality—a league of the Scandinavian powers formed, at the instigation of France, for the purpose of trading freely with France and upholding neutral rights against the British navy. Indeed, a threat by Jay to join the Armed Neutrality would not have impressed Lord Grenville since Alexander Hamilton, without the authorization of President Washington, had already told the British minister that the United States had no intention of associating itself with the Scandinavian powers. Had Jay been disposed to resort to menacing words, Hamilton's action would have undercut him completely, but Hamilton and Jay were agreed that threats would defeat the whole purpose of Jay's mission. They acted throughout on the assumption that only a conciliatory attitude on the part of the United States offered hope of success. And, in truth, the British government would have stiffened its bearing toward Jay had it thought that the Washington administration was hostile to Great Britain. It was precisely because the Federalists seemed to stand as a barrier to "the Torrent of Jacobin Principles" in the United States that Lord Grenville was disposed to make concessions.

It was not Alexander Hamilton but James Monroe who weakened Jay's position in London. Monroe, a Jeffersonian, had been appointed American minister to France at almost the same time Jay was sent to England. Monroe was ardently pro-French, and he gave expression to his sympathies by publicly embracing French leaders and delivering a rousing speech to the National Assembly. Lord Grenville looked suspiciously upon this line of conduct; he told Jay that if Monroe represented the attitude of his government, it would be difficult for His Majesty's ministers to regard the United States as truly neutral. And unless the British government was persuaded that the United States intended to remain neutral, it was not likely to surrender the Northwest Posts or to make a commercial treaty with the Republic.

Conciliation probably accomplished more than threats would have gained for Jay, but, even so, he had to be content with less than Washington and

Hamilton had expected. While he succeeded in making a treaty, his mild-mannered approach did not incline British statesmen to renounce the mastery of the sea and open the British Empire to American trade. The gains achieved by Jay's Treaty were much more modest. He secured a promise to surrender the Northwest Posts, which the British had already promised in the treaty of 1782–1783, a circumstance which provoked some Americans to remark that the United States was buying the same horse twice. He also obtained a very limited right of entry for American ships into the British West Indies. The disputed Maine–New Brunswick boundary was referred to a mixed commission for settlement. By standing firm on the northwest boundary, Jay prevented the British from making the forty-fifth, instead of the forty-ninth, parallel the boundary between the United States and Canada.

In exchange for these concessions, Jay had to abandon the United States' claim to slaves carried off by the British army in 1783 and to agree that the United States government should assume responsibility for the still unpaid pre-Revolutionary War debts that Americans, mostly Virginians, owed to British subjects. He agreed to accept the decision of a mixed commission of British and American citizens regarding American claims for reparations due to British attacks upon American shipping in 1793–1794 and British claims for losses suffered from Genêt's American-based privateers.* In addition, the treaty stipulated that the United States would not export cotton in American ships for ten years, the period of its duration. Nothing was said about impressment of sailors or the rights of American merchant vessels. Indeed, the United States, in effect, renounced the principle of the freedom of the seas by acquiescing to the seizure of American ships carrying contraband, as defined by Great Britain, or cargoes owned by citizens of a nation at war with Great Britain. The effect of this last concession, however, was mitigated by the fact that since early in 1794, the British had permitted American ships to carry to Europe cargoes originating in the French West Indies provided that those cargoes were first brought to the United States, where, presumably, they became American property.

Opposition to Jay's Treaty. In the United States, the initial reaction to Jay's Treaty was shock and dismay. Jay was burned in effigy, and Alexander Hamilton was stoned in New York while trying to make a speech in defense of the treaty. President Washington at first thought that its faults outweighed its merits. Even many northern merchants condemned Jay's handiwork. But when they considered the alternatives to the treaty—and war with Great Britain could not be ruled out—their objections diminished. The Senate ratified Jay's Treaty by a narrow and purely partisan vote but not before it had struck out the section relating to trade with the British West Indies (the tonnage of the ships

*The United States, as a result of the decisions handed down by these commissions, paid about $3 million in satisfaction of the prewar debts, while the British paid over $6 million for the illegal seizures of American ships in 1793–1794.

This engraving shows John Jay being hung in effigy by opponents of the treaty he negotiated with Great Britain. *Picture: New York State Historical Association, Cooperstown, N. Y.*

permitted by Jay's Treaty was too small to be of any value) and the prohibition upon the export of cotton and certain other commodities in American ships.

Even these changes did not reconcile the Republicans to Jay's Treaty. Jefferson declared that Jay's handiwork belonged in the annals of treason rather than of diplomacy. Republicans could not accept a treaty which struck them as an abject surrender of American rights, a virtual alliance with Great Britain, and a long stride toward monarchism. Above all, they deplored the treaty because it deprived the United States of the economic weapons with which the Republicans hoped to compel Great Britain to acknowledge the full complement of the neutral rights claimed by the United States. By giving Great Britain most-favored-nation treatment in United States ports, Jay's Treaty precluded the use of embargoes, nonimportation agreements, boycotts, sequestrations, and the other instruments of peaceful coercion against the island kingdom. Republicans could account for the abandonment of America's freedom of action only by the supposition that Jay had been corrupted by British gold.

Under this conviction, the Republicans made a determined effort to block Jay's Treaty in the House of Representatives, which, they asserted, enjoyed concurrent power with the Senate in approving or disapproving treaties. But when the House demanded to see the papers relevant to Jay's Treaty, President Washington declined on the ground that the disclosure of such papers was not in the national interest. Smarting under this rebuff, the Republican leaders tried to hold up the appropriation of $90,000 necessary to carry Jay's Treaty into execution. The struggle took the form not merely of a contest between Republicans and Federalists but between the President and Congress.

Although the President and the Federalists won—the House finally appropriated the necessary funds—Washington sacrificed his reputation as a president above politics. After Jay's Treaty and Washington's denunciation of the Democratic Societies as a network of subversive clubs modeled upon the Jacobin clubs of France, he appeared to Republicans as a Federalist partisan and much too fond of his "monarchical" prerogatives. It was for this reason that a Republican journalist urged Americans to celebrate Washington's retirement from the presidency as "A Day of Jubilee."

The Rapprochement Between the United States and Great Britain. As Jefferson and Madison feared, Jay's Treaty marked the beginning of a rapprochement between the United States and Great Britain. In 1796 the Northwest Posts were finally transferred to the United States, and until the War of 1812, no British troops occupied American soil. Trade between the two countries brought prosperity to American merchants, and an ever increasing share of the carrying trade of Europe continued to pass into American hands. During the Wars of the French Revolution and the Napoleonic Wars, the assertion of American rights was always less to the financial advantage of American merchants and shipowners than was the policy of acquiescing to the rules laid down by British sea power. With some justice, British shipowners, through their spokesmen in Parliament, pronounced that Jay's Treaty was inimical to their interests. Indeed, the strongest opposition to the rapprochement between the United States and Great Britain came from British shipowners who felt that the ministry was seeking to cultivate good relations with the United States at the expense of the British merchant marine.

The Treaty with Spain, 1795. Jay's Treaty was denounced by Republicans as a victory of northern commerce over the southern agricultural interest. Yet the South, too, received a boon in 1795 with the ratification of the treaty negotiated with the Spanish government at San Lorenzo by William Pinckney. Pinckney's treaty owed more to Jay's Treaty than the Republicans were prepared to acknowledge. The Spanish government was persuaded that Jay's Treaty made the United States and Great Britain virtually, if not in fact, allies

THE GROWTH OF THE MERCHANT MARINE, 1790-1815

VESSELS ENTERING AMERICAN PORTS

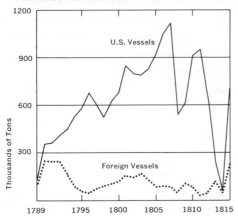

To help the American shipping industry, the First Congress passed discriminating import duties, which imposed higher duties on merchandise imported in foreign vessels and charged higher tonnage taxes for foreign vessels. These advantages and the European war, which increased the demand for American goods and gave American shipping a large carrying trade, caused a rapid growth in the shipping industry. Consequently, the merchants disliked the embargo and the war, which may have defended their maritime rights, but also ruined their booming business. *Source: Historical Statistics of the United States.*

VESSELS CARRYING AMERICAN TRADE

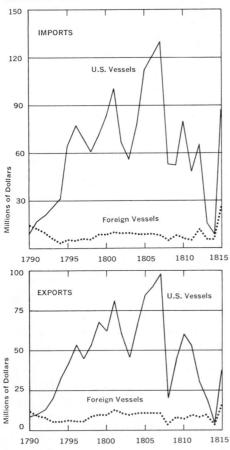

and sought protection of its American frontiers against a joint Anglo-American attack. Spain offered to accept the United States' claim of the thirty-first parallel as its southern boundary from Georgia to the Mississippi River. In addition, it offered American citizens the privileges of navigating the Mississippi through Spanish territory and of maintaining entrepôt at New Orleans. This so-called right of deposit enabled Americans to use the port of New Orleans for the transshipment of goods to Europe. Pinckney's treaty began the long retreat of Spain in the New World which did not end until 1898, when Cuba, "the pearl of the Antilles," gained its independence.

Washington Leaves Office

Political Parties and Foreign Partisanship. Jay's Treaty had been ratified against the opposition of the French minister in the United States as well as that of the Republican party. From the beginning of the French alliance in 1778, French ministers in the United States had interfered in the domestic affairs as well as the foreign policy of their ally. Genêt was by no means the only offender. His successors acted with greater subtlety and decorum, but the fine hand of the French Directory, which came into power in 1795, repeatedly revealed itself in Philadelphia. In particular, Fauchet and Adet, the French ministers in the United States from 1794 to 1797, bent every effort to defeat Jay's Treaty, even going to the length of lobbying in Congress. After the ratification of the treaty, Adet continued to work against it, joining the Republican opposition for that purpose.

President Washington believed that French influence had penetrated even the executive department. Edmund Randolph, Jefferson's successor as secretary of state, was accused of intriguing with the French minister. Although he protested his innocence, Randolph resigned under a cloud. Washington thereupon reorganized his cabinet so as to include only bona fide Federalists. Timothy Pickering of Massachusetts became secretary of state.

The root of the trouble, as the President saw it, was not in France but in the United States. Because the American people had become infected with partisanship for one or the other of the European belligerents, they had opened the door to foreign influence. Until they thought and acted like Americans, he said, rather than as transplanted Europeans, they could not attain the kind of independence to which they had looked forward in 1783. He detected, moreover, a close connection between political parties, sectionalism, and foreign influence in the United States. If the French minister were a power in American politics, it was because the Republican party had made him so.

President Washington himself was almost wholly immune to partisanship between the European belligerents. Throughout his two administrations, he tried to hold an even balance between France and Great Britain. He came as close an any American President has ever come to being neutral in thought as well as in deed.

Washington's Farewell Address. French intervention in American affairs, sectionalism, and the growth of political parties and the partisan feeling to which they gave expression provided President Washington with the text of his Farewell Address to the American people. He and Alexander Hamilton drew up the paper in the summer of 1796 after the President had decided not to stand for a third term. Hamilton, then a practicing attorney in New York, served as the President's collaborator but not as his ghost-writer. Washington took this opportunity to give the American people what he thought to be some badly needed advice. He urged them to renounce partisan politics, sectionalism, and foreign sympathies and antipathies and present a united front to the outside world. He called for an overriding sense of Americanism which would give priority to national interests. Because he believed that the United States had a wholly different set of interests from those of European countries, he recommended that the United States avoid, as a general rule, permanent foreign alliances. The true policy of the United States, he said, was "to be upon friendly terms with, but independent of all, the nations of the earth. To share in the broils of none. To fulfill our own engagements. To supply the wants, and be the carriers for them all."

This address, which was never delivered orally but printed in the newspapers in September 1796, was not as isolationist as it appeared to succeeding generations. Among the engagements Washington advised the American people to fulfill was the French alliance. Moreover, in warning his countrymen against becoming too deeply involved in European affairs, he did not rule out the possibility that future events might make such alliances imperative. Washington was far too experienced in the ways of the world to seek to bind the American people to a certain course of action in all contingencies. On the contrary, he conceded that "temporary alliances for extraordinary emergencies" might be in the national interest.

The Election of 1796

Washington's refusal to run for a third term, which established a tradition in American politics that was not broken until 1940, set the stage for a spirited contest for the presidency, the first of its kind in American history. But contrary to Washington's injunctions, foreign sympathies, sectionalism, and partisan politics all played a conspicuous part in the campaign. John Adams, the Federalist candidate, was described as a pro-British monocrat who aspired to an American throne, whereas Thomas Jefferson, who had been brought out of retirement by the Republicans, was made to appear as a pro-French Jacobin who, if elected President, would rule as a French proconsul. The French minister, although he had no illusions that Jefferson was anything but an American at heart, openly supported the Republican candidate. He even threatened the United States with the dire displeasure of the Great Republic, as the French styled their country, if John Adams should become President.

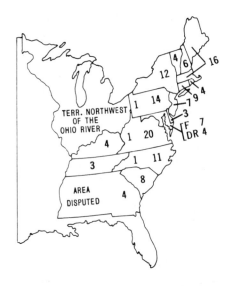

THE ELECTION OF 1796

ELECTORAL VOTE
BY STATE

FEDERALIST
John Adams   71

REPUBLICAN
Thomas Jefferson   68
                             ———
                             139

American voters braved the displeasure of France by electing John Adams to the presidency. But the margin of the New Englander's victory was precariously small. In the electoral college, Adams received 71 votes compared with 68 for Jefferson. As the Constitution directed, Jefferson, having the second-highest number of votes in the electoral college, became vice-president.* This arrangement, which was changed in 1804 by the adoption of the Twelfth Amendment, was due to the fact that the framers of the Constitution had not foreseen the rise of political parties. The leader of the opposition to President Adams was Vice-President Jefferson.

Moreover, the sectional nature of the vote indicated that Americans had not heeded Washington's warnings against sectional rivalries. In the states south of the Mason-Dixon line and the Ohio River, Adams received only two electoral votes. He lost South Carolina, a former Federalist stronghold. His was the most sectional election prior to that of Abraham Lincoln, who received no electoral votes in the South. Jefferson carried Pennsylvania, which made him a less completely sectional candidate than Adams.

The Crisis with France, 1794–1797

From 1793 to the War of 1812, whatever was gained in better relations with one belligerent was usually offset by a worsening of relations with the other. Thus, Jay's Treaty led to a deterioration of relations with France. In addition to Jay's Treaty, the French government was displeased about the election of John Adams and the recall in 1797 of James Monroe as minister to France. Monroe

---

*In the electoral college, or more precisely the state electoral colleges, each elector cast his ballot for two candidates. The individual receiving the largest number of votes became President, the man who stood second in the poll became vice-president. If no candidate received a majority of the total votes cast, the election was transferred to the House of Representatives.

had earned his popularity in France by the ardor with which he took the French side in every dispute, including those with his own country. In consequence, although France was dependent upon the American merchant marine, the French government decreed in 1797 that any neutral carrying any British merchandise whatever was a lawful prize. Under this order, French privateers* began to seize American ships in the West Indies and along the Atlantic seaboard, while the French government confiscated American ships in French ports.

The XYZ Affair. Instead of meeting force with force, as many prominent members of his party demanded, President Adams tried to employ diplomacy to avert war with France. Even though the French Directory refused in 1797 to receive Charles Cotesworth Pinckney as United States minister to France, the President dispatched John Marshall and Elbridge Gerry to join Pinckney in France and demand reparation for damage inflicted upon American shipping and a guaranty that France would respect American neutral rights. But three American ministers proved no more effective than one. The Directory refused to receive the American plenipotentiaries, and the attacks upon American merchantmen continued. Finally Talleyrand, the French foreign minister, acting through intermediaries who later appeared in the American version of these events as X, Y, and Z, gave the American representatives to understand that the United States might procure an accommodation with France by a public apology on the part of President Adams for derogatory remarks he had made about the French Directory, by a loan to France, and by a bribe to Talleyrand.

Although the American envoys were prepared to contribute some sweetening in the form of a bribe to get negotiations started—every nation, including Great Britain, made a practice of paying the Directory a *douceur*—Talleyrand's other demands struck them as extortionate. Marshall and Pinckney demanded their passports, but Elbridge Gerry remained in Paris, fearful that a complete diplomatic break would foreclose all hope of a peaceful settlement. But conflict between the two "allies" seemed inevitable. When the correspondence between the American ministers and Talleyrand's agents was made public by President Adams, the country was swept by a wave of patriotic fervor. "Millions for Defense but not one cent for tribute" became the slogan of the day. The President and the Federalist majority in Congress prepared for war. The Army was increased in size, and three of the six frigates ordered in 1794 but never completed were made ready for action. In 1798 the Department of the Navy was created. George Washington was called out of retirement to command the Army, and Alexander Hamilton, over President Adam's opposition, was appointed a major general and second-in-command.

War Fever. Partisan feeling ran high in the United States. The Reverend Timothy Dwight, a rabid Federalist, said that although every Democrat was not

---

*A privateer was an armed vessel privately owned and operated but licensed by a government at war to capture as prizes merchant vessels belonging to enemy owners, carrying enemy cargoes, or trading with the enemy.

a horse thief, yet every horse thief was a Democrat. Federalists stigmatized the Republican party as a Jacobin faction composed of ingrates, subversives, and traitors who, if they came to power, would repeat the worst excesses of the French Revolution in the United States. Jefferson complained that Federalists cut him on the street and that the atmosphere of every social gathering was poisoned with political rancor. The contagion affected the proceedings of Congress. The Federalist majority not only prepared the country militarily for war: without waiting for a formal declaration of hostilities by Congress, it undertook to muzzle the press, to curtail freedom of speech, to expel foreign-born "agitators," and to proscribe the Republican party as disloyal.

The Alien and Sedition Acts

In July 1798 with these objectives very much in mind, the Federalist-controlled Congress enacted, by a strict party vote, the Sedition, Naturalization, and Alien Acts. The Sedition Act imposed wartime restraints upon freedom of speech and of the press. The use in speech or writing of "false, scandalous and malicious" words which reflected contempt and disrespect upon the President, Congress, or the government, was made punishable by fine of not more than $2000 and imprisonment for a period not to exceed two years. The Sedition Act liberalized common law by allowing truth as a defense in cases of libel and by permitting the jury to decide whether the matter upon which the proceedings were based was actually libelous. But, in practice, these safeguards of the rights of the accused were largely inoperative. Tried by Federalist juries (handpicked by Federalist officials) before Federalist judges, Republicans found that the case was really predetermined against them.

As a result, the list of those convicted, imprisoned, and fined for seditious libel reads like a roster of the prominent Republican newspaper editors. One Republican Congressman, Matthew Lyon of Vermont, was imprisoned and fined $1000, and Dr. Thomas Cooper, an English scientist and scholar, drew a six-month sentence. Despite fifteen indictments brought under the Sedition Act and ten convictions procured in Federal courts, the Federalists did not succeed in silencing the Republican press. On the contrary, two newspapers and a dozen writers seemed to spring up for every newspaper that was muzzled and every journalist who was put behind bars.

The Naturalization Act increased from five to fourteen years the probationary period required of resident aliens who wished to become citizens. The Alien Act gave the President power to order the deportation at his discretion of aliens whose presence he deemed inimical to the security of the United States. These laws were really aimed at the Republican party. Immigrants tended to become Republicans—hence the difficulties placed in the way of naturalization. Moreover, some of the foreigners who had taken residence in the United States were British journalists who, having been hounded out of Great Britain for allegedly subversive activities, came to the United States where they continued their journalistic careers. They simply changed their target from the government of George III to that of President John Adams.

The Alien and Naturalization Acts served little purpose. No foreigner was deported under the Alien Act, although some French émigrés left the country lest they be removed by executive decree. Since the states retained until 1810 the power to grant naturalization, the Naturalization Act had little effect. Some of the more obnoxious British journalists in the United States took out naturalization papers in Pennsylvania and New York and thereby placed themselves beyond the reach of the Alien as well as the Naturalization Acts.

Opposition to the Alien and Sedition Acts. Instead of fostering national union, the quasi war with France exacerbated differences between the Federalists and Republicans over foreign policy and civil liberties. By stigmatizing the Republicans as partisans of France, the Federalists forfeited any chance of converting the struggle with France into a patriotic war.

Jefferson considered the Sedition Act to be as unconstitutional as an order from Congress to bow down and worship a graven image. Even more than the act itself, Jefferson feared the implications of the theory upon which it was based. According to the Federalists, the Sedition Act found sanction not only in the government's right to act for its own preservation but also in its jurisdiction over all cases arising under common law. By extending federal authority throughout the range of the common law, the federal government would be authorized to legislate upon all subjects not specifically excluded by the Constitution itself. In this doctrine, Jefferson foresaw the destruction of the state courts, the annihilation of state sovereignty, and the triumph of Hamiltonian consolidationism and monarchism. Yet Jefferson refused to approve the kind of overt resistance to the federal government contemplated by John Taylor of Carolina and other militants. Jefferson insisted that the remedy must be peaceful: "the reign of witches," he said, would soon be over when the people awakened from the spell cast by the Federalist necromancers.

The Virginia and Kentucky Resolutions. Accordingly, Jefferson took this opportunity to put to the test his theory that when the people were told the truth they would cast aside the error they had impetuously and unwittingly embraced. In 1798–1800 he and Madison drew up a series of resolutions which their friends submitted to the Kentucky and Virginia legislatures without disclosing their authorship. In these resolutions, Jefferson and Madison argued that the Sedition Act went beyond the enumerated powers granted Congress and violated the First Amendment, which prohibited any laws "abridging the freedom of speech or of the press." They took the position that the Constitution was actually a compact between the peoples of thirteen distinct sovereign states, not the people of a single unitary jurisdiction. Among the reserved rights of the states was the power of interpreting the Constitution with a view to determining the constitutionality of measures adopted by Congress or the executive.

To prevent the enforcement of what they regarded as a palpable violation of the Constitution, Jefferson and Madison urged the states to interpose their authority. While Jefferson favored an assertion of the right of a single state to nullify unilaterally an act of Congress which it deemed unconstitutional, Madison thought that the collective action of the states was required. The word nullification did not appear in the first set of resolutions written by Jefferson and adopted by the Kentucky legislature, but the resolutions did declare that each state was to be the judge of the mode of resistance to take. Jefferson's radicalism increased as the crisis deepened. In a second set of resolutions drawn up in 1799 by the vice-president for the consideration of the Kentucky legislature, Jefferson at first intimated that secession ought to be a final constitutional resort. Although Madison dissuaded Jefferson from broaching a doctrine which he feared would recoil upon its sponsors, the second Kentucky resolutions did contain the word *nullification.*

In the minds of their framers, the cardinal purpose of the Virginia and Kentucky resolutions was to preserve the "beautiful equilibrium" established by the Constitution between the states and the general government. Regarded in this light, these documents furnished an answer not only to the Alien and Sedition Acts but to the reports of Alexander Hamilton and to much of the legislation enacted during the Washington administration. Against the permissive or broad interpretation of the Constitution favored by Hamilton, the Virginians put forward the strict, state-rights interpretation together with a theory of the origin and nature of the Constitution which would have forever precluded the exercise by the federal government of many powers which it employs today as a matter of course.

The Virginia and Kentucky resolutions were intended to serve as instructions to the states' senators and as a clarion call to other states. But not a single state took its stand alongside Virginia and Kentucky. Many states simply ignored the resolutions altogether, but Massachusetts went to the trouble of informing the Virginians and Kentuckians that the final interpretation of the Constitution rested with the United States Supreme Court, not with the states.

While the Virginia and Kentucky resolutions suggested a remedy that was too radical for other state legislatures, they did serve the purpose of sowing doubt in the public mind as to the constitutionality of the Sedition Act. Finally, the Virginia and Kentucky resolutions enabled the Republicans to go into the presidential and congressional elections of 1800 as the champions of freedom against the "reign of terror" waged by the Federalists against civil liberties.

The Undeclared War with France

In July 1798 when the Federalists enacted the Sedition, Naturalization, and Alien acts, they assumed that war between the United States and France was inevitable. But war, usually so responsive to the call of statesmen, proved unexpectedly coy and elusive. In Congress, the Federalists lacked a majority in favor of a declaration of war, and President Adams, despite his earlier bellicosity, made no move to take the lead of the war party. In consequence, the Federalists put their hopes in a declaration of war by France. Although the record of the Great Republic in its dealings with smaller powers warranted the expectation of prompt and decisive action, the Directory seemed strangely unmoved by the defiance of the United States. It, too, issued no declaration of war.

Despite the absence of a formal declaration of war, hostilities were carried on at sea. By 1800 fourteen American men-of-war were at sea, and special commissions had been given to the owners of hundreds of private ships authorizing them to capture French armed vessels. As a result, the coastal waters of the United States were quickly cleared of French privateers. Thereafter, most of the fighting occurred in the Caribbean, where ships of the United States Navy clashed with French frigates. Early in 1799 Captain Thomas Truxton met in battle the French frigate *L'Insurgente,* and the Frenchman struck his colors. In February 1800 Truxton so heavily damaged the *Vengeance* that it was put permanently out of action.

War Taxes. To finance the war with France, the federal government resorted for the first time to direct taxation. In 1798 a tax was laid upon land, houses, and slaves. But the actual yield from the tax was disappointingly small. The Federal government lacked the means of collecting the tax, and some states refused to cooperate. No longer was the United States able to borrow money on easy terms from Dutch bankers: in 1795 Holland had been conquered by France. In consequence, the government was obliged to pay a higher rate of interest on its borrowings than at any time since 1789.

While the United States Navy was gaining laurels, the Army was experiencing the boredom of inactivity. No invading French army gave it occupation. Instead, the soldiers marched and drilled and marched and drilled again to prepare to fight a seemingly nonexistent enemy. In fact, the Army's only opportunity to make itself useful came in 1799 when John Fries led a local uprising in Pennsylvania against the federal land tax. Although the disturbance was no more than a riot, it was magnified into an insurrection. President Adams ordered several thousand troops into the area to preserve order. Although Fries and several of his followers were arrested, convicted of treason, and sentenced to death, President Adams, to the chagrin of the Hamiltonian Federalists, gave them an executive pardon.

Adams Acts to End the War. The war had a disruptive effect upon the Federalist party as well as upon the Union. In February 1799 President Adams, resentful of the growing influence of Alexander Hamilton and convinced in his own mind that American victories at sea had brought the enemy to terms, responded to the Directory's peace overtures by submitting to the Senate the nomination of William Vans Murray, the American minister at the Hague, as peace commissioner.

Federalist Opposition to Peace. But Adams' efforts to get out of a war in which he no longer saw political or military profit were opposed by some of the

In the battle between the *Constellation and L'Insurgente*, twenty-nine Frenchmen and one American died before the French commander struck his colors. *Picture: Franklin D. Roosevelt Library*

most powerful members of his party, among them, Alexander Hamilton and Secretary of State Timothy Pickering. Hamilton wished the United States to remain in the war in order to profit from the expected downfall of France, and he even considered an alliance with Great Britain for the liberation of Spanish America. The Federalist-dominated Senate refused to consent to the appointment of William Vans Murray as peace negotiator. The best that Adams could do was to obtain the appointment of a three-man commission headed by Chief Justice Ellsworth of the United States Supreme Court to enter into peace talks with the Directory. Although Hamilton and Pickering succeeded in delaying the departure of these emissaries—it was a mission they devoutly hoped would end in failure—the trio finally set sail for France in November 1799.

The Election of 1800

Even the Federalists who opposed peace had to admit that the war was becoming unpopular. As Jefferson had predicted, the tax-gatherer helped put an end to the "reign of witches" by fostering peace sentiment. In the spring of 1800, therefore, the Federalists began to cut back the size of the armed forces in preparation for the presidential election of 1800. Despite their victories in the congessional elections of 1798, the Federalists could not relax. In 1799 they lost control of Pennsylvania, and in May 1800 Aaron Burr and the Republican party scored a victory over the Federalists by gaining control of the New York legislature, which, like most of the state legislatures, controlled the state's vote in the electoral college.

Hamilton's Opposition to Adams. Despite this reverse, Alexander Hamilton widened the breach within the Federalist party by intriguing in several state legislatures to put Charles C. Pinckney, the Federalist vice-presidential candidate, ahead of John Adams in the electoral college. When Hamilton's maneuvers were exposed, he wrote a pamphlet which was intended only for the eyes of the party leaders but which was given to the press by Aaron Burr, who accidentally obtained a copy. In it he subjected the character of President Adams to a devastating psychological analysis. After pronouncing Adams to be a man of distempered jealousy and of weak character, Hamilton lamely concluded that Adams ought to be supported for reelection. But the real purpose of Hamilton's pamphlet was to make Pinckney appear the better man.

The Federalists could ill afford this division within their ranks. The Republicans were pressing them hard on every side. In contrast to the strife-torn Federalists, the Republicans united behind Thomas Jefferson and Aaron Burr. The party stood for peace with France, economy in the government, strict observance of states' rights and of the First Amendment. John Adams sat out the campaign in Braintree, Massachusetts, where, indeed, he had spent most of his presidency. Nor did Jefferson actively solicit votes. When not rusticating at Monticello, he attended to his duties as vice-president. Yet Jefferson had working for him a large number of devoted Republicans. In the final results, the dedication of the Republicans and their superior organization proved decisive: Jefferson received 73 electoral votes compared with 65 for Adams and 64 for Pinckney. In the congressional elections, the Republicans won control of both houses of Congress. In the House of Representatives on March 4, 1801, there would be 65 Republicans to 41 Federalists.

The election results revealed that the Jeffersonian Republicans had succeeded in forming a national party. Although Adams won a scattering of electoral votes in Delaware, Maryland, and North Carolina and carried all of the New England states, Jefferson and Burr garnered most of the electoral votes of Pennsylvania and New York together with all the votes of South Carolina, Virginia, Georgia, Kentucky, and Tennessee. Yet the election was closely contested: the Republicans' victory was won in the key states of New York and South Carolina.

In the election, President Adams ran better than his party. Like Jefferson, he was a peace candidate. Later he said that he wished to have the fact that he had sent emissaries to France put on his gravestone. But peace did not come in time to help Adams: it was not until after the election that France and the United States agreed to a convention which put an end to the undeclared war. Ratified by the United States Senate in 1801, this convention abrogated the Franco-American treaty of alliance of 1778 and made the United States government financially responsible for most of the depredations suffered by American shipowners and merchants during the undeclared war. As a result,

Jefferson became the first President of the United States who was wholly free of an entangling alliance.

A Tie Vote. Decisive as it was, the Republican victory created a dilemma which no other political party has ever been obliged to face. To demonstrate his party loyalty, every Republican elector who voted for Jefferson also voted for Aaron Burr. As a result, Jefferson and Burr were tied in the electoral college with 73 votes apiece.* In case of a tie, the Constitution provided that the election should be made by the House of Representatives, each state voting as a unit and casting one vote. In February 1801, accordingly, the House of Representatives began balloting for a President and vice-president of the United States.

Efforts to Elect Burr. Imbued with fear and hatred of Jefferson, the Federalists tried to defeat the will of the majority of the people of the United States by making Aaron Burr President. Despite Hamilton's warnings that they were admitting the Grecian horse into the federal Troy, every Federalist in the House of Representatives voted for the New Yorker. To them, Burr seemed manageable, reasonable, and devoid of the principles which made Jefferson dangerous. Moreover, Burr was not a Virginian. He was born in New Jersey, educated at the College of New Jersey, and after distinguished service in the American Army, settled in New York to practice law. Burr was descended from Jonathan Edwards, the eminent Congregationalist divine.

Fortunately for Jefferson and for the peace of the country, the Federalists lacked the power to make Burr President. Although numerically preponderant in the House, the Federalists controlled the votes of only six states. When the first ballots were taken, Jefferson had eight states, Burr had six and two were divided. While Jefferson had to gain the vote of only one additional state, Burr had to pick up three. In terms of individual members of Congress, Jefferson could win by securing the vote of one Federalist—James Bayard of Delaware, the sole representative of his state–whereas Burr needed to change the votes of at least four Republican members of Congress. Burr was told by his Federalist supporters that three of these key congressmen presented no problem: one was a blockhead and the other two were willing to be corrupted. Yet Burr made no move. He remained in Albany, New York, leaving the corruption, if it proved necessary, to his Federalist friends. On the other hand, Burr did not take himself out of the race by declaring that he would not serve if elected.

Jefferson's Election. With the inauguration only two weeks away and despite threats of civil war, the Federalists persisted in their course until the thirty-fifth ballot when James Bayard of Delaware, disgusted by Burr's refusal to cooperate and convinced in his own mind that Jefferson had given assurances—later denied by Jefferson—that he would administer the govern-

---

*It proved to be the last time a political party has suffered from an embarrassment of votes in the Electoral College. The Twelfth Amendment, adopted in 1804, directed electors to designate their choice for President and vice-president.

THE ELECTION OF 1800

ELECTORAL VOTE
BY STATE

REPUBLICAN
Thomas Jefferson   73

FEDERALIST
John Adams   65
                                   ___
                                   138

ment in a manner agreeable to the Federalists, announced that he would vote for Jefferson on the next ballot. His defection meant that, for the Federalists, the game was up. Yet, rather than vote for Jefferson, the Federalist members of the evenly divided Vermont and Maryland delegations simply abstained from voting on the thirty-sixth ballot, thereby delivering the votes of those states to Jefferson. Not a single Federalist congressman, not even Bayard who had broken the impasse, voted for Jefferson. Ten states voted for Jefferson, the New England states, with the exception of Vermont, continued to vote for Burr, and two states declined to vote. The Federalists went down to defeat with their prejudices and antipathies nailed proudly to the masthead.

SUGGESTED READING

Political developments, especially the rise of political parties, have attracted the attention of a number of scholars. Among the books particularly relevant to the Jeffersonian period are Lisle A. Rose, *Prologue to Democracy: The Federalists in the South, 1789–1800* (1968); Roy F. Nichols, *The Invention of the American Political Parties* (1967); Richard Hofstadter, *The Idea of a Party System: The Rise of Legitimate Opposition in the United States, 1780–1840** (1969); David Fischer, *The Revolution of American Conservatism** (1965); Shaw Livermore, Jr., *The Twilight of Federalism* (1962); Morton Borden, *Parties and Politics in the Early Republic, 1789–1815** (1967); John P. Roche, ed., *Origins of American Political Thought: Selected Readings** (1967); Paul Goodman, ed., *The Federalists vs. the Jeffersonian Republicans** (1967). William Nisbet Chambers and Walter Dean Burnham have edited *The American Party Systems: Stages of Political Development** (1967).

*Available in a paperback edition

Some recent biographies of prominent political figures of the period are Robert Ernst and Rufus King, *American Federalist* (1968); Winfred E. Bernhard and Fisher Ames, *Federalist & Statesman, 1758–1800* (1965); Lynn W. Turner, *William Plumer of New Hampshire, 1759–1850* (1962); Frank Monaghan, *John Jay: Defender of Liberty* (1935).

Since 1950—the era of Senator Joseph McCarthy—the Alien and Sedition Acts and the Virginia and Kentucky Resolutions have attracted the attention of historians. Among the fruits of the investigations made by historians in the past two decades are James Morton Smith, *Freedom's Fetters: The Alien & Sedition Laws & American Civil Liberties** (1956); J. C. Miller, *Crisis in Freedom: The Alien & Sedition Acts ** (1951); Dumas Malone, *Thomas Jefferson and the Ordeal of Liberty** (1962); Marshall Smelser, "George Washington and the Alien and Sedition Acts," *American Historical Review,* LIX (1954).

Foreign affairs during the Federalist period are examined by Samuel F. Bemis in *Jay's Treaty: A Study in Commerce and Diplomacy** (revised ed., 1962) and *Pinckney's Treaty* (1926). Other important studies are Gerald S. Graham, *Sea Power and British North America, 1783–1820: A Study in British Colonial Policy* (1941); Bradford Perkins, *The First Rapprochement: England and the United States, 1795–1805* (1955); Alexander De Conde, *The Quasi-War: The Politics & Diplomacy of the Undeclared War with France, 1797–1801** (1966); Felix Gilbert, *To the Farewell Address: Ideas of Early American Foreign Policy** (1961); Arthur P. Whitaker, *The Spanish-American Frontier, 1783–1795* and *The Mississippi Question, 1795–1803* (1934); H. G. Barnby, *The Prisoners of Algiers: An Account of the Forgotten American-Algerian War, 1785–1797* (1966); A. T. Mahan, *The Influence of Sea Power upon the French Revolution and Empire, 1793–1812,* 2 vols (1898).

The politics of the Adams administration are examined by Stephen G. Kurtz, *The Presidency of John Adams** (1957); Manning J. Dauer, *The Adams Federalists** (1953); Page Smith, *John Adams,* 2 vols., (1962); Gilbert Chinard, *Honest John Adams** (1933); Octavius Pickering and Charles W. Upham, *The Life of Timothy Pickering,* 4 vols., (1867–1873); Henry Cabot Lodge, *The Life and Letters of George Cabot* (1877).

CHAPTER FIVE

JEFFERSON'S PRESIDENCY

THOMAS JEFFERSON DESCRIBED the election of 1800 as a revolution which deserved to rank with that of 1776. Yet, clearly, it was a political revolution only if judged by Jefferson's standards. In his opinion, the true republicans had wrested control of the government from a monarchical faction which had established itself in power while the people slept. It was not a case of "turning the rascals out," which would have brought the election within the normal American frame of reference, but of "turning the monarchists out," which put it in the realm of revolution or counterrevolution.

The Harmonious Revolution

Jefferson's Inaugural. Jefferson's first inaugural address did not indicate a revolutionary spirit. He made clear that he intended to follow the foreign policy laid down by Washington: neutrality in the European war and peace and commerce with all nations. Jefferson went beyond Washington in warning Americans against the baneful effects of "entangling alliances," a phrase not used by Washington. In the spirit of Washington's Farewell Address, the new President urged Americans to bury their political differences and to display the "harmony and affection," without which, he asserted, "liberty and even life itself are but dreary things." Fortunately for Americans, he said, they were in agreement upon fundamentals, an agreement which made republican government possible in the United States. "We are all Federalists, we are all Republicans," he declared. And to prove his point, he promised that his administration would be dedicated to the payment of the national debt, the "sacred preservation of the public faith," and a "wise and frugal government, which shall restrain men from injuring one another, which shall leave them otherwise free to regulate their own pursuits of industry and improvement, and shall not take from the mouth of labor the bread it has earned. This is the sum of good government, and this is all that is necessary to close the circle of our felicities." Within this ample orbit, Jefferson hoped to establish the republican consensus.

Jefferson explicitly disclaimed any sectional bias. He was, he said, an American President, not a southern man in the President's House. Herein lay one of the sources of his strength: he promised to bind up the sectional wounds left by the Federalists' overzealous efforts to centralize power in the United States and to curtail civil liberties. His cardinal purpose, he said, was to make Americans "one people, acting as one nation." He did not repudiate Hamilton's objectives so much as Hamilton's methods of attaining them. Jefferson believed that Americans could be better united by an ideology—a sense of the uniqueness of America and devotion to the ideals upon which the Republic had been founded—than by converting stocks, bonds, and the national debt into a "cement" for the union.

Thomas Jefferson in a portrait by Rembrandt Peale. *Picture: "White House Collection"*

As Jefferson privately admitted, Americans could not be made into one people until Federalism had been sunk "into an abyss from which there will be no resurrection." In this context, federalism meant monarchism. Jefferson distinguished between the rank and file of the party and its leaders. As he saw it, the common run of Federalists were republicans, whereas the leaders hankered after the fleshpots of monarchism. He saw no hope for them. They were, he said, hopeless cases fit only for the madhouse.

Political Patronage. Nevertheless, when making appointments to political office, he did not act upon the dictum "We are all Federalists, we are all Republicans." When he came to the presidency, he found the government staffed almost exclusively by Federalists. Since wholesale removals from office would be certain to inflame party spirit, he adopted the policy of removing incumbents only for flagrant partisan activity. At the end of his second administration, he asserted that he had never deprived a man of office simply because he was a Federalist or because he voted for Federalist candidates. Nevertheless, in some states, notably Connecticut, where the Federalist regime had made a clean sweep of Republicans in the state civil service, Jefferson retaliated by ordering a purge of Federalist officeholders who held their appointments from the federal government.

To Jefferson's way of thinking, the special felicity of the American people was that at last they had a government of republicans by republicans and for republicans. The spirit by which the government was animated after 1800, he asserted, was very different from that which had prevailed under the Federalists: for the first time, the elected officials of the federal government fully trusted the people and their wisdom.

Jeffersonian Simplicity. To signify the triumph of true republicanism, President Jefferson abolished all the monarchical "pomp and parade" introduced by the Federalists and inaugurated the reign of republican simplicity. As the president of a republic of plain farmers, Jefferson affected the garb of a farmer. When Anthony Merry, the British minister, made his first official call, he found the President sitting on a sofa throwing up his slipper and catching it on his toe. But even more egregious departures from protocol were in store for the British minister. At a dinner party at the President's, Merry was left to escort Mrs. Merry to the dinner table while Jefferson, Madison, and the congressmen present gave their arms to the more attractive women.

Despite this carefully contrived air of rusticity, the President's table was loaded with choice viands prepared by a Parisian cook. Jefferson often served as many as eight different wines. No President of the United States surpassed Jefferson as a gourmet. Not only good food but good conversation made dining at President Jefferson's a treat.

The Party Leader. These dinners at the President's also served a political purpose. One of the most revolutionary aspects of his presidency was the success with which he guided congressional legislation into channels marked out by the administration. For the first time in American history, the President became the leader of Congress by being the leader of his party. It was not the first time that the executive department had provided leadership. Hamilton, as secretary of the treasury, had made himself to all intents and purposes the head of a party in Congress, but neither Washington nor John Adams had injected the power of the presidency into the legislative process as did Jefferson. While Jefferson rewarded deserving Republicans with political office—he found that there were not nearly enough to go around—he also counted upon his weekly dinner parties, at which congressmen were usually present, to plant ideas in the legislators' minds and to bring them round to his way of thinking.

Jefferson made clear that his administration was to be a return to the pristine purity of a simple republic rather than an attempt to strike out in a new direction. As he conceived it, the revolution of 1800 was primarily an undoing of Federalist-inspired legislation. His only regret was that he could not undo more of the Federalists' work.

The Heritage from Federalism

The Survival of the Bank. Jefferson was compelled to admit that the scope of the revolution of 1800 was limited by the prior work of Alexander Hamilton. The Hamiltonian gloss seemed to have become part of the Constitution, and the institutions which Hamilton had brought into being seemed to be indistinguishable from the government itself. For example, although Jefferson had vowed that one of his first acts as President would be the liquidation of the unconstitutional Bank of the United States, he received from Secretary of the Treasury Albert Gallatin the unwelcome news that the Bank was essential to the fiscal operations of the government. The Bank, therefore, survived the revolution intact. Jefferson did no more than to sell the government's shares in the Bank to the Baring Brothers, an English financial house, thereby augmenting foreign ownership of the Bank's stock, already a source of concern to Republicans.

While his doubts regarding the constitutionality of the Bank of the United States persisted, Jefferson was not an enemy of all banks. All he asked of them was that they be founded and staffed by Republicans and that they make their resources available to Republicans. In the early Republic, banks became accessory not only to political parties but to individual partisans. Alexander Hamilton, for example, was closely associated with the Bank of New York, while his archrival, Aaron Burr, owed a large measure of his political influence to the Manhattan Bank, which he helped found.

Frugality and Debt Reduction. Although the debt had actually increased only a little over $3 million since 1791, Jefferson estimated the increase at $31 million. After such a "saturnalia" of deficit financing under the Federalists, Jefferson believed that economy in government was essential to save republicanism from the big spenders. He confidently expected that an examination of the Treasury records would disclose Hamilton's defalcations, which, to the

FEDERAL GOVERNMENT FINANCES, 1792-1815

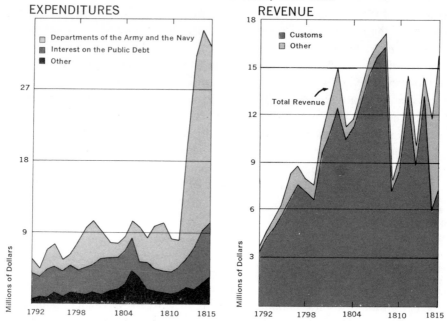

Source: Historical Statistics of the United States.

President's regret, it did not. Although the academy at West Point was established in 1802, the Army provided the President with an opportunity to use the paring knife freely. Nor did the diplomatic service escape. The ministers to Holland, Portugal, and Prussia were recalled, and no successors were appointed.

The President and his Cabinet acted upon the belief that the Republic was in desperate financial straits. In actuality, Jefferson had inherited a good estate from the Federalists. The government's revenues exceeded expenditures, and the Treasury contained a balance of $3 million. Yet Jefferson did not feel that republicanism would be secure until the national debt was totally extinguished. He took no stock in the idea that the growth of the economy and the steady increase in governmental revenue made the payment of the debt relatively unimportant. Jefferson took a doctrinaire position regarding the national debt, but, as the event proved, he did not permit doctrine to prevent the expansion of the territorial boundaries of the United States when a bargain came along.

Jefferson and Civil Liberties. One of the first acts of the Jefferson administration was to repeal the Naturalization Act of 1798 and to reduce the probationary period for aliens from fourteen to five years. The President was denied the satisfaction of repealing the Alien and Sedition Acts: the Alien Act expired in 1800, and the Sedition Act ceased to have effect after March 3, 1801. As regards civil liberties, Jefferson took a much less revolutionary position than might be supposed from a reading of the Virginia resolutions. He had no intention of removing all restraints upon freedom of the press and of speech. To adopt such an extreme position would, he warned, produce licentiousness rather than freedom. Accordingly, while denying cognizance over libel to the federal courts, Jefferson made no move to deprive the state courts of jurisdiction over actions for libel brought by individuals and by the state governments. Every private citizen and government official could take his complaints into a state court where, Jefferson believed, he would find complete justice. In 1804 without doing violence to his principles, Jefferson advised his supporters to institute libel suits in the state courts in order to discipline Federalist journalists.

One of the revolutionary features of his administration, as Jefferson saw it, was the active concern shown by the federal government after 1800 for the welfare of farmers. In keeping with his principles, this concern was manifested mainly by a restriction of governmental functions rather than by an expansion of government services. Jefferson acted upon the belief that the common economic denominator in the American Union was agriculture. A farmers' Republic, he thought, ought to give primacy to the interests of agriculture. But he recognized that Americans, particularly New Englanders, were a seafaring people who could not be kept down on the farm. Jefferson was a political realist, who acted upon the principle that "what is practicable must often control what is pure theory, and the habits of the governed determine in a great degree what is practicable." He saw that the commercial and manufacturing interests of Pennsylvania and New York could not be ignored without destroying the coalition to which the South owed its ascendancy in the federal government.

A New Power Base: The South and West

The election of 1800 resulted in a shift of political power from New England to the South and West, a fact sufficient to make New England Federalists agree with Jefferson's view that it was truly a revolution. For over a generation to come, a succession of Virginia Presidents—the Virginia dynasty—would hold power. The West and the South constituted the power base of the Republican party. The Federalists let the West go virtually by default. Except in the region north of the Ohio River beginning to be settled by New Englanders—Ohio was admitted to statehood in 1803—Federalism made few converts in the West. Indeed, Federalists made no effort to conceal their distrust of the West. In 1796 they opposed the admission of Tennessee. Federalism was a political vintage which did not travel well, particularly if the direction was West.

Although New Englanders found the rule of southern planters quite as insupportable as Jefferson had found the "reign of witches" in 1798–1800, the planters were not as firmly situated in the saddle as the Federalists supposed. Their ascendancy was qualified by the fact that they had to retain the support of New York and Pennsylvania as well as that of the western states. Jefferson said that with Pennsylvania on their side the Republicans could defy the universe, but the interests of Pennsylvania were not necessarily those of Virginia. The Old Dominion furnished much of the political leadership of the early republic, but no southern President was able to pursue purely southern policies without risking the disruption of the party. Jeffersonian democracy was based upon a sectional coalition. The Virginia dynasty existed because the Virginians were able to hold this coalition together.

For this reason, Jefferson admitted that a policy based solely upon agrarianism was not politically feasible. As an astute politician, he strove to strengthen his party where it was weakest—in the business community. Despite the strong Federalist bias of most northern businessmen, Jefferson believed that they belonged within the Republican fold: "a merchant," he said, "is naturally a Republican."

Yet he did not neglect his agrarian allies. In 1802 to the delight of whiskey drinkers everywhere and of the western farmers in particular, the excise was repealed by Congress. But this concession to political expediency did not advance the cause of wine drinking or of sobriety which Jefferson had at heart. Reducing the price of whiskey, he discovered, increased consumption and turned Americans away from wine to the stronger potation.

Jefferson and the Judiciary

Jeffersonian democracy revealed most clearly its revolutionary bent in its encounters with the federal judiciary. Such a collision could hardly have been foreseen in 1788–1789, when Hamilton, writing in the *Federalist,* observed that the judiciary was the weakest of the three departments and was far more likely to suffer encroachments from the other departments than to encroach upon them. And, in fact, during the Federalist period, the judiciary appeared to be much the weakest sister of the three. Two Chief Justices resigned to accept diplomatic and gubernatorial posts, and Washington and Adams had difficulty in filling the bench with competent men.* From 1790 to 1800, the Supreme Court decided only six cases involving important questions of constitutional law. The first United States attorney-general worked only part time for the government because there was not enough work to keep one lawyer fully occupied.

Chisholm v. *Georgia.* When the Supreme Court challenged the power of a state, the judges came off the field ignominiously with their robes trailing in the dust. In 1793 in the case of *Chisholm* v. *Georgia,* the Court upheld the right of a citizen to institute in the Supreme Court an original suit for breach of contract against a state of which he was not a resident. The Georgia legislature

---

*In 1795 President Washington named John Rutledge of South Carolina to the Supreme Court. Rutledge was in disfavor with the Federalists because of his outspoken opposition to Jay's Treaty. His nomination was rejected by the Senate 10–14. The Senate therewith established a precedent which it has frequently followed. Of 129 presidential nominations for positions on the Supreme Court, 28 have failed to obtain Senate confirmation.

proceeded to prevent the execution of the Court's decision. The issue was not resolved until 1798 when the Eleventh Amendment to the Constitution was adopted. This amendment represented a victory of the states over the Court. It provides that "the Judicial power of the United States shall not be construed to extend to any suit in law or equity, commenced or prosecuted against one of the United States by a citizen of another State, or by Citizens or Subjects of any foreign State." The justices of the Supreme Court thereupon beat a strategic retreat from the high ground to which they had laid claim in 1793. In the case of *Calder* v. *Bull* (1798), the Court acknowledged that it had no power to declare a state law unconstitutional on the ground that it was in conflict with the state constitution.

On the other hand, in 1796 the Supreme Court asserted the supremacy of national treaties over state laws and upheld the constitutionality of a tax imposed upon carriages by the federal government. Yet in 1800 former chief justice John Jay declined reappointment to the bench because, he said, the Court was wholly lacking in "energy, weight and dignity."

In 1801, however, the federal judiciary was girded for battle with Jeffersonian democracy. President John Adams appointed John Marshall chief justice of the Supreme Court after Marshall had served a brief tour of duty as secretary of state. At the same time, faced with the impending loss of the executive and legislative departments to the Republicans, the Federalist-controlled lame duck Congress enlarged the jurisdiction of the federal courts, increased the number of district courts and judges, and relieved the justices of the Supreme Court of the necessity of presiding over circuit courts in all parts of the Union—a requirement which, Gouverneur Morris observed, obliged them to combine the agility of jockeys with the erudition of savants. Since such paragons were not readily found, the administration of justice in federal courts was slow and expensive. Prisoners were sometimes confined in jail for months waiting trial.

The Question of Judicial Review. As the Federalists well knew, the Judiciary Act of 1801 was certain to bring down the wrath of the incoming President and his party. A onetime defender of the doctrine of judicial review, Jefferson had become sharply critical both of the practices of the justices of the Supreme Court in declaring acts passed by the state legislatures unconstitutional and of the evident enthusiasm with which the justices enforced the Sedition Act. After the passage of the Judiciary Act of 1801, Jefferson felt certain that the Federalists intended to use the judiciary to create a consolidated, monarchial government.

Accordingly, in March 1802 the Judiciary Act of 1801 was repealed, and a new judiciary act was adopted which cut back the number of judges to the pre-1801 figure, confined the jurisdiction of the federal courts to the limits authorized by the Judiciary Act of 1789, and again required the justices of the Supreme Court to ride circuit. Not until 1875 did the federal courts regain the powers they had briefly enjoyed in 1801–1802.

President Jefferson and his party had made their decision with regard to the federal judiciary. It remained to be seen whether Chief Justice Marshall and his colleagues would permit them to enforce it. Yet, instead of declaring the Judiciary Act of 1802 unconstitutional, as the Federalists expected, Marshall bided his time. In 1803 to the astonishment of the Republicans and the mortification of the Federalists, the Supreme Court upheld the constitutionality of the Judiciary Act of 1802.

Marbury v. *Madison.* John Marshall, as adroit a politician as Jefferson himself, fought only on ground of his own choosing. In 1803 he chose a relatively unimportant case to deliver a lecture to the President and the secretary of state on their constitutional duties and to assert the right of the Supreme Court to declare acts of Congress unconstitutional.

The case arose from the Judiciary Act of 1801. In order to fill the offices created by that act, President Adams labored until nine o'clock of the night of March 3, 1801. Despite this exemplary industry, not all the commissions could be delivered before he vacated the presidency the next day. When Jefferson took office, Secretary of State Madison, at the President's orders, refused to deliver the commissions to these so-called midnight judges. William Marbury, whose commission as justice of the peace had been withheld, instituted suit in federal court to compel the delivery of the commission by the secretary of state. The case was carried to the Supreme Court where Marshall was faced with a dilemma. If he declared Marbury's claim invalid, it would be a victory for Jefferson; if he ordered Madison to deliver the desired commission, there was a possibility that Madison would refuse to obey the Court's order, which would discredit the Court and thus also be a victory for Jefferson. So Marshall astutely shifted the main question from the validity of Marbury's claim to the correctness of Marbury's procedure in bringing the case directly to the Supreme Court. The Judiciary Act of 1789 authorized bringing the case in this way, but Marshall questioned the constitutionality of that part of the act, since the Constitution defined the original jurisdiction of the Court in a different way. Marshall ruled that Congress could not give the Court this jurisdiction, that the section of the act giving it was void, and therefore Marbury would have to take his case to another court. In this way Marshall was able simultaneously to avoid rendering a decision which he could not enforce, to assert that Marbury was right and Madison and Jefferson wrong on the merits of the case, and to set the tremendously important precedent that the Supreme Court had power to determine whether an act of Congress was constitutional and declare it void if it were not.

Much as President Jefferson resented the strictures passed upon his conduct by Marshall, he did not make a major issue of the Supreme Court's claim of the right of judicial review. After all, the section of the Judiciary Act of 1789 which Marshall declared unconstitutional was a piece of Federalist legislation which the Republicans were not sorry to see expunged from the statute book. But the decision which rid the Republicans of an unwelcome piece of legislation also gave the judiciary, which Jefferson did not control, power of review over the acts of the legislature and the executive, which he did control.

Impeachment. Despite Marshall's circumspection, President Jefferson held a measure of power in Congress which seemingly made him the master of any court. The President was determined to use this power to the full'. In 1803 impeachment proceedings were instituted by the House of Representatives against John Pickering, a New Hampshire federal judge. Although obviously a mentally unbalanced alcoholic, Pickering was found guilty of "high crimes and misdemeanors." The Republican majority moved next against Justice Samuel Chase of the United States Supreme Court, a rabidly partisan Federalist, who, while presiding over several trials of Republican editors accused of sedition, had conducted himself more like a prosecuting attorney than an impartial judge. If Chase were found guilty, the President and his party hoped to pluck Chief Justice John Marshall himself from the bench. But the prosecution of Chase fell short of the necessary two-thirds majority. Marshall and the rest of the federal judges were saved, as the Federalists exultingly said, from "the fangs of Jefferson."

The Barbary Pirates

Not only were Jefferson's plans for effecting sweeping changes in the institutions of the Republic thwarted by Hamilton and the federal judiciary but the President found himself similarly constrained in the field of foreign policy by the Barbary pirates. Jefferson had said that "peace is my passion," and he was prepared to believe that the United States Navy was potentially a cause of war, since its presence on the high seas exposed the United States to the risk of attack. Both his passions for peace and for economy led him to deplore a strong navy. He yearned to use the sharp axe of Republican cost cutting on the Navy by laying its ships up in dry dock and by building gunboats for coastal defense.

But the corsairs of Tripoli, outraged by the refusal of the United States government to pay them the same tribute given the Algerians since 1795, declared war upon the United States early in 1801. Much against his inclinations, Jefferson perforce became a war President and was obliged to strengthen the Navy even though he detested it. The President sent a squadron to the Mediterranean, and Congress appropriated money for the construction of additional fighting ships.

Both as governor of Virginia during the Revolution and as President of the United States, Jefferson proved to be an indifferent war leader. In the first years of the struggle with Tripoli, he deferred far too much to Congress, and he could not bring himself to commit a large naval squadron to the Mediterranean. Instead, he tried to win the war with a minimal use of force; consequently, little was accomplished. Even in time of war, the President did not forget the necessity for frugality and economy. In October 1803 the United States suffered its worst reverse of the war. The U.S.S. *Philadelphia*, Captain Bainbridge commanding, ran aground while chasing a Tripolitan vessel. The American warship and its crew of 307 officers and men were captured. But the Tripolitans were not permitted the use of the *Philadelphia* against the United States. In 1804 Captain Stephen Decatur entered the harbor of Tripoli and burned the *Philadelphia.*

William Eaton, the American representative in Egypt, marched at the head of a ragtail army, accompanied by a claimant to the throne of Tripoli, from Cairo across a thousand miles of desert to Derna. However, his only accomplishment was to raise the United States flag for the first time in Africa. It was not until 1804 after Congress imposed new taxes to build additional ships and to carry on large-scale operations in the Mediterranean that the corsairs sued for peace. In 1806 a treaty was approved by the United States Senate which, while it committed the United States to pay tribute to Tripoli, gave the Americans more favorable terms than any western power had yet received. Not until 1815, after another war with the Barbary pirates, were these payments discontinued.

The Great Annexation

President Jefferson's unwillingness to divert the entire striking force of the United States Navy to the Mediterranean was partly occasioned by the menacing situation which had developed on the North American continent. In 1801 the Peace of Amiens brought a temporary halt to the European war and with it a recession in the United States. Under peacetime conditions, France and Spain regained their colonial trade, and the United States lost its privileged position as a carrier of the produce of the French and Spanish colonies which had been the most lucrative branch of American commerce.

Napoleon's Plans for an American Empire. Even more ominously, Napoleon, now First Consul of the French Consulate, turned his attention from Egypt, where the French army and fleet had met with disaster, to the western hemisphere where he hoped to create a new French colonial empire based upon Haiti, the French part of the island of Santo Domingo, and Louisiana. In 1800 as the first step toward the fulfillment of this grand design, Napoleon acquired title to Louisiana from Spain by the secret treaty of San Ildefonso. His second step was to reconquer Santo Domingo from the black insurgents who had successfully resisted British as well as French efforts to occupy the island. Accordingly, two French armies were committed to the western hemisphere— one for the reconquest of Santo Domingo, the other for the occupation of Louisiana.

Although the secret treaty of San Ildefonso was known to Jefferson and his advisers, they were not seriously alarmed until October 1802, when the Spanish intendant at New Orleans abruptly suspended the right of deposit. To Americans, this event seemed to portend not only a French take-over of Louisiana but the closure of the Mississippi to American shipping.

While they had left no doubt of their hostility to western interests, Federalists felt an even greater hostility to France. Accordingly, they called for military action to prevent the French occupation of Louisiana. For almost the first time, Federalists found themselves in agreement with westerners, many of whom saw war as the only alternative to French control of the lower Mississippi and domination of the heartland of the American continent.

Rather than see the French in Louisiana, Jefferson declared that he would marry the United States to the British fleet and nation. He would have found the British receptive to such an alliance: the London government viewed French actions in the Caribbean as a threat to Jamaica and other British-held islands. But before rushing into John Bull's embrace, Jefferson began to prepare the country for war. In 1803 Meriwether Lewis and William Clark were ordered to make a quasi-military reconnaissance of the region beyond the Mississippi. But his first objective was to explore the possibility of buying New Orleans from Napoleon. The President's territorial ambitions were relatively modest. All he asked was that the French sell the United States New Orleans and the land lying immediately to the east of the city including a small segment of West Florida. Possession of this strategic area would ensure the United States the free navigation of the Mississippi River and a port at its mouth.

Early in 1803 James Monroe was sent to Paris as minister plenipotentiary to back up Edward Livingston, the resident United States minister. He was instructed to pay up to $10 million for New Orleans and the adjacent territory. Even before Monroe's arrival, however, it had become apparent that Napoleon was prepared to do business with the Americans and on a scale far beyond their expectations.

In Santo Domingo, the French army under the command of General Leclerc met with heroic resistance from the blacks led by Toussaint L'Ouverture, Jean Jacques Dessalines, and Henri Christophe. These reverses blighted Napoleon's hopes of making that island one of the pillars of a new French empire. General Leclerc came to restore slavery to Santo Domingo. Rather than give up their freedom, thousands of blacks waged a guerrilla war against the French army. "The men die with unbelievable fanaticism; they laugh at death," General Leclerc reported to Napoleon. "It is the same with the women." On both sides, it was a war of atrocity: prisoners were killed in cold blood, Negro-hunting dogs were trained by the French, and civilians, including women and children, were massacred. General Leclerc concluded that only genocide would enable the French to rule the island. Even after Toussaint was captured by a ruse and sent to die in a Swiss prison, the struggle was carried on by Dessalines and Christophe. "General Disease" fought on the side of the blacks: thousands of French troops died of yellow fever.

The Louisiana Bargain. Abandoning all hope of empire in the western hemisphere, Napoleon decided to resume the war in Europe, which meant that he would be cut off from Louisiana by the British navy. Rather than see his colony fall to the British or Americans as a prize of war, Napoleon decided to sell the entire province to the United States. Although the price demanded by Napoleon, $15 million, was more than Monroe and Livingston were instructed to pay, they closed the deal without waiting for authorization from Washington. By any reckoning it was a bargain: a domain of imperial extent for about two cents an acre.

Jefferson as a Loose Constructionist. When on July 4, 1803, President Jefferson received the draft of the treaty concluded by Monroe and Livingston, his first impulse was to delay ratification until a constitutional amendment giving the federal government the right to acquire territory had been adopted. But any delay, he quickly realized, might jeopardize the agreement made at Paris. Napoleon was quite capable of changing his mind about selling Louisiana. Moreover, the necessity of a constitutional amendment failed to impress itself upon the President's closest friends. Accordingly, Jefferson laid the treaty before the Senate without mention of a constitutional amendment. Instead, he advised his supporters to avoid becoming involved in "metaphysical subleties" regarding the Constitution. If this was Hamiltonianism, Jefferson justified it on the ground that he was acting for the people's good and that it would be so regarded by the people themselves.

The Federalists as Strict Constructionists. In actuality, however, strict Jeffersonian construction of the Constitution was not dead: it had simply changed parties. The Federalists opposed the acquisition of Louisiana on the ground that it was unconstitutional. The Federalists, not the Republicans, now delved into metaphysical subleties in order to prove that the United States government did not have the power to purchase and administer territory under the conditions laid down by the Louisiana treaty. But in fact the Constitution had little to do with it. In opposing the acquisition of Louisiana, the Federalists were giving vent to their fears that the growth of the West was to the political and economic advantage of the South. Their real objection to the Louisiana treaty was the commitment to admit Louisiana as a state of the Union, equal in every respect to the original states. Federalists were willing to accept the entire Louisiana Purchase if they were assured that it would be governed forever as a colonial dependency of the United States.

In taking this stand, the Federalists were not playing politics. Rather, they were engaged in digging their own political graves. It was futile to oppose the ratification of the Louisiana treaty, and only a party bent upon self-destruction would have done so. The treaty was ratified by the Senate by a large majority, and the House of Representatives appropriated the money required to carry out the terms of contract made with Napoleon. The total amount which changed hands was $11,250,000; the remainder represented the debts owed by France to United States citizens which the United States government assumed.

Explorations of the New Acquisition. After the purchase of Louisiana, the Lewis and Clark expedition, originally planned as a quasi-military operation, was changed into a scientific and geographical mission. In 1804 Meriwether Lewis and Captain William Clark left St. Louis. The expedition consisted of

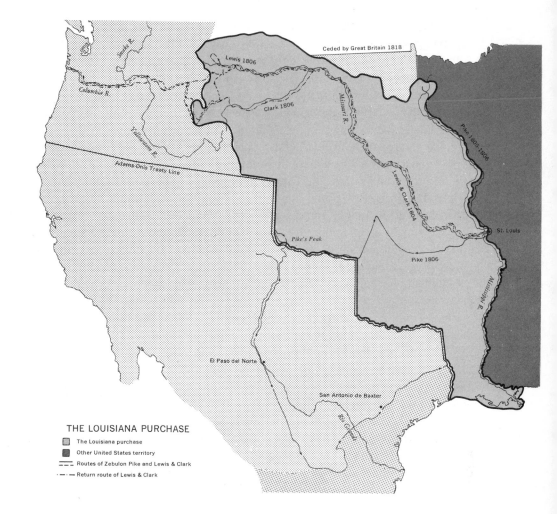

THE LOUISIANA PURCHASE

- [shaded] The Louisiana purchase
- [shaded] Other United States territory
- ===== Routes of Zebulon Pike and Lewis & Clark
- ·—·— Return route of Lewis & Clark

thirty-one men, the Indian woman guide Sacajawea, and Captain Lewis' Newfoundland dog. After ascending the Missouri River and crossing the Rocky Mountains, it followed the Snake and Columbia Rivers to the Pacific. This was not the first overland crossing of the continent. In 1793 Alexander Mackenzie, a Scot, had reached the Pacific at 52 degrees north, but Lewis and Clark were the first to make the journey by way of the waterways that flowed east and west from the Rockies. After traveling over eight thousand miles by boat, horseback, and on foot, and with the loss of only one man, Captain Lewis ended his journey at Washington, D.C., on December 28, 1805, twenty-seven months after leaving St. Louis.

Although neither Lewis nor Clark had scientific training, they followed closely the instructions of President Jefferson, a man of wide-ranging scientific interests. As a result, they were able to gather a wealth of miscellaneous scientific information about the hitherto unknown western part of the North American continent. Packages containing skins, skeletons of animals, plants, and Indian robes and pottery were sent to the President. Among the curiosities were two grizzly bears which were kept in cages on the President's lawn.

In 1805–1806 Jefferson, the most western minded of American Presidents with the possible exception of Theodore Roosevelt, sent Zebulon Pike on two expeditions: first to explore the upper Mississippi, and second to locate the source of the Arkansas and Rio Grande Rivers. In the course of his explorations, Pike discovered the peak in Colorado which bears his name. In 1810 after traversing the region between the Missouri and the Rockies, Pike reported that much of the area was too arid for agriculture. Jefferson concluded that because of these "deserts," the Pacific Coast would probably become an independent English-speaking republic and that a large part of the intervening space would remain forever an Indian hunting-ground. He hoped, too, that the Louisiana Purchase would help solve the Negro problem in the United States. He seriously considered the possibility of colonizing part of the region with free blacks. There, removed from proximity to whites, they could attain a far fuller development, he believed, than if they remained alien outcasts in a white community.

The Independence of Haiti. The Jefferson administration poorly repaid the blacks of Santo Domingo for their part in changing Napoleon's mind about the feasibility of a new French empire, thereby inadvertently helping to bring about the sale of Louisiana. President Jefferson, hopeful of gaining more territory from Napoleon, cooperated with France's efforts to blockade the island. Nevertheless, American shipowners, without governmental permission, brought military supplies to the beleaguered blacks. Without aid from the United States government, the blacks succeeded in making Santo Domingo—or Haiti, as it is now called—an independent monarchy and later a republic. Haiti became the second state in the New World to free itself from European domination. Its independence was not recognized by the United States until 1864.

The Downfall of the Federalists

Federalist Rigidity. By opposing the purchase of Louisiana, the Federalists cut themselves off from the most rapidly growing and the most nationalistic section of the Union. The party leaders ceased to function as politicians seeking to create the conditions under which political power can be exercised in the United States, that is, by a coalition of sections. Instead, they placed the narrow interests of their economic group and their section above all other considerations and adopted an inflexible position of ideological dogmatism. The Federalist leaders had discovered an infallible method of destroying a political party, and they followed it implicitly.

Secessionism and the Burr-Hamilton Duel. Even without their own considerable efforts, the Federalists seemed headed for political extinction. By 1804 as a result of Jefferson's conciliatory attitude toward the Federalist rank

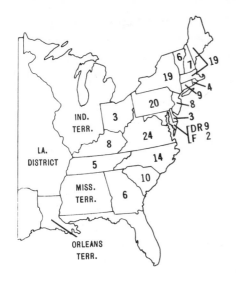

THE ELECTION OF 1804

ELECTORAL VOTE
BY STATE

REPUBLICAN
Thomas Jefferson   162
FEDERALIST
Charles C. Pinckney   14
                                        ───
                                        176

and file and his adoption of some of the basic Federalist policies, the Federalists had lost ground even in New England. In desperation, former Secretary of State Pickering and a few other New England Federalists sought salvation for the good, the wise, and the rich, as the Federalists described themselves, in a resort to secession. They planned to establish an independent northern confederacy consisting of the New England states and New York, in which all the virtue of the country would be concentrated, leaving vice, irreligion, and democracy a clear field in the remainder of the truncated Republic. The success of the plot required that Vice-President Aaron Burr, now at odds with Jefferson, be elected governor of New York. But Burr failed to win the governorship, and the conspiracy—it had never been divulged to the people—collapsed. Its only concrete result was the duel between Burr and Hamilton, occasioned by Hamilton's outspoken efforts to prevent Burr's election. The two adversaries met in July 1804 at Weehawken, New Jersey. The former secretary of the treasury was mortally wounded by the vice-president of the United States.

The Election of 1804. Plotting secession was hardly the way to win a presidential election, and in 1804 the Federalists went down to an ignominious defeat at Jefferson's hands. Aaron Burr was dropped by the Republicans as their candidate for vice-president. Since he had lost his standing with the Federalists by killing Hamilton—indeed, he was under indictment for murder in New Jersey—Burr was ostracized from both parties. Like many another man down on his luck, Burr decided to go west.

Scheming for West Florida

In 1805–1807 the West offered extraordinary opportunities to political adventurism. Despite the purchase of Louisiana, the United States was not a territorially satisfied power. Control of the rivers flowing into the Gulf of Mexico was essential to the economic growth of the Southeast. This necessitated in turn the acquisition by the United States of the Spanish province of West Florida, especially Mobile Bay. President Jefferson believed that in buying Louisiana the United States had obtained title to West Florida and Texas—the boundaries of the French province of Louisiana. While East Florida had never been a part of Louisiana, Jefferson claimed it as compensation for Spanish spoliations of American commerce.

Since Napoleon seemed to hold the keys to West Florida and other Spanish territory claimed by the United States—Spain had been reduced to the status of a French client-state—Jefferson adopted the strategy of propitiating Napoleon, despite the fact that he regarded the Corsican as the betrayer of the French Revolution. In 1805–1806 he tried to buy West Florida from Napoleon. Jefferson's deviousness precipitated a revolt within his own party. John Randolph of Roanoke and a group called the Quids broke away from Jefferson's leadership and demanded that a straightforward effort be made to secure the province from Spain. Meanwhile, the French Emperor declined to engage in any more real estate transactions with the United States. After this rebuff, advocates of a forcible solution to the problem of West Florida and Texas made their voices heard. James Monroe, for example, advocated an armed attack upon those provinces. President Jefferson continued to rely upon diplomacy, but it was doubtful if he could keep westerners under control.

The Burr Adventure. Into these troubled waters entered Aaron Burr with the most grandiose scheme ever conceived by an American filibusterer. Upon graduating from Princeton, Burr had delivered an oration entitled "Building Castles in the Air." Thirty years later, still incurably romantic, he was still building them.

Whatever castle Burr was engaged in building in the West in 1805–1806, he invested it with an air of mystery. To enlist money and support, he described his enterprise at various times and to various people, including the British and Spanish ministers, as an effort to settle lands west of the Mississippi to which he claimed title, to seize Texas, to conquer Mexico, to break up the Union, and to hang Thomas Jefferson. Of all these projects, Burr seemed to be most partial to the idea of conquering Texas. He connived with General James Wilkinson, the commander of the United States forces in the West, to invade Texas and thereby give himself the chance to play the conquering hero. But Wilkinson proved to be an unreliable ally. He was already in the pay of the Spanish government and at a critical moment in Burr's fortunes, Wilkinson betrayed him to President Jefferson.

From the evidence supplied by Wilkinson and other informants, Jefferson concluded that Burr was trying to break up the Union by creating an independent western confederacy. He therefore issued orders for Burr's arrest. The former vice-president was apprehended on his way to New Orleans and brought to Richmond, Virginia, to stand trial on a charge of treason. Presiding over the trial was Chief Justice John Marshall.

In actuality, as Jefferson admitted, the government lacked sufficient evidence to procure a conviction. Even so, the Chief Executive took personal charge of assembling the evidence against Burr and instructed the government attorneys how to conduct the case.

When in August 1807 the trial of Aaron Burr and his associates opened, the weakness of the government's case quickly became apparent. Even the testimony of General Wilkinson, the government's star witness, did not carry conviction to the jury. Indeed, Wilkinson himself narrowly escaped being presented to the grand jury. Nor did Chief Justice Marshall neglect this opportunity to pay off his score against Jefferson: at the request of defense counsel, Marshall issued a subpoena ordering the President to appear and give testimony to the court at Richmond. Jefferson refused to comply with an order that would have clearly established the supremacy of the judicial over the executive branch of the government.

Although he failed to bring the President to Richmond, Marshall in effect put an end to the trial by charging the jury that the prosecution had not proved Burr's presence, upon the testimony of two witnesses, at the scene where the act of treason was alleged to have taken place. The jury promptly returned a verdict of not guilty on the charge of treason. Burr was likewise acquitted on a technicality of the lesser charge, a misdemeanor, of having attempted to raise men on United States territory for the purpose of invading Spanish territory.

President Jefferson called the verdict rendered at Richmond a miscarriage of justice and a defiance of public opinion which, he believed, had already convicted Burr. In a message delivered to Congress in 1807, the President recommended changes in the law to preserve the government from "destruction by treason." But the President knew only too well that as long as Marshall and his Federalist colleagues were on the bench to interpret the law, no statutory changes would suffice. He therefore also recommended to Congress that a constitutional amendment be proposed to the states authorizing the President to remove federal judges at the request of both houses of Congress. The amendment was introduced into Congress but failed of passage. Despite all that Jefferson could do, the Supreme Court continued to stand as a Federalist citadel in a Republican government.

SUGGESTED READING

Henry Adams' great *History of the United States During the Administrations of Thomas Jefferson and James Madison* (1930 edition) contains an admirable survey of

*Available in a paperback edition

the United States in 1800 as well as a detailed account of the political events of the years 1800–1816. An important new interpretation of Jeffersonian democracy is made by Noble F. Cunningham, *The Jeffersonian Republicans: The Formation of a Party Organization, 1789–1801** (1967) and *The Jeffersonian Republicans in Power: Party Operations, 1801–1809** (1963). Other significant monographs are Paul Goodman, *The Democratic-Republicans of Massachusetts: Politics in a Young Republic* (1964); Carl E. Prince, *New Jersey's Jeffersonian Republicans* (1967); Marshall Smelser, *The Democratic Republic, 1801–1815* (1968); Raymond Walters, Jr., *Albert Gallatin: Jeffersonian Financier and Diplomat** (1957); Charles M. Wiltse, *The New Nation, 1800–1845** (1961); Max Beloff, *Thomas Jefferson and American Democracy** (1962); Dumas Malone, *Jefferson the President* (1970); Leonard D. White, *The Jeffersonians** (1950); Merrill Peterson and Aida D. Donald, eds., *Thomas Jefferson, A Profile** (1967); Leonard W. Levy, *Jefferson and Civil Liberties: The Darker Side* (1963); Dumas Malone, *Thomas Jefferson as Political Leader* (1963); William A. Robinson, *Jeffersonian Democracy in New England* (1916); Henry M. Tinkcom, *The Republicans and Federalists in Pennsylvania, 1790–1801** (1950); John H. Wolfe, *Jeffersonian Democracy in South Carolina** (1940).

New light is cast upon the election of 1800 by Morton Borden, *The Federalism of James A. Bayard* (1954); Charles O. Lerche, "Jefferson and the Election of 1800," *William and Mary Quarterly,* Third Series (1948).

The social scene during the period of Jeffersonian democracy is seen in Constance M. Green, *Washington: Village and Capital, 1800–1878* (1962); Sir Augustus John Foster, *Jeffersonian America* (1954); Anne Hollingsworth Wharton, *Social Life in the Early Republic* (1902).

For *Marbury* v. *Madison,* see John P. Roche, ed., *John Marshall: Major Opinions and Other Writings** (1967); W. Melville Jones, ed., *Chief Justice John Marshall* (1956); Ernest Sutherland Bates, *The Story of the Supreme Court* (1936); Samuel J. Konefsky, *John Marshall and Alexander Hamilton* (1964); Raoul Berger, *Congress v. The Supreme Court* (1969); Albert J. Beveridge, *The Life of John Marshall,* 4 vols (1916–1919); Charles Warren, *The Supreme Court in United States History,* 2 vols., (1937); Edward S. Corwin, *John Marshall and the Constitution* (1919).

For the Louisiana Purchase, the following books are recommended: Irving Brant, *James Madison: Secretary of State, 1801–1809* (1953); Hubert Cole, *Christophe, King of Haiti** (1967); and E. W. Lyon, *The Man Who Sold Louisiana: The Life of Francois Barbe Marbois* (1943) and *Louisiana in French Diplomacy* (1934).

On the far west explorations, see John Bakeless, *Lewis and Clark: Partners in Democracy** (1947); Bernard De Voto, ed., *The Journals of Lewis and Clark** (1953); S. H. Hart and A. B. Hulbert, eds., *Zebulon Pike's Arkansas Journal* (1937). The advance of the American frontier during this period is chronicled by Dale Van Every, *Ark of Empire: The American Frontier, 1784–1803** (1963); E. E. Rich, *The Fur Trade and the Northwest to 1857* (1968); and Reginald Horsman, *The Frontier in the Formative Years, 1783–1815** (1970).

For the embargo, see Louis M. Sears, *Jefferson and the Embargo* (1927); G. W. Daniels, "American Cotton Trade Under the Embargo," *American Historical Review,*

XXI (1916); Bradford Perkins, *Prologue to War: England and the United States, 1805–1812** (1961); Henry Adams, *History of the United States During the Administrations of Thomas Jefferson and James Madison** (1930).

The Burr conspiracy has proved to be a source of controversy among historians. The question whether Burr was guilty of treason is by no means settled despite his acquittal in 1807 on that charge. Among the historians and biographers who have taken positions in this controversy are W. F. McCaleb, *The Aaron Burr Conspiracy* (1903); Nathan Schachner, *Aaron Burr: A Biography** (1937); Thomas P. Abernethy, *The Burr Conspiracy* (1954); Francis F. Beirne, *Shout Treason* (1959).

Meriwether Lewis. *Picture: Independence National Historical Park Collection, Philadelphia*

Lewis and Clark / Pictorial Essay

Careful planning and foresight on the part of the commanders prepared the Lewis and Clark expedition to meet the dangers and difficulties of their journey. They carried an ample supply of such essentials as gunpowder and firearms, which were needed to supply food as well as protection; camp supplies; medicines; and presents for the Indians. In addition, they also carried such useful, but nonessential, items as a forge and a violin. The forge was used to manufacture tomahawks for trading with the Indians, who were also delighted with the violin music and the square dances the men performed. But even more important to the success of the journey was the care with which the members of the expedition were selected. Included in the Corps of Discovery, as it was called, were experienced hunters, a blacksmith, a house-joiner, and a man who had lived with the Indians and was acquainted with sign language.

As they moved up the lower Missouri River, the expedition's main problem was dealing with the Indians. Lewis and Clark tried to convince the Indians that their mission was peaceful, that the Indians should recognize the American government, and that they should end their wars with other tribes. In exchange,

William Clark. *Picture: Independence National Historical Park Collection, Philadelphia*

the United States government promised its protection. Lewis signed agreements to this effect with many chiefs. He also gave them medals as a sign that the United States government recognized their status.

The expedition spent its first winter in what is now North Dakota in a fort which the explorers built and named Fort Mandan after the nearby Mandan Indian villages. Sacagawea, a Shoshone Indian girl, and her French–Canadian husband Charbonneau, joined the expedition at Fort Mandan. Both were hired as interpreters. Sacagawea's knowledge of Shoshone enabled the expedition to buy horses with which to cross the Rocky Mountains.

When they continued their journey up the Missouri in the spring, travel became more difficult, as they were moving against the current and in swift water. The boats often had to be towed from the river bank with men wading in the water to steady them. On the upper Missouri, they began to encounter numerous grizzly bears which amazed the explorers with their ferociousness and their capacity to withstand bullets before giving up the attack.

As they approached the Continental Divide, they attempted unsuccessfully

to locate Indians in order to buy horses so that they could abandon river travel, which was becoming ever more difficult. Finally, Lewis went ahead overland and succeeded in contacting, by a quirk of fate, the same band of Indians in which Sacagawea had been reared. From the Shoshones, they obtained horses and guides to cross the mountains. The crossing was difficult. The weather was cold and food was scarce. At the worst period, they subsisted on whale oil and candles.

On the other side of the Rockies, they were happy to build dugout canoes and return to water travel. Although they were going downstream, the trip was not as easy as they had hoped. They frequently encountered rapids which on occasion caused accidents damaging to the canoes or which forced them to make portages.

Two of the illustrations from Sergeant Patrick Gass' journal, published in 1812, are shown at the left. The top picture shows Lewis and Clark at one of the many councils they held with Indian chiefs along the way. The picture below shows the difficulties the expedition had with their canoes. However, the well–dressed men in the picture bear no resemblance to the men in dirty buckskins who actually ascended the Missouri. *Pictures: The New York Public Library, Astor, Lenox & Tilden Foundations.* On this page is Charles Bodmer's painting of the Mandan Indians and their bullboats. It was in such a craft that Sergeant Pryor managed to rejoin Clark on the return trip down the Missouri. *Picture: The Newberry Library, Ayer Collection*

When they finally cited the Pacific Ocean on November 7, 1805, their happiness was tempered by the cold, wet weather of Pacific Northwest winters. Everything was wet, their clothing was rotting, and game was scarce. They spent the winter on the Pacific Coast. Clark drew maps; Lewis worked on his botanical notes; and everyone hoped that they would find a trading ship on which to return home. When this hope was unfulfilled, they began their second transcontinental journey the following March. The high prices the Indians along the lower Columbia had charged for food had almost exhausted their supply of trading goods. On the return trip Clark was obliged to barter medical treatment for the food or other goods the expedition needed.

After recrossing the Rocky Mountains, the expedition separated, with Lewis and Clark each leading a group of the men. Lewis went overland to the Great Falls. There he left most of his men to portage the supplies they had cached by the Falls on their westward trip. Taking only three men he rode north to explore Maria's River. There he and his men became involved in a fight with Indians who tried to steal their guns and horses. Two Indians were killed.

At the left is Clark's elk-skin bound field book in which he recorded rough notes that he later used in making his diary entries. In addition to Lewis and Clark, at least five other members of the expedition kept journals. *Picture: Missouri Historical Society.* The horned toad pictured below was drawn by C. W. Peale. It was one of the many specimens that Lewis preserved and brought back with him to Washington. *Pictures: The American Philosophical Society*

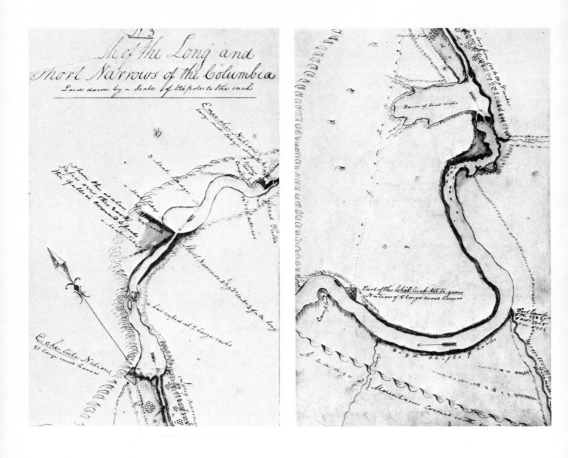

Fearing Indian vengeance, they rode 120 miles in 24 hours to the Missouri River where they luckily encountered part of Clark's group. Clark had sent these men down the Missouri with the canoes that the expedition had cached on the east side of the Rockies on their westward trip. It was intended that they would pick up Lewis and his men.

Meanwhile, Clark and the rest of his party had gone overland to the Yellowstone River and built canoes to go down that river to the Missouri. He left three men to take the horses overland. However, two days after they started, the horses were stolen by Indians. Hurrying on foot to the river, they found that Clark had already passed. The men then shot enough buffalo to build boats similar to the Mandan bullboats they had seen at Fort Mandan. Clark was surprised several days later to find them coming down the river after him. Shortly thereafter, Lewis caught up with Clark on the Missouri. The members of the expedition returned together to St. Louis on September 23, 1806. They were greeted with great excitement. They had been given up as dead long before, since no word had been heard of them since they had left Fort Mandan in April 1805.

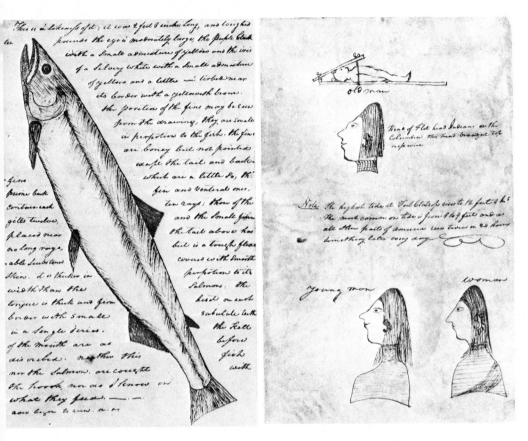

Clark was the expedition's artist and cartographer. On the opposite page is his map of the long and short narrows of the Columbia River. Above left is a picture of a salmon that he drew in his diary. The appearance of salmon in the Columbia River convinced Clark that they were nearing the Pacific. Clark also drew the picture at the right showing how the Chinook Indians used a special cradleboard for their infants in order to flatten their foreheads. *Pictures: Missouri Historical Society*

CHAPTER SIX

TWELVE YEARS
OF ECONOMIC AND
MILITARY CONFLICT

British Trade Restrictions

W HILE THE RESUMPTION of the war between Great Britain and France in 1803 restored American prosperity, it also immensely complicated the government's efforts to uphold neutral rights, that is, to enjoy the privilege of trading freely with both belligerents. Caught between the upper and nether millstones of French and British maritime policy—Jefferson likened those two powers to the tiger and the shark—neutral rights were ground exceedingly small. In 1805 in the *Essex* decision, British admiralty courts imposed restrictions upon the privilege granted to Americans of carrying supplies from Britain's enemies to Europe. Previously the doctrine of continuous voyage had been construed to mean that continuous voyages between Europe and the French and Spanish West Indies, the Philippines, the East Indies, and other colonies of belligerents were forbidden; however, such traffic had been allowed if the goods were imported into the United States and then reexported, thus becoming part of a separate voyage. When this procedure was followed, it was held that the goods became neutral property protected by the American flag. In the *Essex* decision, however, the admiralty court required the American shipowner to prove that the goods were genuinely imported into the United States in good faith and did not merely touch at an American port. This was difficult since the cargoes were seldom intended for import into the United States. Failure to prove good faith meant seizure and condemnation by British courts. In such cases, shipowners were charged with violating the British Rule of 1756, which declared that trade illegal in time of peace could not be made legal in time of war. Unfortunately for the United States, its trade with the French and Spanish possessions was illegal in time of peace and therefore subject to the restrictions imposed by the Rule of 1756.

In 1806 the British aggravated the injury already done American neutral rights by declaring a paper blockade of the coast of northern Europe. A paper blockade was a blockade of a port, coast, or country declared by a belligerent to be in existence but not enforced by sufficient naval strength to make it effective. Its purpose was not actually to close a given port but to make fair game of any ship anywhere that might have such a port as its destination. The United States maintained that to be binding, blockades must be effective; it must be hazardous to ships to attempt to run the blockade.

Most serious of all, the British navy redoubled its efforts to impress British seamen aboard American ships, and the officers in charge of British landing parties seemed less able than before to discriminate between Americans and Englishmen. By 1812 over 2500 seamen in the Royal Navy claimed to be American citizens forcibly pressed into British service.

The Failure of Negotiations. In 1806, as in 1794 Republicans demanded economic reprisals against Great Britain. Since Jay's Treaty had expired in 1805, the United States was free to take whatever action it pleased. Yet, although the United States imposed a brief embargo in the spring of 1806,

The Battle of Queenston, October 13, 1812. *Picture: Royal Ontario Museum, Toronto, Canada*

President Jefferson, like President Washington in 1794, tried to ease the crisis by diplomacy.

To help save the peace, Jefferson chose William Pinkney, one of the ornaments of the Maryland bar, to lend support to James Monroe, the resident United States minister at the British court. Pinkney and Monroe were instructed to secure American rights at sea, including the absolute immunity of American ships from search by boarding parties. But, while the British agreed to renew the provisions of Jay's Treaty, they would not renounce the right of impressment. To Jefferson and James Madison, this was a fatal flaw: they refused even to submit the treaty to the Senate.

The Chesapeake Affair. President Jefferson believed that there could be no genuine accord between the United States and Great Britain as long as impressment continued. This view seemed vindicated in June 1807 by the attack upon the U.S.S. *Chesapeake* by the H.M.S. *Leopard,* which acted under orders from Admiral Berkeley to remove deserters from the American man-of-war. When Captain James Barron of the *Chesapeake* refused to permit a British party to come aboard, the *Leopard* opened fire, killing or wounding several members of the crew. Four men were taken off and the *Chesapeake* limped back to port. Captain Barron was court-martialed for his failure to prepare the *Chesapeake* for action.

Although the British had regularly seized American merchant vessels, they had never claimed the right to board a ship of the United States Navy, much less fire upon her without provocation. To the American people, the "Chesapeake outrage" meant war: Jefferson declared that not since 1775 had he seen his countrymen so stirred by hatred of Great Britain. The President said that he had only to raise his finger to produce a declaration of war.

But the President did not give the signal. Even while directing the militia to hold itself in readiness and ordering British warships out of American waters, he initiated diplomatic moves designed to keep the dispute within bounds. Jefferson did not believe that the attack upon the *Chesapeake* had been authorized by the British government, and he expected a prompt disavowal and apology. Under these circumstances, he refused to plunge the country into war. Yet he took a very firm diplomatic line toward Great Britain. He insisted not only upon an apology but also upon the recall of the *Leopard*'s commander, the punishment of Admiral Berkeley, the return of the impressed seamen, and full reparation to the families of the dead and wounded seamen. He went further: tying the *Chesapeake* outrage to the question of impressment, he demanded a renunciation by the British government of its assertion of the right to impress seamen from American ships.

Although His Majesty's government, recognizing that it was clearly in the wrong, was willing to go far toward meeting American demands, it would not renounce impressment. With equal obstinacy, the United States government refused to budge from its position that impressment was a violation of its sovereign rights. As a result, it was not until 1811 that the three American citizens impressed from the *Chesapeake* were restored to their ship and the incident was officially closed. The fourth man, a British subject, had been hanged as a deserter.

French Retaliation and British Counterretaliation

The Berlin Decree. Meanwhile, finding an invasion of England impossible, Napoleon adopted the strategy of strangling the great "sea serpent" by cutting off its trade. Inevitably, this involved a struggle with the neutrals who were the monster's source of food, raw materials, and shipping. On November 21, 1806, after winning a decisive victory over the Prussians, Napoleon promulgated at Berlin a decree declaring the British Isles to be in a state of blockade. Neutral vessels were warned to stay out of British ports on pain of seizure by French warships and privateers. Coming after Lord Nelson's great victory over the combined French and Spanish fleets at Trafalgar (1805), it seemed that Napoleon might quite as effectively have declared the moon to be in a state of blockade. By ordering the confiscation of all British merchandise upon the European continent, the French emperor revived, under the name of the Continental System, the self-blockade originally imposed by the French revolutionaries. It was now useful for seizing any shipments that might ultimately be destined for Britain or any ships that might have stopped at a British port.

Orders in Council. Against the Berlin Decree, the British issued two orders in council. The first, dated January 1807, prohibited American ships from engaging in the European coastal trade. In November 1807 a second order forbade neutral ships from going directly from their home port to any part of the European continent under French control. In effect, the British ministry thereby withdrew permission to the United States to carry on trade even under the doctrine of continuous voyage; the Rule of 1756 was now invoked in its full rigor. But the British had no intention of putting an end to all trade with the European continent. They simply prohibited commercial intercourse between the United States and France, including its satellites, *except through Great Britain.* The British objective was to increase the sale of British merchandise on the Continent through neutral shipping. The order in council of November 1807 was intended to make Great Britain the entrepôt of neutral, particularly American, trade with Napoleonic Europe. These maneuvers by the British and French left the American trade in a situation where the French would confiscate anything that went to Europe by way of Britain, and the British would confiscate anything that did not go by way of a British port.

The Embargo

When the President learned of the order in council of November 7, 1807, he concluded that Great Britain intended to claim absolute dominion of the ocean and to prescribe the terms and conditions under which other nations might navigate upon it. It was the kind of high-handed outrage he had come to expect from "the Great Robber of the Sea." His response to this crisis was to put into effect his long cherished plan of using economic pressure to coerce Great Britain into showing a decent respect for the rights of neutrals. He believed that the United States could reduce to starvation the white workers in Great Britain and the black slaves in the British West Indies. Great Britain's economy would show it how dependent it was upon the shipping, markets, and commodities of the United States.

Accordingly, late in December 1807 in a secret message to Congress, the President recommended that an embargo be imposed upon all American ships. Congress responded promptly and affirmatively to the President's message, and the embargo went into effect late in December 1807. In January 1808 enforcement machinery was established.

The Milan Decree. The necessity of taking action to protect American shipping was augmented when in November 1807 Napoleon issued the Milan Decree, which subjected to confiscation all neutral ships carrying British merchandise and all ships which had put in at a British port. Even a handkerchief marked "Made in Britain" was sufficient to blacklist the ship and its whole cargo.

Without fully foreseeing the consequences, President Jefferson had involved the United States government in a struggle not only against the European powers but against a large number of its own citizens. The mercantile and shipping communities had no desire to wage economic war with Great Britain and France in order to establish neutral rights. New England shipowners and businessmen who believed that Great Britain was fighting the battles of the United States against Napoleonic France were not disposed to sacrifice their own trade in order to resist British sea power. After all, the British orders in council did not deny American shipowners and merchants the possibility of profit. Indeed, by accepting the protection of the British navy against French warships and privateers, American shipowners could turn a handsome profit. Sailing in the wake of a British man-of-war was the course of prudence as well as profit. Nothing would be lost save the right to trade with the Continent, which could not be enforced in any event without war.

To these merchants and shipowners, it seemed that the Republican leaders regarded commerce as an expendable counter in the struggle with Great Britain. Even if commerce were ruined, the politicians would account it a victory if American rights to trade with belligerents in wartime were established.

The Profits of a Dangerous Trade. Certainly American shipowners had a heavy stake in the outcome of a commercial war with Great Britain. From 1792 to 1807, the tonnage of the American merchant marine had increased almost threefold, and the value of goods transported in American ships was thirteen times greater than in 1792. The combined imports and exports of the United

AMERICAN FOREIGN TRADE, 1790-1815

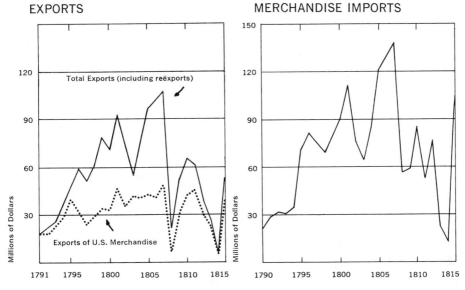

EXPORTS

MERCHANDISE IMPORTS

DESTINATION OF EXPORTS

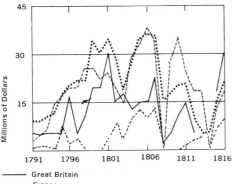

Great Britain
France
Other European Nations
Non-European Nations

Events in Europe had a direct effect on American foreign trade, most of which was with Western Europe. The Napoleonic wars increased the demand for American products and gave the United States a larger share of the carrying trade. The brief peace in Europe during 1802 caused a depression in the United States; however, the resumption of hostilities brought an even greater growth in American trade. Even the British Orders in Council and Napoleon's Continental System could not destroy it. *Source: Historical Statistics of the United States.*

States rose from $52 million in 1792 to $246 million in 1807. Part of this increase had been at the expense of Great Britain. By 1800 American ships handled 95 percent of the trade between the United States and Great Britain, up from less than 50 percent in 1792. The stars and stripes were becoming a common sight in India and China. So brisk was the demand for sailors that the average pay rose from $8 to $30 a month.

A commensurate increase was registered by the federal government's revenue. Tonnage and import duties accounted for a jump in revenue from

$12,935,000 in 1801 to $17,160,000 in 1807. Much of this money was ploughed back into the redemption of the national debt which, despite the Louisiana Purchase, was pared from $83,000,000 in 1801 to $45,200,000 in 1813.

To the Federalists, the embargo meant not only the end of American wartime prosperity but the first step toward war with Great Britain and an alliance with France—the consummation, as they saw it, of Jefferson's Francophilism. For the embargo promised to hurt Great Britain far more than it did France, since France had virtually no open and direct trade with the United States. Inevitably, the embargo would be mainly directed against the nation which by virtue of its control of the sea dominated trade with the United States.

Violations of the Embargo. The embargo created a wholly new kind of violation of the law—smuggling goods out of the United States. Congress passed three enforcement acts, each progressively more severe in the fines and other penalties inflicted upon violators. Such a multitude of regulations were imposed upon American citizens that it was humorously said that a baby could not be born without a clearance from the customs house. Attempts to violate the embargo were made punishable by the confiscation of the ship and cargo and a fine of four times their value. No ship could be loaded without a revenue officer on hand to inspect the cargo and certify the manifest, and clearance papers were given only by the special permission of the President. Collectors of the United States customs were authorized to conduct searches without warrants or any other legal authorization. These officials could seize property if they suspected an intention to violate the embargo. Naval officers were instructed to stop and search American vessels to determine if they carried cargo that might be sold to foreign buyers.

The Embargo and Centralized Power. These laws represented a longer stride toward consolidated government and the concentration of power in the presidency than the Federalists themselves had dared to take. In fact, the enforcement of the embargo violated every precept laid down by Jefferson when he was leader of the opposition to the Federalists. Yet Jefferson justified his actions on the ground that the embargo was the only way to avoid war, which would be certain, he believed, to produce a far more dangerous concentration of power in the federal government and the executive.

Despite these punitive measures, large quantities of goods were smuggled both in and out of the United States. The focal points of this kind of activity were Lake Champlain and the St. John's River in the North and the St. Mary's River, which marked the boundary between the United States and Spanish Florida in the South. Even the United States Army proved unable to stop the traffic through these loopholes. Supplies continued to reach the British West Indies, thereby easing the pressure which President Jefferson had hoped to apply to the economy and the slave population of those islands.

Effects of the Embargo on Agriculture and Manufacturing. Napoleon, meanwhile, turned the embargo to his advantage; he seized and confiscated American ships that entered French ports and cynically justified his action by alleging that he was helping President Jefferson enforce the embargo. George Canning, the British foreign secretary, said that His Majesty's government stood ready to aid in the removal of the embargo "as a measure of inconvenient restriction upon the American people."

And, indeed, it was undeniable that this self-blockade, resembling, in many respects, the self-blockade Napoleon was attempting to impose upon French-controlled Europe, injured the United States more than the belligerents. The government's revenue, for example, shrank from $17 million to $7,773,000. The effects were equally disastrous upon shipping and agriculture. Cotton, wheat, and tobacco, denied their usual markets overseas, fell sharply in price. During 1808 the value of cotton exported from the United States dropped from $14,232,000 to $2,221,000 while exports of tobacco declined from $4,476,000 to $838,000.*

The plight of the planters was aggravated by the fact that unlike northern businessmen, they were obliged to feed and clothe their slaves and pay the fixed charges inseparable from the maintenance of large landed estates. Nevertheless, the southern planters remained loyal to President Jefferson. They seemed to account their economic well-being of little consequence compared with the great objective of asserting American rights at sea and vindicating national honor. The people who went down to the sea in ships, on the other hand, seemed to the Jeffersonian Republicans ready to jettison neutral rights in order to preserve their trade.

Disastrous as were the effects of the embargo upon commerce and agriculture, it proved a boon to manufacturing. The high price or unavailability of British merchandise forced Americans to manufacture for themselves. Although most of this manufacturing was of the household variety, factories using the latest machinery began to spring up in the North, particularly in New England. Prior to the embargo, the United States had fifteen cotton mills. By 1810 eighty-seven mills had been established, and sixty-five were in operation. Thus the efforts of a southern President to use the commerce and economy of the United States as a weapon in the struggle with the European belligerents served to aggravate the already existing imbalance between an industrializing North and an agricultural, staple-producing South.

The unpopularity of the embargo in the North recoiled upon the Republican party. In 1807 Federalism seemed to be dying on the vine even in New England, but a few months after the embargo had gone into effect, the party began to send forth new shoots all over the North. The mercantile interest, which President Jefferson had seemed on the point of detaching from Federalism, was now largely arrayed against him. In 1808 he picked as his successor Secretary of State James Madison, but the election did not prove to be the routine affair

*These, of course, are official figures which do not take into account the large quantity of agricultural produce smuggled out of the country. The fact that there were any exports at all was owing partly to the permission granted state governors by President Jefferson to license exports of flour. Jefferson himself gave hundreds of permits. Moreover, exports by land were not banned until March 1808.

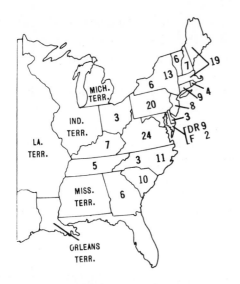

THE ELECTION OF 1808

ELECTORAL VOTE
BY STATE

REPUBLICAN
James Madison 122

FEDERALIST
Charles C. Pinckney 47

INDEPENDENT-REPUBLICAN
George Clinton 6

NOT VOTED 1

176

the Republicans had expected. Federalism showed remarkable strength in New England, New York, New Jersey, and Delaware. But the South and the West carried the day, and Madison won over Charles C. Pinckney, the Federalist candidate, by an electoral college vote of 122 to 47.

The Embargo Abandoned. Even so, the embargo could not be sustained without ruinous consequences to the country and the Republican party. Late in 1808 the New England Republicans threatened to revolt against executive leadership, and some Federalists talked openly of secession. The President bowed to the impending storm. In February 1809 he signed a bill which terminated the embargo on March 3, 1809, the day before he relinquished the presidency to James Madison. It had been in effect for almost sixteen months.

Other Attempts to Secure Neutral Rights

The Nonintercourse Act. The repeal of the embargo did not mean that Republicans had abandoned the policy of economic coercion. On March 3, 1809, the embargo was replaced by the Nonintercourse Act which, while it permitted American ships to put to sea, prohibited them from trading with either of the belligerents and forbade the entry of British and French merchantmen into American ports and the importation of any merchandise originating in those countries. The way was left open, however, for France and Great Britain to restore themselves to the good graces of the United States government: the Nonintercourse Act authorized the President to reopen trade with all nations which ceased to violate American neutral rights. The main difference between the embargo and the Nonintercourse Act, however, was not in the trade which they legalized—for trade with Britain and with France was illegal under both—but in their enforceability. The embargo could prevent ships from putting to sea, but the Nonintercourse Act, having allowed them to put to sea, could not control them once they left port.

In the spring of 1809, by complying with this provision of the Nonintercourse Act, Great Britain temporarily reopened trade with the United States. The British government modified the orders in council in favor of American shipping—among other things, the Baltic was opened to American trade—and in Washington David Erskine, the British minister, signed a treaty by which the British government pledged to repeal the orders in council altogether provided that the United States withdrew nonintercourse against Great Britain while continuing it against France. Even though nothing was said in the Erskine agreement about impressment, President Madison jubilantly proclaimed that nonintercourse, as applied to Great Britain, would be terminated on June 10, 1809. Scores of American ships headed for British ports. During a single week in June 1809, more cotton was landed at Liverpool than had been received at that port during the entire year of 1808.

But George Canning, the British foreign minister who during the Napoleonic Wars figured as the evil genius of Anglo-American relations, repudiated Erskine's agreement on the ground that Erskine had violated his instructions. In truth he had, but he had also aligned the United States economically with Great Britain in its war with France. Punctilio prevailed and the Erskine agreement was consigned to the wastebasket and the offending minister recalled.

In August 1809, angry and crestfallen, President Madison was obliged to withdraw his proclamation and to reinstate nonintercourse against Great Britain as well as against France. But this measure, like the embargo, inflicted greater damage upon the United States than upon Great Britain and France. Once at sea, American ships proceeded to go to the country where prices were highest, which usually meant Great Britain. Moreover, the British navy enforced the nonintercourse act against France far more effectively than did the United States itself. Nonintercourse, in short, worked to the advantage of Great Britain—the last thing the Republicans wanted.

Macon's Bill. In lieu of strong leadership from the executive—and it was obvious that President Madison was at a loss for a policy—Congress took over the direction of American foreign policy. In 1810 Congress passed Macon's Bill #2, which reopened trade with all countries for one year. However, if either Great Britain or France rescinded its regulations in restraint of American trade before March 3, 1811, and the other country did not follow suit within three months, nonimportation would go into effect against the noncomplying country.

Like the Nonintercourse Act, Macon's Act #2 favored the nation which controlled the sea-lanes. But against British sea power, Napoleon could bring an almost inexhaustible store of cunning and guile. In Macon's Act #2, the French emperor saw an unprecedented opportunity for the exercise of this particular talent. In 1810 in the hope of forcing Great Britain to repeal the orders in council or, failing that, to provoke war between the United States and Great Britain, Napoleon assured President Madison that the Berlin and Milan Decrees had been revoked insofar as they affected American commerce. Although Napoleon failed to back up his words with deeds, President Madison declared that the French emperor had satisfied all the requirements stipulated by Macon's Act #2. The American President was himself playing a deep game. He believed that if the restrictions were lifted against France, Great Britain would be forced to follow by repealing the orders in council.

But the British government refused to play either Napoleon's or President Madison's game. Before rescinding the orders in council, it insisted upon proof that France was acting in good faith. No such proof was forthcoming. Accordingly, in February 1811, Macon's Act #2 went into effect. American ports were open to the ships of France, and American ships were permitted to trade with French-controlled Europe. British ships, on the other hand, were excluded from American ports, and Great Britain placed beyond the reach of American commerce.

Even though Napoleon continued to seize and condemn American ships and their cargoes in French ports, the United States government solemnly maintained that the Milan and the Berlin Decrees had been rescinded and that the British must, therefore, repeal the orders in council. From the vantage point of London, however, President Madison seemed to be either the dupe or the accomplice of Napoleon. The President, of course, was neither. He was taking a calculated risk which, if successful, would mean that the freedom of the seas would be established without the necessity of firing a shot.

Public Impatience with Economic Coercion. Nevertheless, the failure of economic coercion to accomplish the results confidently predicted by Jefferson and Madison created a mood of disillusionment in the country. Embargoes, nonimportation, nonintercourse, and, indeed, all other measures short of war began to seem wholly inadequate. Even Thomas Jefferson, in retirement at Monticello, admitted in 1811 that the policy of palliating and enduring no longer held out hope of redress of grievances. War promised to resolve all the doubts and dilemmas produced by the fruitless and interminable controversy over neutral rights. The peaceful diplomacy of Jefferson and Madison had tried the souls of many American patriots more than war itself.

The War Hawks. This shift in public opinion was clearly manifested in the congressional elections of 1810, when over sixty incumbent Republicans were replaced by new members most of whom were War Hawks. Chief among them were John C. Calhoun of South Carolina, Henry Clay of Kentucky, Felix Grundy of Tennessee, and Peter B. Porter of New York. Clay, although a freshman member, was elected speaker of the House of Representatives, an election more far-reaching in its consequences than some presidential elections. For Clay converted the office of speaker into one of the most powerful positions in the United States government. He appointed members of committees, planned legislation, shepherded bills through Congress, and, in general, took direction of the country's foreign and domestic policy.

Clay's rapid rise to power resulted not only from his ability and his forceful and magnetic personality but from the lack of strong leadership on the part of President Madison. Jefferson said that Madison was "the greatest man in the world," but his talents were those of a parliamentarian and student of government rather than those of an inspiring public leader. From the beginning, his Cabinet was disrupted by factionalism. The Smith faction of Maryland headed by Senator Samuel Smith and his brother Robert, later appointed secretary of state by Madison, feuded with Albert Gallatin, the secretary of the treasury.

The Expiration of the Bank. Dissension within the Republican party contributed to the downfall of the Bank of the United States. Although the recharter of the Bank (its charter was due to expire in 1811) was strongly recommended by Gallatin, the anti-Gallatin forces in Congress and within the administration were strengthened by the large number of Republicans who had never been reconciled to the constitutionality of the Bank, by the state banks which wished to escape from the restraints imposed upon the amount of paper money they could safely circulate, and by those who argued that since two thirds of the stock of the Bank was held by foreigners, it would weaken the United States in time of war. Against these arguments, President Madison had no convincing answers. As a result, the bill to recharter the Bank of the United States was defeated in Congress by the votes of many members who were already clamoring for war against Great Britain.

The Road to War

The British and the Indians. In the American West, war had already begun. The fighting, it is true, was between Americans and Indians, but behind every hostile Indian, westerners saw an Englishman, guiding the hand that wielded the gun and the scalping knife. True, the scalping knives, guns, and ammunition were made in Britain and traded to the Indians for furs. Yet the British government did not incite the Indians to take up the hatchet against the American settlements. Its policy was to conserve the tribesmen's strength until war between Great Britain and the United States made their services indispensable.

Tecumseh and the Prophet. The fact that, from the British point of view, the Indians struck prematurely, was due to the presence of the most remarkable twin brothers produced by any Indian tribe in recorded history. Tecumseh and his brother, the Prophet, were Shawnees. Had they been fighting in any other cause than that of resisting white settlement, they would have gone down in history as heroes in mankind's struggle for freedom. Tecumseh was the orator and warrior. The Prophet supplied the mysticism and the fervor that inspired the tribesmen to fight with reckless courage. Claiming to hold direct communication with the Great Spirit and to possess miraculous powers, the Prophet called upon all Indians to abjure the white man's firewater and firearms and to take up the ancestral weapons of the bow, arrow, and tomahawk. Tecumseh organized the Indians in accord with his brother's directives: all Indians, he declared, were one people, all lands belonged to the tribes in common, and no lands could be sold without the consent of all.

Disdaining the Prophet and the Great Spirit, William Henry Harrison, the governor of the Indiana territory, "bought" three million acres of tribal lands in a single transaction and at a price which, by comparison, made the Louisiana Purchase seem extortionate. By so doing, he invited an Indian War, but it was the British who were accused of having incited the Indians.

The Battle of Tippecanoe. When Harrison threatened to uphold these land cessions by military force if necessary, Tecumseh took his case for an Indian confederacy to the southern tribes. Meanwhile, the northern Indians began to concentrate at Tippecanoe, the Prophet's town, near the confluence of the Wabash and Tippecanoe Rivers. In the autumn of 1811 in order to break up this concentration before Tecumseh returned, Harrison moved his army of one thousand men up the Wabash River to Tippecanoe. But the Indians struck first, and Harrison's men were forced to withstand a day of heavy enemy fire. They drove off the attackers and burned the Indian village. The heavy Indian losses weakened the Indian confederacy on the eve of the war for which the British had been holding back their Indian allies. In the telling and retelling, however, the battle of Tippecanoe became an epic of heroism and consummate generalship. Nearly thirty years later, on the strength of this myth and copious quantities of hard cider, Harrison was swept into the presidency of the United States.

The battle of Tippecanoe convinced westerners that the Northwest would know no peace until the British were driven from Canada. Andrew Jackson exclaimed that "the blood of our murdered heroes must be revenged!" But he did not believe that killing Indians would be sufficient. Britons, as well, must bite the dust.

The Southern Frontier: West Florida. On the southern frontier, Americans' territorial ambitions brought them into conflict with Spain and its tributary Indians, especially the Cherokees and the Choctaws, some of the most formidable warriors on the North American continent. But Spain itself was far too deeply involved in the war in Europe—in 1810–1812 French and British armies were fighting for control of the Iberian Peninsula—to play an active part in North America. Since Spain denied that West Florida was part of the Louisiana Purchase and refused to sell it to the United States, the Americans determined to take it by force. In 1810 American settlers and adventurers in West Florida staged an insurrection, declared their independence, and asked to be incorporated in the United States. The "republic" of West Florida was annexed in 1811, the expenses incurred by the revolutionaries were paid by the United States government, and the territory was made part of Louisiana. Even so, not all the territory supposedly acquired from France in 1803 was "redeemed." The republic of West Florida extended only to the Pearl River, whereas the United States claimed everything, including Mobile Bay, to the Perdido River. In 1813 this region too became United States territory when American troops occupied Mobile and the surrounding area.

In the meantime, President Madison was becoming the victim of his own diplomatic finesse. By portraying Napoleon as an honest man who was dealing fairly and aboveboard with the United States, he severely strained credulity. Worse, he had put himself and the country in a position which required the British government to accept Napoleon's probity or face the consequence of war with the United States.

Prowar and Antiwar Factions. In contrast to the President's devious diplomacy, the War Hawks advocated a straightforward policy which promised to deliver the United States from the perplexities and frustrations occasioned by economic coercion. They stood for patriotism, national honor, freedom of the seas, sailors' rights, and the pacification of the Indians. In short, they proposed to accomplish by war everything that economic pressure had failed to do.

Even the most pugnacious War Hawks could hardly fail to see that the country was not united in support of war. They themselves were a minority of their own party. With few exceptions, the merchants and shipowners opposed a war from which they foresaw only financial loss. Repeatedly, President Madison and the War Hawks rebuked American businessmen for putting profit above national honor. Yet the War Hawks believed that if the flag were flung forward, the American people would rally around, resolved to do or die for Old Glory. President Madison thought that even New Englanders would give their all to the country. They were, he said "determined republicans."

Whatever the attitude of New Englanders, there was no doubt of the loyalty of westerners and their ardor for war. The most national-minded section of the Union keenly resented British disregard of American rights at sea. Moreover, their material interests were directly affected: the loss of British markets and the withdrawal of the British merchant marine from American trade tended to depress the price of commodities which westerners sold and to increase the cost of manufactured goods which they bought. Finally, the depredations committed by the Northwest Indians gave them a special reason for hating Great Britain.

Had neutral rights been the sole reason for going to war, the United States might well have engaged either Great Britain, France, or both simultaneously in hostilities. For ever since the resumption of the war in 1803, the French had taken a heavy toll of American ships, heavier, in fact, than had the British. As Nathaniel Macon said, "the Devil himself could not tell which government, England or France, is the more wicked."

A Choice Between Two Enemies. But the War Hawks did not weigh degrees of wickedness; their objective was to vindicate American rights and honor and, in the process, to expand the territory of the United States by military victory. Such calculations led inescapably to the conclusion that Great Britain was both the prime and the logical enemy. The reason for preferring Great Britain rather than France as an antagonist was put succinctly by Henry Clay: "The one we can strike, the other we cannot reach." The United States had already fought an undeclared war with France and found that it yielded no material profit. War with Great Britain, on the other hand, offered hope of tangible rewards. While the hope of acquiring Canada was not the paramount cause of war—without the orders in council and impressment there would have been no armed conflict—Canada did provide the theater upon which the War Hawks expected to engage the enemy and did offer a potential indemnity for the losses in ships and cargoes Americans had sustained from the operation of the orders in council. Moreover, Canada was expected to offer little resistance to the "liberating" American army. Thomas Jefferson predicted that the conquest of Canada as far as Quebec would be "a mere matter of marching," and Andrew Jackson told the Tennessee volunteers that they could look forward to a "military promenade."

Territorial aggrandizement was certain to raise the question of sectional balance. If the North acquired Canada from Great Britain, at whose expense was the South to procure corresponding gains? Many southerners regarded East Florida as an acceptable counterweight to Canada. But the full implications of the problem created by the possibility of incorporating Canada in the Union were not squarely faced in 1812. Such difficult decisions were usually evaded by saying that if Canada were conquered, it would be retained for bargaining purposes at the peace table. By thus leaving indefinite the final disposition of Canada, an open breach between North and South was avoided.

The Decision for War. Before yielding to the clamor for war, President Madison was resolved to exhaust every resource of diplomacy and economic coercion. By the spring of 1812, however, he was convinced that the British could never be persuaded that Napoleon had really revoked the Berlin and Milan Decrees. On June 1, therefore, the President sent a message to Congress recommending not that it declare war but that it consider whether the United States ought to remain passive or resort to the use of force. In this message, the President gave some inkling of his own inclinations. In deference to the War Hawks, he put impressment, which since the settlement of the *Chesapeake* affair, had been relegated to a secondary position, at the top of American grievances.

Despite the War Hawks' assertion that a vote against war was "a vote for England against America," the vote in Congress was not overwhelmingly in favor of a declaration of hostilities. In the House, 79 members favored a declaration while 49 were opposed; in the Senate, 19 votes were cast in favor and 13 against. While almost half the votes cast for war in the House of Representatives came from states south of Mason and Dixon's line, it was not as sectional as it appeared. Six affirmative votes came from Massachusetts

Republicans. Pennsylvania voted 16 to 2 in favor of war. The entire West, by contrast, possessed only nine votes in the House. Without the votes cast by northern Republicans, the declaration could not have been carried. It was not, as Federalists said, "Mr. Madison's War"; it was the Republican party's war. Party regularity, more than public opinion or sectionalism, produced the war. Most of the party moderates or doves went over to the Hawks. Almost 90 per cent of the Republican members of Congress present on June 18, 1812, voted for war. But the Federalist minority exhibited even greater cohesion: not a Federalist broke ranks to vote for war with Great Britain.

No Republican admitted that the United States was acting in any sense as an ally of France. Yet their protestations did not alter the fact that the United States entered the war in England's darkest hour. Although President Madison and the War Hawks had no inkling of Napoleon's intentions, a few days after the American declaration the French army began the invasion of Russia, the one country on the European continent which Jefferson regarded as the true friend of the United States. The War of 1812 ranks as one of Napoleon's most notable diplomatic triumphs. At the time most critical for his own fortunes, he had played an important role in precipitating war between the two English-speaking countries.

A War for Objectives Already Gained. At the very time that the United States was declaring war, economic coercion was achieving belated results. On June 23 responding to pressure from British merchants and manufacturers, the British government revoked the orders in council on condition that the United States repeal the Nonintercourse Act against Great Britain. The ships carrying the news of the war declaration and of the conditional withdrawal of the orders in council passed each other in mid-Atlantic.

For the British, however, it was a case of too little and too late. The ministry said nothing about impressment, about incitement of the Indians, or about compensation for American losses suffered under the orders in council. Although the British navy held off from engaging in hostilities until October 1812, in the hope that the United States would reconsider its declaration of war, President Madison decided to let the conflict go on. The United States, it appeared, would settle for nothing less than the total freedom of the seas.

The War of 1812

Declared but Unprepared. Anticipating an easy victory, the United States had hardly troubled to prepare for war. By abolishing the Bank of the United States in 1811, the government had disarmed itself financially. The small United States Army was fully occupied in guarding the frontiers against the Indians. Except for gunboats, which proved completely useless, the Navy was scarcely larger than when it had fought the Barbary corsairs. Since 1806 in consequence of Republican economizing, no large ships had been built. Americans expected to fight the war with *élan:* armored with a sense of righteousness and imbued with hatred of British "despotism," scores of thousands of mettlesome militiamen and volunteers for the regular army were expected to spring to arms overnight, that is, if they could find the arms. There was even a shortage of fifes and drums with which to stir the martial enthusiasm of prospective volunteers. At the outbreak of the war, only about 7000 men were in uniform out of the 35,000 authorized by Congress. Although West Point had been established in 1802, the country as yet possessed no organization for the training of military officers other than engineers. To command its meager army, the government called upon veterans of the first war with Great Britain. American revolutionary generals did not fade away; they were resurrected to fight the battles of the War of 1812. West Point's contribution was mainly in engineers: not a single fort constructed by West Pointers during the war was captured by the British or the Indians.

Military Defeats. For Americans, the war proved to be almost wholly a succession of unpleasant surprises. The invasion of Canada did not turn out to be the walkover predicted by Andrew Jackson. Instead, in July 1812 General William Hull surrendered an American army at Detroit to a combined force of British and Indians. A few months later, another American army that had crossed into Canada near Niagara was forced to surrender, while a large body of New York militiamen watched from the American side of the river. Their orders did not permit them to fight outside the territorial limits of the United States. At the end of 1812, the British controlled the Great Lakes. Several important American posts, including Detroit and Fort Dearborn, the site of Chicago, had fallen to their attack, and the only Americans in Canada were prisoners of war. Americans were defeated by their own overconfidence, the better generalship of the British, the superior discipline of the British regulars, the hostility of the Canadians to the American invaders, and the inability of the American Army to solve the logistic problems involved in maintaining operations hundreds of miles from the American bases.

Economic Distress. Driven from office by the machinations of the Smith faction, Albert Gallatin left the finances of the United States to far less expert hands. Although taxes were increased slightly in 1813, the government's principal financial resource was loans. These could be floated only at a high rate of interest because the government's credit was seriously impaired as a result of the reverses suffered in the war and of the refusal of New England bankers to cooperate. Moreover, since the state banks no longer were subject to the controls formerly exerted by the Bank of the United States, they issued paper money freely. An inflationary spiral was thereby set in motion which caused hardships to wage earners and increased the cost of the war.

The Election of 1812. For President Madison, the war had become a political liability. Realizing that the President was in trouble, De Witt Clinton of New York entered the presidential contest as an antiadministration Republican. Although Clinton did not run as a peace candidate—his campaign was directed chiefly against "Virginia influence"—he received the enthusiastic

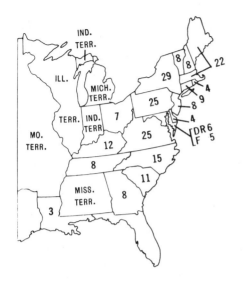

THE ELECTION OF 1812

	ELECTORAL VOTE BY STATE
REPUBLICAN James Madison	128
FUSION De Witt Clinton	89
NOT VOTED	1
	218

support of antiwar Federalists to whom Madison had become anathema. Madison won reelection with 128 votes to Clinton's 89. At best, the President had received a tepid endorsement of his handling of foreign policy and his conduct of the war.

End of the War in Europe. Because Napoleon's army perished in the snows of Russia in 1812–1813, 1813 promised to be a year of decision for the United States. When the war in Europe ended, thousands of seasoned British regulars would be released for service in North America. Presumably, the British would then attempt to use Canada as a base from which to mount an invasion of the United States. In 1813 the best the United States could do to prevent this thrust into its own territory was to regain control of Lake Erie, an indispensable chain in the British line of communications with the West. Late in the summer of 1813, a jerry-built American flotilla, under the command of Oliver Perry, defeated a British flotilla. As laconic as Caesar, Perry merely reported that "we have met the enemy, and they are ours." Tecumseh's death and the ruin of the Indian confederacy, which followed closely upon the British loss of Lake Erie, permitted American forces to regain temporary control of the West. Moreover, in October 1813 the Americans finally won an important land battle when General Harrison defeated the British at the Battle of the Thames. Later that year, in one of their brief and inglorious forays into Canada, American troops burned the parliament buildings at York (Toronto).

No American army could maintain itself in Canada. At the end of 1813, the British still retained the initiative. In December 1813 Niagara fell to the British who controlled it until the end of the war. The small American fur-trading settlement at Astoria on the Columbia River surrendered to a rival British fur-trading company and was renamed Fort George. And early in 1814 the British regained control of Lake Ontario.

American Victories at Sea. During the darkest days of the war, the Americans' morale was sustained by naval victories. American and British frigates and sloops engaged each other in single-ship actions. These duels testified to the sporting spirit of British naval officers and sailors. Because of its numerical strength, the British fleet in North American waters was under no compulsion to throw away its advantage by taking on individual American ships, particularly since American frigates carried more guns and were more maneuverable than their British counterparts. Even so, victory did not always go to the Americans. Before the war was over, the United States lost two of its best frigates and several of its sloops in single-ship actions. And in 1814 the British admiralty prohibited further duels. Henceforth, the British navy concentrated its attention upon blockading the American coast, a blockade which in the spring of 1814 was extended to New England. This action was forced upon the government by the heavy losses incurred at the hands of American privateers. Before the British tightened the blockade and instituted the convoy system, they had lost over one thousand ships to enemy action.

Federalist Opposition to the War. The ill-success of the war merely intensified the Federalists' opposition to it. They viewed American defeats as a vindication of their prophecies, not as calls to action to save the country. In their opinion, the United States was fighting the wrong nation. From every point of view, the real enemy of the United States was Napoleonic France. For this reason, they celebrated Russian victories over the French. "In the redemption of the world, by the arms of Russia," declared Robert G. Harper, a South Carolina Federalist, "all nations must rejoice."

Insofar as it was within their power, the New England Federalist leaders succeeded in taking their section out of the war. Government war loans were boycotted; illegal trade with the enemy was carried on; and several state governors withheld their militia from service in the field on the ground that they were needed for home defense. But not all New Englanders were antiwar Federalists. The section contributed more volunteers to the United States Army than did either the South or the West.

Economically, the war proved more injurious to the economy of tidewater Virginia than to any other section. Already decaying as a result of generations of wasteful and destructive agricultural practices, the tidewater was abandoned by hundreds of planters. Travelers found deserted country houses, desolate and tumbledown churches, and careworn, disheartened people. Yet, in general, the planters supported the war as loyally as they had the embargo. No state of the Union was as ill served economically by the presidents it gave to the country as was Virginia.

The British Three-Pronged Offensive. In April 1814 Napoleon abdicated and thereby brought about the event most dreaded by the Madison administration: the freeing of thousands of veteran British troops and scores of ships for service in North America against the United States. The British took full advantage of this turn of fortune. A three-pronged attack upon the United

States was planned. A British army was to move down from Canada by way of the Lake Champlain waterway; a British fleet and army were to conduct combined operations against the United States coastal cities; and a large British force was ordered to capture New Orleans.

At first, everything went according to the British plan. In the Chesapeake, the British army and navy met with astonishing success. Overcoming brief American resistance at Bladensburg, the army marched to Washington. The Madisons were not at home. The President had been carried away in the crush of panic-stricken militiamen after the defeat at Bladensburg, and Mrs. Madison, setting an example of courage to her countrymen, left the President's House shortly before the British arrived, carrying with her Gilbert Stuart's portrait of George Washington. Ostensibly in retaliation for the American burning of York, the British put to the torch the President's House, the Capitol, and other public buildings.

But at Baltimore, where the British next turned their attention, they encountered unexpectedly stiff resistance. The Maryland militia, before retreating to the city, inflicted heavy casualties upon the enemy, including the loss of the British commander, General Ross. After failing to silence the shore batteries guarding the approaches to Baltimore, the British fleet sailed away. It was during this bombardment that Francis Scott Key, held a prisoner aboard a British ship, wrote the words to "The Star-Spangled Banner."

In the North, a British army under General Prevost failed to penetrate south of Lake Champlain. At Plattsburg on that lake a British flotilla was destroyed by a fleet built of green timber, manned by equally green crews, and commanded by a young officer, Commodore Thomas Macdonough, who had seen action in the Mediterranean during the war with Tripoli. Macdonough's victory, one of the truly decisive engagements of the war, convinced General Prevost that he had no alternative but to retreat to Canada. The threat to the North was over.

Secession Sentiment in New England. But the internal threat to the integrity of the Union was by no means over. Some New England Federalists, among them Timothy Pickering the seasoned old secessionist, were ready to secede from the Union over Mr. Madison's War. The justification for secession was political rather than economic. These men were estranged primarily by the shift in political power which had occurred since 1800. The war brought to the surface all the latent discontents, jealousies, and animosities which had been rankling New Englanders for years: the three-fifths rule, the succession of Virginia-born presidents, the Louisiana Purchase, the admission in 1811 of Louisiana as a state, the "jealousy and hatred of commerce" manifested by the government in Washington, and a war, ostensibly for free ships and sailors' rights, which compelled shipowners to abandon the sea and put the sailors on the beach.

However gratifying to the pride and prejudices of New England, secession entailed political and economic sacrifices which gave pause to many moderate

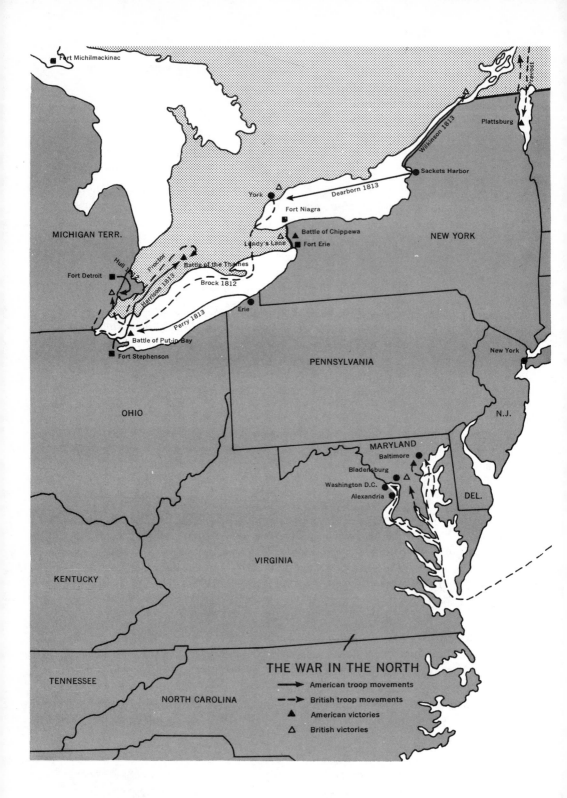

Fort Michilmackinac

Wilkinson 1813

Plattsburg

Sackets Harbor

York

Fort Niagra

Dearborn 1813

MICHIGAN TERR.

Battle of Chippewa

Lundy's Lane

Fort Erie

NEW YORK

Hull

Proctor

Battle of the Thames

Fort Detroit

Harrison 1813

Brock 1812

Perry 1813

Erie

New York

Battle of Put-in Bay

Fort Stephenson

PENNSYLVANIA

OHIO

N.J.

MARYLAND

Baltimore

Bladensburg

DEL.

Washington D.C.

Alexandria

VIRGINIA

KENTUCKY

THE WAR IN THE NORTH

→ American troop movements

- - → British troop movements

▲ American victories

△ British victories

TENNESSEE

NORTH CAROLINA

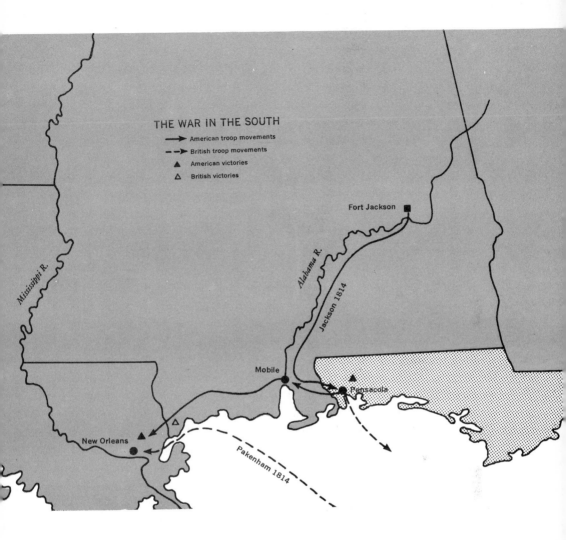

THE WAR IN THE SOUTH

→ American troop movements
--→ British troop movements
▲ American victories
△ British victories

Fort Jackson

Mississippi R.

Alabama R.

Jackson 1814

Mobile

Pensacola

New Orleans

Pakenham 1814

Federalists. In the first place, Federalism was staging an unprecedented comeback in New England. In the elections of 1814, Federalists carried 43 out of 45 congressional districts east of the Hudson. Secondly, of all the banks in the United States, only those of New England remained on a specie basis, with the result that specie tended to gravitate toward that area. With capital abundant and supplies of European-manufactured goods running low, manufacturing burgeoned in New England. Under these circumstances, moderates pointed out, by seceding New England would be cutting itself off from its customers, its debtors, and its source of riches.

While the radicals at first favored a convention of delegates from the New England states, the meeting which was held in Hartford, Connecticut, from December 1814 to January 1815 was actually summoned by conservatives who hoped to avert secession. They succeeded in confining the work of the convention to the recommendation of amendments to the Constitution designed to improve New England's position in the Union. Armed with these recommendations, delegates from Massachusetts arrived in Washington in January 1815 only to be greeted by the news that Andrew Jackson had won a great military victory at New Orleans. The commissioners folded their tents and silently stole away. But nothing could undo the damage the Federalist party had inflicted upon itself. In the hour of the Republic's trial, the party leaders had thought not of how they could serve their country but of how they could convert the Republic's distress into sectional advantage.

Defeat of the British at New Orleans. The British attack upon New Orleans, which was expected to deprive the United States of the use of the Mississippi River, ended in one of the worst disasters in proportion to numbers engaged ever suffered by a British army. In this expedition, the element of surprise was wholly lacking except insofar as the British themselves were surprised by the resistance they encountered. But they had received strong intimations that it was not to be an easy victory. In March 1814 Andrew Jackson and his army of frontiersmen broke the power of the Creek Indians, who had been armed and supplied by the British, and in November 1814 Jackson invaded Spanish Florida and captured Pensacola. Despite these signs that the Americans planned to fight at New Orleans, Sir Edward Pakenham, the British commander, ordered his troops to make the kind of stand-up, frontal attack upon strong American positions which his father-in-law, the Duke of Wellington, would have considered suicidal. And so, indeed, it proved. With a motley army made up from the waterfront population of New Orleans, Jean Lafitte's pirate crew from Barataria, townspeople, two regiments of regulars, several companies of militia, and a band of free Negroes, Andrew Jackson defeated the British. By means of rifle fire from protected positions upon an enemy advancing across an open field, the Americans inflicted crushing casualties upon the British force of 6000 men. In less than half an hour, 2600 British soldiers had been killed or wounded, among them three major generals and eight colonels. Pakenham himself was killed. The Americans lost only 13 men killed and 58 wounded.

It was a famous victory, the anniversary of which was long celebrated as a holiday, but it had no bearing whatever upon the peace settlement. The battle was fought only because of the slowness of communications across the Atlantic. The treaty of peace had already been signed when Jackson and his men mowed down the British regulars. Nevertheless, the battle of New Orleans gave Americans the comforting illusion that they had won the war. A generation of English travelers in the United States was forced to listen to American boasting about New Orleans, which, together with tobacco-chewing and spitting, was accounted one of the worst trials faced by English visitors in the United States.

Negotiations for Peace. Even while the delegates were meeting at Hartford, the British and American representatives at Ghent in the Netherlands, were bringing the war to an end. As early as 1813, the Madison administration had extended peace feelers. The Russian czar was the first to respond. Eager to bring the war between Great Britain and the United States to a halt, the czar offered his good offices as mediator. The British government rejected his offer, but direct negotiations between the belligerents began in the early summer of 1814. The British at first insisted upon the creation of an Indian buffer state and a redrawing of the boundary between the United States and Canada that would have cost the United States approximately one third of its territory. But as reports of the fighting in North America reached London, it became apparent to the British that they were not in a position to dictate peace. The Duke of Wellington declined to take command of the British army in North America, pointing out that nothing could be done until control of the Great Lakes had been ensured.

The military stalemate was reflected in the treaty of peace signed by the British and American commissioners on December 24, 1814. Both sides were compelled to recede from their maximum demands and to restore the prewar boundaries of the United States and Canada even though this necessitated the evacuation by the British of a part of Maine. Other boundary questions were referred to commissions, and the conflicting claims of the United States and Great Britain to the Oregon territory were left to later discussion. In effect, these provisions of the treaty gave the United States time to consolidate its position upon the North American continent.

Results of the War. The clear intent of the treaty was to return to the prewar status quo. The United States failed to achieve any of the objectives for which it had gone to war. No mention was made of impressment, freedom of the seas, and blockades. The only territory gained by the United States as a result of the war was the eastern part of West Florida, which was taken from Spain, a country with which America was at peace. As for the Indians, they received a mere promise on the part of the United States to restore to Tecumseh's warriors their tribal lands. Few of the warriors remained alive to enjoy this felicity. In fact, the Indians were the only real losers by the war. No longer assured of British protection, firearms, and supplies and decimated by the war, they were left to the mercy of expansionist-minded Americans.

Some Long-Term Consequences. Even though the second war with Great Britain was marked by defeat and humiliation quite as much as by victory and glory, Americans discovered a hitherto unprobed depth of national feeling. Seemingly, Americans had to prove their independence, their national identity, and their title to the rank of a great power, by fighting Britons. The words of the national anthem were inspired by the British attack upon Fort McHenry at Baltimore. Americans gained from the war a new sense of self-confidence, self-sufficiency, and national purpose. The fact that the war produced no territorial conquests except West Florida meant that the sections had nothing to quarrel about. The cardinal objective of the War Hawks, "the establishment of the national character," was achieved even beyond their most sanguine expectations. Yet within a decade of these events, the nationalism which characterized the Era of Good Feelings began to be eroded by the controversy over slavery and the sectional balance of power.

For almost the first time since independence, the almost simultaneous ending of war in Europe and in the western hemisphere liberated Americans not only from foreign entanglements but from the foreign sympathies which had divided them and weakened the nation. In the long interval of peace which followed the Napoleonic Wars, the sources of friction between the United States and the European powers largely disappeared. Except for brief flare-ups, neutral rights ceased to embroil belligerents and neutrals. Moreover, in 1861–1865, the roles were reversed. The North upheld the rights of belligerents while Great Britain advocated the cause of neutral rights without, however, going to the length of fighting for them.

While the War of 1812 did not mark the end of animosity, prejudice, and ill will in Anglo-American relations, powerful countervailing influences began to make their influence felt. Many Britons accepted the result of the war as the beginning of a decisive change in the relations between the two countries. Eight years after the Peace of Ghent, George Canning, who prior to the War of 1812 had made Americans the butt of his sarcasm and ridicule, proposed a virtual alliance between his country and the United States for the defense of the western hemisphere against the aggressive designs of the Holy Alliance. Blood did prove thicker than water, but it required the shedding of blood to make it so. On the American side, over 2200 men died in battle during the War of 1812.

The United States in Peace and War. At the time of the Treaty of Ghent, the United States had existed for almost forty years as a republic under either the Articles of Confederation or the Constitution. During most of this period, the era of the Wars of the French Revolution and the Napoleonic Wars, Europe had been the scene of unremitting international strife, and the conflict had spilled over into Africa, Asia, and the western hemisphere. This worldwide struggle of the great European powers had jeopardized the existence of the United States in several ways. It had created a profound division in the Republic between French and British sympathizers, and it had threatened to involve the United States directly in the war at a time when the country was too new and too weak to endure such involvement. This danger had come very close to fulfillment. New England and the South were at odds most of the time, and a group of New England Federalists had actually advocated the secession of their section from the Union. Moreover, the country was informally at war with France in 1798–1801 and formally at war with Great Britain in 1812–1815. But internal disruption had been averted, and the War of 1812 was too brief to put an unbearable strain upon the ligaments of union.

For twenty years of this period, the most important public questions had concerned the trading rights of a neutral carrier on the high seas in wartime. Neither the War of 1812 nor any other event which occurred during this time span brought these questions closer to settlement. However, the restoration of peace in Europe—a peace which, except for the Crimean and Franco-Prussian Wars, lasted for a century—made the assertion of the rights of neutrals at sea seem far less relevant to the preservation of national dignity and independence. As a result, the questions which had been raised by the slogan "the freedom of the seas" were permitted to lapse but not, as 1914–1917 was to show, wholly to expire.

After 1815, consequently, the United States was free to concentrate its attention almost entirely upon its internal development. By so doing, the people of the United States were brought face to face with a problem far more intractable than the rights of neutrals—the existence of Negro slavery in a republic dedicated to the principle of human equality and to the amelioration of the human condition.

With the election of 1800, a political party and a political philosophy which emphasized the virtues of an agricultural economy, the decentralization of authority, and the derogation of the functions of government had come into power in the United States. Seemingly, Hamilton's policies calling for centralization of power and economic diversification had been irrevocably defeated. Yet, while the majority of the American people approved of Jeffersonianism and gave it their suffrage, circumstances worked in favor of Hamiltonianism. Ironically, it was the Jeffersonians who gave the central government strength by purchasing Louisiana, by imposing rigid controls on American shipping, and by exercising the powers of war from 1812 to 1815. At the same time, they pushed the country toward economic diversification by cutting off European trade and forcing New England capital and manpower to turn toward manufacturing during the embargo and the war with Great Britain. By 1815 having survived the vicissitudes of both peace and war, the United States possessed a heritage of Jeffersonian ideals and Hamiltonian methods of meeting internal problems.

SUGGESTED READING

J. W. Pratt in his *Expansionists of 1812* advances the view that the war was produced primarily by the desire of northwestern frontiersmen to acquire Canada and of southwestern frontiersmen to take Florida. These frontiersmen, in Pratt's view, were actuated by a strong urge to acquire territory and to eliminate the Indian menace. The tendency of recent scholarship has been to downgrade this motive and to emphasize the importance that Americans attached to the freedom of the seas. Among the more important books that deal with the origins of the War of 1812 are A. L. Burt, *The United States, Great Britain, and British North America from the Revolution to the Peace after the War of 1812* (1940); Bradford Perkins, *Prologue to War: England and the United States, 1805–1812* (1961); Reginald Horsman, *The Causes of the War of 1812* (1962); J. F.

*Available in a paperback edition

Zimmerman, *Impressment of American Seamen* (1923); Irving Brant, *James Madison, the President* (1958); Roger H. Brown, *The Republic in Peril* (1964); Albert Z. Carr, *The Coming of the War* (1960); Dennis Gray, *Spencer Perceval* (1963); J. Steven Watson, *The Reign of George III* (1960).

Books relevant to the *Chesapeake* incident are Irving Brant, *James Madison: Secretary of State* (1954); Henry Adams, *History of the United States During the Administrations of Thomas Jefferson and James Madison** (1930); Leon F. Guttridge and Jay D. Smith, *The Commodores* (1969).

Congressional diplomacy is adequately treated by Alfred W. Crosby, Jr., *America, Russia, Hemp, and Napoleon: American Trade with Russia and the Baltic, 1783–1812* (1965); Bernard Mayo, *Henry Clay: Spokesman of the New West* (1937); Charles M. Wiltse, *John C. Calhoun: Nationalist, 1782–1828* (1944).

Henry Adams, *The History of the United States During the Administrations of Thomas Jefferson and James Madison** (1930) contains an excellent account of the military and naval events of the war. Irving Brant's *James Madison: Commander-in-Chief, 1812–1836* defends Madison's course of action. A. T. Mahan, *Sea Power in Its Relations to the War of 1812,* 2 vols. (1905) is a classic. Theodore Roosevelt, *The Naval War of 1812* (1882), was the maiden historical effort of a future President of the United States; Marquis James, *Andrew Jackson: The Border Captain* (1933), is highly readable. *See also* Leonard F. Guttridge and Jay D. Smith, *The Commodores: The U.S. Navy in the Age of Sail* (1969) and Colonel Vincent J. Esposito, ed., *The West Point Atlas of American Wars* (1959). For the peace negotiations of 1814, see F. L. Engelman, *The Peace of Christmas Eve* (1962); Samuel F. Bemis, *John Quincy Adams and the Foundations of American Foreign Policy* (1949); Bradford Perkins, *Castlereagh and Adams, 1812–1813* (1963); James R. Jacobs, *Tarnished Warrior: Major General James Wilkinson* (1938).

The Hartford Convention is best approached through Samuel Eliot Morison, *The Life and Letters of Harrison Gray Otis, Federalist,* 2 vols. (1913); Henry Cabot Lodge, *Life and Letters of George Cabot* (1877); James M. Banner, Jr., *To the Hartford Convention* (1970).

Tecumseh
and Indian Resistance
to the White Man /
Pictorial Essay

Tecumseh's attempt to unite the Indian tribes in concerted resistance to the expanding white population failed mainly because of the insular feelings of the individual tribes. The weaknesses of his British allies and the determination of the United States government to rid the frontier of the "Indian menace" also helped to defeat him.

Tecumseh, a Shawnee Indian, was born and raised in southwestern Ohio. His hostility toward the white man was intensified by two incidents in his youth. First, white men murdered his father when he refused to serve as their guide. A few years later the Shawnee war chief Cornstalk was shot at an American garrison. He had gone to the garrison to warn the commander that many of the Ohio Indians were drifting to the British. Although he was almost certainly innocent, the Americans believed Cornstalk guilty of the death of a white man.

After 1793, white settlers began to move into the area north of the Ohio River, although settlement was forbidden by treaty. As the number of whites increased, border warfare with the Indians resulted. Tecumseh took part in these forays and in 1792 became the leader of all the Shawnee warriors in Kentucky and Tennessee. After the Indians had defeated two earlier American expeditions, "Mad" Anthony Wayne was sent with an American army to settle the Indian problem in the Northwest territory. Tecumseh distinguished himself by his courage and boldness at the ensuing Battle of Fallen Timbers (1794), in which the Indians were defeated. When Wayne invited the Indians to a peace meeting at Greenville in Ohio, Tecumseh refused to go

On the opposite page is George Catlin's drawing of Tecumseh and the Prophet. *Picture: from* LETTERS AND NOTES ON THE MANNERS, CUSTOMS, AND CONDITION OF THE NORTH AMERICAN INDIANS, *Vol. II, by George Catlin, 1857.* Above is a picture of Tecumseh saving the lives of white prisoners. Known as one of the most humane Indian leaders, Tecumseh attempted, during the War of 1812, to prevent his followers from slaughtering white prisoners. *Picture: This item is reproduced by permission of The Huntington Library, San Marino, California*

LOVIE

On the opposite page is a picture of the peace council at Vincennes to which Governor Harrison invited Tecumseh in 1810. When the governor asserted that the United States had always been fair in its dealings with the Indians, Tecumseh shouted, "It is false! He lies!" Whereupon Harrison drew his sword, the Indians raised their tomahawks, and a fight seemed imminent. But Harrison adjourned the council, and the incident ended. *Picture: from* HISTORY OF INDIANA *by John B. Dillon, Indianapolis, Bingham and Doughty, 1859.* On this page is a picture of Tecumseh dressed in a British uniform. *Picture: The Filson Club*

and would not recognize the Treaty of Greenville (1795), which ceded to the United States almost two thirds of the Ohio territory, including the area in which Tecumseh lived. But as more settlers moved into the territory, Tecumseh decided that resistance was pointless and moved with his followers to Indiana. His resistance to the Treaty of Greenville endeared him to other warriors who were also unhappy with it, and made him the dominant Indian leader in the Northwest territory. The peace established by the Treaty of Greenville proved to be only a truce of about ten years.

During this time Tecumseh met a white girl named Rebecca Galloway. From her, he acquired a better knowledge of English and a deeper understanding of the white mentality. A romantic attachment developed between them, and Tecumseh eventually asked her to marry him. She consented on the condition that he agree to live with her as a white man, but Tecumseh would not leave his people.

Whiskey had been introduced to the Indians of the Northwest, and Tecumseh's younger brother, who was later known as Tenskwatawa or The Prophet, became a notorious drunkard. In 1805 he experienced the first of many trances. Following the trance, he gave up alcohol and preached against its use. His preaching, which he expanded to include support for Indian ways and an attack upon the evils brought by the white man, attracted many followers among the Indians. When he joined Tecumseh, his preaching furnished the philosophical and emotional basis for Tecumseh's fight against the encroaching white settlers. As The Prophet drew followers from many tribes, he began to alarm Governor William Henry Harrison, who in 1806 challenged him to perform a miracle, if he were really a prophet. Tenskwatawa obliged with a solar eclipse, which greatly increased his following.

As tensions between Indians and whites increased, Tecumseh realized that the only way the Indians could preserve their lands was to present a united front against the white intruders. To this end, he visited the tribes of the Northwest and the South. Everywhere he exhorted the Indians to unite in a confederacy against the white man. While young braves rallied to his cause, many older chiefs were reluctant to unite with old enemies or to pursue a course which they felt would lead only to defeat.

While Tecumseh was on his second southern trip, Harrison attacked and burned Tippecanoe, The Prophet's Town. The Battle of Tippecanoe came

Tecumseh's brother Tenskwatawa, "the Prophet," is pictured at the right. After the defeat at Tippecanoe, Tecumseh dismissed the Prophet in disgrace. *Picture: Library of Congress.* The picture on the opposite page shows the mounted riflemen under Colonel Richard Johnson attacking the British and the Indians at the Battle of the Thames. Johnson himself killed Tecumseh. *Picture: Anne S. K. Brown Military Collection, Brown University Library*

before Tecumseh had been able to forge an Indian alliance and touched off the sporadic warfare he had tried to avoid. Instead of a united Indian confederacy fighting to preserve Indian lands, each tribe struck out on its own without any coordination. Three months after Tippecanoe, the War of 1812 began, and Tecumseh allied himself with the British. He and his followers helped the British to capture Detroit. After Perry's victory on Lake Erie, the British decided to withdraw and abandon the Detroit region to the advancing American army under Harrison. Tecumseh was angry at the willingness of the British to give up the region he had fought to secure for his people. He finally extorted a promise from the British to retreat no further than the Thames River. There 700 British troops and 1000 Indians fought 3500 Americans under Harrison. At the end of the day, Tecumseh was dead, and the Indians dispersed. With Tecumseh died his dream of a united Indian confederacy.

CHAPTER SEVEN

PATTERNS OF LIFE AND SOCIAL VALUES

An Era of Equalitarian Democracy

POLITICALLY, IF THE progress of democracy seemed uncertain in the Republic between 1787 and 1815, it was because the Federalists believed that national power could be built only upon the basis of a program designed to gain the support of men of property and influence, a program which the Jeffersonians, when they attained power, did not wholly repudiate. But, actually, while endorsing the exercise of national power, the Jeffersonians were demonstrating that this power could be most firmly established on a broad base of democratic support rather than on a narrow base of aristocratic influence. In the United States, nationalism found an ally in the plain people rather than exclusively in "the wise, the good and the rich," as the early Federalists had supposed. Thus, if the era was one of increasing governmental power, it was also an era of increasing equalitarian democracy.

At first, the democratic tendency, especially in politics, was restrained by fear of unbridled popular government. Thus, in 1789–1790 the states which adopted new constitutions or revised their old constitutions tended to emphasize checks and balances designed, like those of the federal Constitution, to protect the opulent minority against "popular licentiousness." In 1790, for example, Pennsylvania adopted a new constitution which abandoned the single-chamber legislature of 1776 for a bicameral legislature and a strong executive. Even the frame of government adopted by Kentucky in 1791 required that the governor and the senate be chosen by an electoral college.

But toward the end of the period 1783–1815, the foundations were laid for the advent of Jacksonian democracy. Virtual manhood suffrage was achieved in several states, notably Pennsylvania and the new western states. Property qualifications for office holding were reduced. The choice of electors for the electoral college was taken from the state legislatures and given to the people. Political parties engaged increasing numbers of people in political campaigns by means of caucuses, party "tickets," and devices to "get out the vote." Even before 1815, Federalists were complaining that the United States was rushing into democracy before the people had been sufficiently prepared for the responsibilities thrust upon them. But, in general, conservatives in the United States realized that they must seek political power within an increasingly democratic political framework.

Social Democracy. Political democracy was a reflection of the social democracy which grew more and more characteristic of the United States. One of the features of American life which most forcibly struck Europeans was its insistence upon equality. Except for Negroes and the poorest white laborers and seamen, everyone was addressed as Mister. Servants were referred to as help; to call them servants to their face was to risk having them quit without notice. The only people who rejoiced in the name of servant were politicians who wished to be known as public servants. It was noted that even day laborers

A bridge over the Mohawk River. *Picture: The Newberry Library* advanced their opinions upon religious and political matters "with as much freedom as the gentleman or the scholar." An American workman or domestic servant expected to be treated with all the respect due a free, white citizen of the Republic.

While a patrician order did not exist in the United States, there was an aristocracy composed of planters, merchants, physicians, clergymen, and lawyers. Because of the extreme litigiousness of Americans, lawyers abounded. It was said that there were more lawyers in the Republic than beggars in Great Britain. More importantly, lawyers were replacing the clergy as the most influential body of men in America. But the American aristocracy, composed as it was of diverse elements, was always open to talent, and it could assert none of the prerogatives of a long-established aristocracy. Nor did upper-class Americans generally claim such distinctions. In public, at least, they chose to be regarded simply as conspicuously successful, but representative, figures of a society in which many members were also engaged in climbing the economic and social ladder.

Democracy in Religion. The pervasive influence of democracy extended to religion. Eighteenth-century intellectuals, among them the founding fathers of the American Republic, broke with orthodox Christianity and embraced Deism and later Unitarianism. Deism emphasized reason rather than emotion in religion. Deists believed in the essential goodness, instead of the depravity of men, and they discovered the essence of the Deity in benevolence, rationality, and good will toward men.

But such religion did not satisfy the emotional hunger of many of the common people. To them, Deism was a religion for tepid intellectuals and those who had arrived socially, not for those who sought God in ecstasy and felt in anticipation the delights of Heaven or the flames of hellfire. And so, revivalism began to sweep the American West, beginning in Kentucky in 1800. The gospel was carried by itinerant preachers, many of them unordained, who made stumps substitute for pulpits at large, open-air camp meetings. The effect of these hot-gospelers upon their audiences was electrifying: men, women, and children shrieked, frothed, groveled, and prostrated themselves in the dust as the Spirit moved them.

The foursquare gospel, as preached by the revivalists, restored the reality and the sense of immediacy of Heaven and hell. And the open book from which they drew inspiration promised an open road to salvation. Heaven was portrayed not as an exclusive residence for saints, far from the madding crowd in hell, as the early Puritans had imagined, but as a crowded, bustling place in which even sinners, if they had accepted Christ and repented of their sins, were sure of accommodations. Thus was American religion democratized even before the doctrine of equality and natural rights had fully democratized American politics.

The Methodist and Baptist churches profited most from this outpouring of the spirit. Both churches were already active in the areas where the revival had its greatest impact; both were frontier churches equipped with lay preachers, circuit riders, and proselyting zeal. American Methodism, ultimately the most numerous and powerful of the American Protestant denominations, owed its early success to Francis Asbury. In 1771 Asbury had been sent to America by John Wesley, the founder of Methodism. In 1784 he became the first bishop of the Methodist Episcopal Church of America. Almost his entire life was dedicated to evangelical preaching and to the expansion and organization of his church. The "pioneer bishop," as he was called, was rarely out of the saddle. He successfully surmounted every hazard of the frontier, including bugs, hostile Indians, and drunken, trigger-happy frontiersmen.

Among the most important social effects of the labors of Asbury and other itinerant preachers was the impetus they gave to the establishment of order, morality, and self-discipline among backwoodsmen. That westerners did not become white savages, as some Federalists feared, was owing in large measure to the civilizing influence exerted by the frontier churches.

In contrast to the evangelical churches, the Roman Catholic Church made few converts among frontiersmen. On the frontier it had better success with the Indians. However, its strength lay in the cities, particularly in New York and Philadelphia among Irish and German immigrants. In 1789 John Carroll was ordained as the first bishop of the Roman Catholic Church in the United States, and thereafter its growth was rapid. In 1776 there had been fewer than twenty thousand Roman Catholics in the country; by 1800 the number had increased to one hundred thousand.

Democracy and Education. The democratic spirit of the age was also reflected in concern for education. In a society where all men were "created equal," it was crucial that all should have an equal chance to develop their own potentialities and to make the most of their opportunities. It was no less crucial that where the people ruled, they should be competent to rule. Thus, Americans adopted earlier than the countries of Europe a democratic belief in widespread public education. New England had developed a school system during the colonial period. Jefferson envied this system and drew up for Virginia a comprehensive plan of education from the elementary grades to the university. The system he devised was highly competitive, and it did not provide for free schools, except in the elementary grade. It did give the children of the poor scholarships in the upper grades and at the college level if they showed exceptional ability. He stipulated that these natural aristocrats should devote their careers to public service. But, as Jefferson learned, Americans were more disposed to build canals and highways than to lay out their money on schools. In this respect, the New England states, where since colonial times each town had been obliged by law to maintain a school and a schoolmaster, were far ahead of other parts of the Union. The realization of the demand for free, universal, compulsory education awaited the growth of cities and the emergence of a large number of wage earners and dedicated educational reformers.

At the level of higher education, plans for the creation of a national

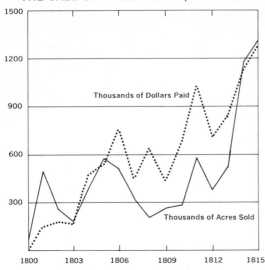

THE SALE OF PUBLIC LAND, 1800-1815

By 1795 Jay's treaty, Pinckney's Treaty, and the Treaty of Grenville had cleared the way for the rapid settlement of the Appalachian Plateau. Speculators' advertisements and new roads tempted thousands of people to leave the seaboard states because of overcrowding, poor soil, or encroaching plantations. *Source: Historical Statistics of the United States.*

university were recommended by the first six presidents of the United States, but Congress declined to act affirmatively. Nevertheless, during the period 1783–1815, almost forty colleges were founded in the United States. Many were denominational schools whose faculties attested to the dominant position still enjoyed by clergymen in American higher education. But even the denominational schools competed with each other for students and reached out beyond their own denominational bounds for bright young men capable of paying tuition. Some of the colleges founded during the colonial period began to expand beyond the teaching of undergraduates. Harvard, Pennsylvania, and Columbia added faculties of law and medicine.

Independently of the colleges, educated Americans were coming into closer intellectual association with one another. The founding of the American Academy of Arts and Sciences in 1780—Boston's answer to Philadelphia's American Philosophical Society founded by Benjamin Franklin in 1743—gave the United States two national organizations dedicated to the advancement of the arts and sciences. Moreover, the cultural life of the nation was enriched and the sense of nationality reinforced by the growth of public libraries, theaters, state and local historical societies, medical societies, musical and artistic groups, and by the publication of national magazines, some of which were devoted to literary criticism.

Frontier Democracy. In some respects, the democratic forces of the age were probably strengthened by the rapid settlement of the West. The frontiersmen left behind them the social distinctions of the East, and everyone's circumstances were much alike, inasmuch as all had to fend for themselves against the wilderness, and few started with special advantages. In other respects, however, these conditions were not quite as democratic as they have

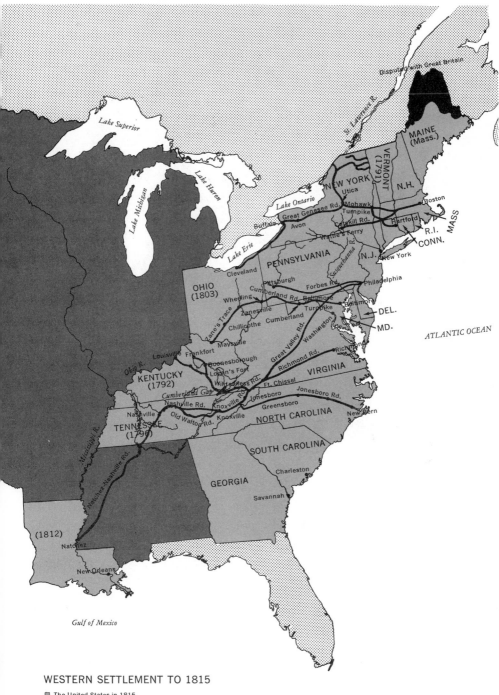

Lake Superior

Lake Michigan

Lake Huron

Lake Ontario

Lake Erie

St. Lawrence R.

Disputed with Great Britain

MAINE
(Mass.)

VERMONT
(1791)

N.H.

NEW YORK

Utica

Mohawk
Turnpike

Boston

MASS

Great Genesee Rd.

Avon

Catskill Rd.

Hartford

R.I.

Buffalo

CONN.

Susquehanna R.

N.J.

New York

PENNSYLVANIA

Cleveland

Pittsburgh

Forbes Rd.

Philadelphia

OHIO
(1803)

Wheeling

Cumberland Rd.

Baltimore

DEL.

Zanesville

Turnpike

MD.

Zane's Trace

Chillicothe

Cumberland

Washington

Ohio R.

Louisville

Frankfort

Maysville

Great Valley Rd.

Richmond

ATLANTIC OCEAN

Boonesborough

Richmond Rd.

KENTUCKY
(1792)

Logan's Fort

VIRGINIA

Cumberland Gap

Wilderness Rd.

Ft. Chissel

Nashville Rd.

Knoxville Rd.

Jonesboro

Jonesboro Rd.

Nashville

Knoxville

Greensboro

New Bern

TENNESSEE
(1796)

Old Walton Rd.

NORTH CAROLINA

Mississippi R.

SOUTH CAROLINA

Natchez-Nashville Rd.

GEORGIA

Charleston

(1812)

Savannah

Natchez

New Orleans

Gulf of Mexico

WESTERN SETTLEMENT TO 1815

▨ The United States in 1815

▣ Territories of the United States

■ Areas disputed with foreign powers

Standing on land he has cleared by the log house he built, a settler watches a wagon carrying another group of pioneers west. *Picture: Culver Pictures*

been made to appear, for on the frontier each man was expected to sink or swim according to his own strength; there was little effort to work out public solutions to social questions. An aristocracy consisting of entrepreneurs, landowners, and politicians quickly emerged. Racial prejudice, directed against Indians rather than against blacks, was likewise a characteristic of the frontier. Nevertheless, many Americans regarded the frontier as democratic and acclaimed its growth as a blow to aristocracy.

Whether democratic or not, the West was certainly growing in population and influence. Ohio, which before the Revolution had not contained a single white inhabitant, by the early 1800's was being converted into an annex of Connecticut, then the most thickly populated state in the Union. Every year, ten thousand or more Connecticut Yankees packed their families, household furniture, and farming utensils into a wagon, shouldered their axes, whistled

Yankee Doodle, and set off for the wilderness. To them, however, it was not the wilderness but the promised land.

Even Daniel Boone had difficulty in keeping ahead of the torrent of pioneers that poured into Kentucky and beyond. In 1775 he had settled in the wilderness on the site of Boonesboro, Kentucky. Twenty-five years later Kentucky had a population of about 200,000, and Boone was complaining of overcrowding and the scarcity of game. By 1815 Boone had moved on to the Missouri, but by that time it was clear that no matter how far west he might travel, he never could be sure of enjoying the solitude he sought. If Boone lived long enough, it was predicted, he would eventually reach the mouth of the Columbia River "and there, perhaps, sit down, like another Alexander of Macedon and weep, because there are no more worlds to settle."

The Great Anomaly: Slavery. The inescapable paradox of the American Republic was that the freest white society in the world lived in juxtaposition to a large and ever increasing population of black slaves. In a nation dedicated to

This water color by Benjamin Latrobe, called "Overseer Doing His Duty," purports to show the hard life that field hands in the South led. *Picture: From the Collections of the Maryland Historical Society*

the realization of the ideals of the Declaration of Independence, skin color determined to whom these ideals applied. The census of 1810 revealed that almost every sixth American was in bondage. And despite the act of Congress of 1808 which prohibited the importation of slaves from Africa, they continued to be smuggled into the country. Fears of "Africanizing" the southern states were allayed by the belief that slavery offered a permanent solution of the "color problem" by keeping the Negro "in his place."

Yet slavery was only part of the larger problem created by the presence of the black man in white America. Even when the Negro became free, he was not accorded the full enjoyment of his rights as a citizen. Nor did he achieve any marked improvement in his economic position. One of the arguments commonly advanced against emancipation was that the lot of free Negroes was worse than that of slaves. Few whites were willing to consider emancipation without the simultaneous removal of the free blacks to Africa. In 1816 the Society for Colonizing the Free People of Color in the United States was organized for the purpose of resettling free Negroes in Africa. Under its auspices, Liberia came into existence, but the colonization society never succeeded in removing more than a fraction of even the annual increase of the black population. The society read its total failure in the census returns. Slavery and racial discrimination remained the great flaws in an otherwise democratic society.

Despite the crushing disabilities imposed upon the blacks, they produced during this period several extraordinarily talented individuals. Among them was Benjamin Bannecker, a self-taught mathematician, who, under happier circumstances, might have become as renowned a scientist as his white contemporary, David Rittenhouse of Philadelphia. There was no color line in genius, however rigidly it was drawn in society, in civil rights, and in ways of making a living.

Cultural Nationalism

In the twentieth century, historians are inclined to measure the progress of American society by the extent to which it was democratized. However, during the period 1783–1815, many contemporaries would have equated progress with the development of the arts and letters in the Republic. As former colonists, sensitive about their parochialism and resentful at being snubbed by the "effete sophisticates" of London, Americans regarded independence as an explosive force which would release the creative talents of the country, prove the superiority of free men over the oppressed peoples of Europe, and usher in a new Augustan age of literature. Since freedom was supposed to offer the most favorable environment for the development of genius, the United States would produce "poets, orators, critics, and historians, equal to the most celebrated of the ancient commonwealths of Greece and Italy," said Dr. David Ramsay of South Carolina, the author of a history of the American Revolution.

Nationalistic Writers. Animated by this spirit, several generations of American men of letters addressed themselves to the task of crowning the Revolution with a truly republican literature. Only an epic on the order of the *Aeneid,* it was felt, could do justice to the grandeur of the American promise. A coterie of Yale graduates, John Trumbull, Timothy Dwight, David Humphrey, Joel Barlow, and Lemuel Hopkins—the so-called Hartford Wits—vied with each other for the honor of composing this masterpiece. Joel Barlow spent eight years writing *The Vision of Columbus* (1787), which he later rewrote and published under the title of *The Columbiad.* But instead of receiving critical acclaim, he was accused of committing a libel upon the memory of Columbus.

With the exception of Joel Barlow, all the Wits became pillars of the Federalist establishment. Timothy Dwight, later president of Yale University, was a staunch champion of orthodoxy against the "heresies" of Deism and Unitarianism. In *The Triumph of Infidelity* (1788), he recounted in verse Satan's efforts to subvert Christ's kingdom by means of his favorite instrument for effecting this purpose, the Roman Catholic Church. The Wits had high aspirations for themselves and America, but their vision was totally uncritical, and instead of developing a distinctively American literary style, they merely imitated the rhapsodical effusions of debased eighteenth-century European epic poetry.

The tone of self-congratulation assumed by the Wits was considerably muted in Hugh Henry Breckinridge's *Modern Chivalry* (1792–1815). In form a picaresque novel dealing with the adventures of Teague O'Regan and Captain Farrago, it was actually a satire upon many facets of American life. In describing the antics of Teague and the even more reprehensible follies of the American people, Breckinridge meant to reveal what he believed to be the fundamental defects of democracy. His message was that the United States could not afford incompetence and ignorance either in its electorate or in its elected officials and that levelism, if given free rein, would destroy excellence. Like many later American idealists, Breckenridge expressed his ideal by scolding America for failure to fulfill its promise, rather than by indulging in indiscriminate praise of its merits.

Washington Irving was the first American professional writer to win a reputation abroad. A native New Yorker, Irving began his career as an essayist. In 1807 he and a group of friends commenced the publication of *Salmagundi,* a magazine devoted to satirizing the foibles of the *bon ton* of Gotham (*Salmagundi* was the first to apply this name to New York City), reviewing plays, and purveying gossip. Later, Irving turned the legends dating from the days of Dutch rule into such enduring works of literature as *The Legend of Sleepy Hollow* and *Rip Van Winkle.* Irving's contribution was neither in eulogizing or in criticizing America, but in proving that an American author and American themes could enjoy universal appeal.

Among American poets, Philip Freneau and William Cullen Bryant, like Irving, drew inspiration from distinctively American scenes and experiences.

In 1817 Bryant published *Thanatopsis,* a poem celebrating the "noble" rivers, lakes, and mountains of the United States. It was said that "whoever saw Bryant, saw America."

Phillis Wheatley, the black poetess (the second poetess in the history of American literature), had been brought from Africa as a slave and educated by her white owners in Boston. She celebrated the events of the American Revolution in heroic couplets, eliciting the praise of General George Washington to whom she addressed some laudatory lines. She said nothing in verse about the oppressions suffered by her people, but in her last poem, *Liberty and Peace, A Poem,* published in the year of her death (1784), she commemorated her country's freedom and the emancipation of her people in Massachusetts:

Auspicious Heaven shall fill with fav'ring Gales,
Where e'er Columbia spreads her swelling Sails:
To every Realm shall Peace her Charms display,
And Heavenly *Freedom* spread her golden Ray.

Some American playwrights were also concerned with native themes and drew their plots and characters from the American Revolution. Royall Tyler's *The Contrast,* a play designed to exhibit the superiority of plain, down-to-earth American men and manners over the "decadent fops" and over refined manners of Europe, was first presented in 1787. William Dunlap, "the father of the American Drama," produced an entire repertoire of box-office successes, among them *The Glory of Columbia—Her Yeomanry* and *André.*

Despite the addiction of men of letters to epic poetry, the novel became the most popular literary art form in the early Republic. Charles Brockden Brown, the first creative writer in America to make literature a full-time career, produced six novels between 1798 and 1801. Although Brown fell victim to the cult of horror popularized by English novelists in the eighteenth century, he succeeded in domesticating the novel at least superficially by giving it an American setting. Brown was fascinated in an erratic way by abnormal psychology. In *Wieland* he dealt with a case of religious melancholia aggravated by ventriloquism. He explicitly renounced Gothic castles, clanking chains, and all other appurtenances of the Gothic novel. Instead, he said, "the incidents of Indian hostility, and the perils of the Western wilderness, are far more suitable; and for a native of America to overlook these would admit of no apology."

To achieve the goals of the Revolution, some Americans felt that it was necessary to break away from the English language altogether. Writing in the *North American Review* in 1815, Walter Channing urged his fellow countrymen to adopt the language—he did not specify which one—of the Indians. In contrast to the enervated, sterile, and decadent language of Englishmen, Channing believed that the Indians spoke an "elevated and soaring language" upon which a great literature could be built.

Despite all these efforts to create a truly distinctive literature, it was apparent, as Henry Adams later observed, that Americans had not gotten off their literary knees to Europe. The bonds of language, taste, and fashion resisted the best efforts of American men of letters to produce a literary declaration of independence. Without a literary metropolis of their own, Americans inevitably looked to London. In 1837 Ralph Waldo Emerson lamented that in literature, the United States had not fulfilled "what seemed the reasonable expectation of mankind," much less the optimistic expectations of Americans themselves. Literature, he said, remained derivative and uninspired. At the best, it was characterized by "a certain grace without grandeur."

American Art. But in the fields of art and architecture Americans succeeded in emancipating themselves more decisively from contemporary English and European influences. In the early Republic, art, like literature, was directed toward inculcating patriotism, morality, and "republican virtue." John Adams called on painters and sculptors to "assist in perpetuating to posterity the horrid deeds of our enemies," and he himself drew up a design for a medal commemorating the evacuation of Boston by the British in 1776. In 1810 the Society of Artists of the United States was organized for the purpose of promoting the "prosperity, glory and independence of the United States" by establishing art schools, holding public exhibitions of the work of American artists, and commemorating upon canvas the events of the American Revolution.

John Trumbull's painting *The Declaration of Independence* was certainly one of the finest exemplifications of this aspiration. But even more effective in inculcating patriotism were portraits of George Washington. Americans, wrote a Russian visitor, kept a likeness of Washington in their homes "just as we have images of God's saints." Charles Willson Peale of Philadelphia made so many copies of his portraits of Washington that it was said he was "peeling" the father of his country. Gilbert Stuart dashed off copies of his portraits of Washington for $100 apiece to pay his numerous creditors.

American artists were not less bound than writers to a narrow and self-conscious commitment to hortatory and patriotic themes, but they succeeded better because their work to some extent transcended this badly overworked vein. To a greater extent than their literary contemporaries, they produced real works of art which subtly revealed character and went beyond a mere self-assertive nationalism. The demand by well-to-do Americans for portraits seemed insatiable. In 1810 ten portrait painters found employment in Philadelphia alone. By their work in this field, Gilbert Stuart, John Singleton Copley, Thomas Sully, Charles Willson Peale, and S. F. B. Morse raised the reputation of the United States high in the artistic world. Benjamin West, a Pennsylvania farm boy who had studied art in Italy, was elected president of the Royal Society—the highest honor that England could bestow upon an artist.

American Architecture. America's architecture, like its literature and its painting, was at first heavily imitative of European forms. Thomas Jefferson,

The first Roman Catholic cathedral in the United States is shown in this drawing made by Benjamin Latrobe while he was working on the cathedral. *Picture: From the Collections of the Maryland Historical Society*

who made architecture one of his numerous hobbies, found inspiration in the architecture of the Roman Empire. His design for the Virginia State Capitol was an eclectic version of the Maison Carrée at Nimes, France, which Jefferson had observed while serving as minister to France in 1785–1789. Jefferson established the national style in public buildings. Based upon the temple form, these structures were intended to give stability, dignity, and permanence to the public edifices of the Republic. To achieve this effect, Americans looked not only to Rome but to Greece as well. The Roman revival in the United States was followed by the Greek revival.

But Jefferson was almost the last of the gentlemen amateur architects who dominated the colonial period. The coming order was represented by Charles Bulfinch of Boston, a professional architect, who designed the Massachusetts State House and the Massachusetts state prison at Charlestown. Patronized by wealthy Boston merchants and manufacturers, Bulfinch built so many mansions in the onetime Puritan metropolis that he was said to have found Boston a city of wood and left it a city of brick.

The Structure of Society

Rural America. If, as Thomas Jefferson said, farmers were the chosen people of God, the United States was richly blessed. The massive exodus from the farms to the cities was still far in the future. In 1810 of seven million Americans, only about 6 per cent lived in towns of over 5000 inhabitants. Nevertheless, the towns were increasing rapidly in population. Between 1790 and 1810, rural population grew approximately 40 per cent, whereas urban population increased approximately 60 per cent. New York City with a population of 96,373 was the largest city in the United States, closely followed by Philadelphia with 92,247. The most rapid rate of growth was attained by Baltimore. Before the Revolution, it was a straggling village of a few houses; by 1810, it contained 13,000 more inhabitants than Boston. Its rapid growth was due to its position as an entrepôt for the export of wheat and tobacco and to the dredging of the harbor in 1794 by large machines worked by oxen.

Cities and Transportation. Before the advent of rail transportation, a navigable waterway was the prime requirement for a city. In the age of water transport, roads rarely made cities, nor could an eastern seaport that had no water communication with the West hope to partake fully of the general prosperity. Boston, lacking a navigable river connecting it with the West, was doomed to suffer comparative commercial stagnation. Lancaster, Pennsylvania, was the only large inland town without any important navigation. Its prosperity was due to its manufactures and to the turnpike which made it a distributing center for the western part of the state.

Samuel Slater founded the first successful cotton-spinning mill in America. He used a treadmill like this one to run it. *Picture: The New York Public Library, Astor, Lenox and Tilden Foundations*

POPULATION IN THE UNITED STATES, 1790-1815

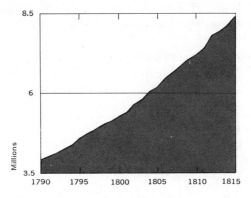

Source: Historical Statistics of the United States.

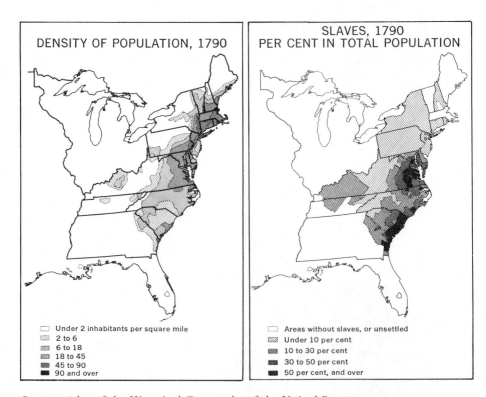

DENSITY OF POPULATION, 1790

☐ Under 2 inhabitants per square mile
▨ 2 to 6
▩ 6 to 18
▦ 18 to 45
▩ 45 to 90
■ 90 and over

SLAVES, 1790
PER CENT IN TOTAL POPULATION

☐ Areas without slaves, or unsettled
▨ Under 10 per cent
▩ 10 to 30 per cent
▦ 30 to 50 per cent
■ 50 per cent, and over

Source: Atlas of the Historical Geography of the United States.

BLACK POPULATION

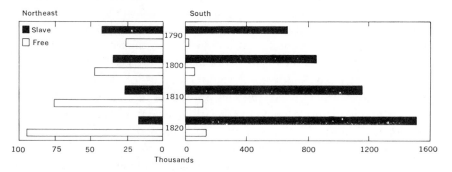

Source: *Historical Statistics of the United States.*

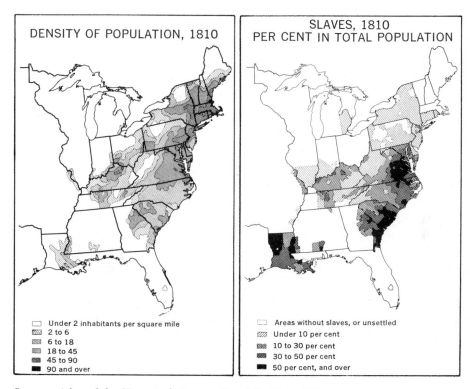

Source: *Atlas of the Historical Geography of the United States.*

Manufacturing. A regional pattern had taken shape in manufacturing. In New England, where waterpower, capital, and skilled labor were comparatively plentiful, cotton factories sprang up in the old maritime centers and farming towns. This process was greatly stimulated by the embargo in 1808 and the War of 1812, which cut off the supply of manufactured goods from England and forced the United States to develop factories of its own. By 1815 Pawtucket, Rhode Island, had thirteen thread or cotton cloth factories. Twenty-five textile factories, employing nearly twelve thousand persons, were in operation in Connecticut. Shoes were turned out by the scores of thousands at Lynn, Massachusetts. Although Paterson, New Jersey, which enjoyed both water power and access to the sea, failed to become the great manufacturing center envisaged by Alexander Hamilton, a few cotton mills survived the depression that descended upon the place after 1795. Rifles were the specialty of Lancaster, Pennsylvania, and Harper's Ferry, Virginia. As early as 1817, citizens of Pittsburgh were complaining that smoke blackened the houses and gave the town a gloomy appearance, and an English visitor to Richmond, Virginia, was oppressed in 1810 by the cloud of smoke hanging over the city, making it reminiscent of an English factory town. On the Brandywine River in Delaware, Du Pont de Nemours established a powder works, a paper mill, and a cluster of textile factories.

The Industrial Workers. The development of industry meant inevitably that a part of the American population would become factory workers, a situation which, according to Thomas Jefferson's philosophy, could only be a change for the worse. England was already beginning to present a foretaste of what an industrialized country with an urban proletariat would be like, but Alexander Hamilton had assured Americans that they could avoid the evils of industrialism by the use of laborsaving machinery and the employment of women and children. This, of course, was a time when almost all children worked on the farm. The novelty of child labor in factories was not that children worked, but that they worked away from home.

Just as the abundant land of the frontier offered a new dimension in the economic lives of men, the opportunity for employment in the textile mills opened up a new dimension in the lives of women and children. In New England, about 90 per cent of the hands were women, young girls, and boys. Captain Basil Hall, an English traveler, remarked that "an urchin, before he is an inch bigger than a cotton bobbin, is turned to some use." A sail factory in Boston employed fourteen young girls, "the daughters of decayed families": no child of bad character or dubious antecedents need apply. At David Humphreys' wool factory in Connecticut, most of the labor force consisted of boys from the New York almshouse and poor boys from neighboring villages. The carpet factory in Philadelphia that supplied the Senate chambers in Philadelphia gave employment to a number of poor women and children.

Some American factory owners tried conscientiously to apply in their mills the humanitarian ideals of the Enlightenment. It did not follow, said the *Gazette*

This watercolor by the Baroness Hyde de Neuville shows New York City in 1809. *Picture: Museum of the City of New York*

of the United States in 1792, that "because the European artificer received but a mere pittance for his labor, the American manufacturers should be a meagre, pale, starveling crew of emaciated wretches." The American solution to the problems created by industrialism was to turn the factories into finishing schools for instruction in religion and good manners as well as for turning out saleable merchandise. David Humphreys' youthful employees were obliged to attend evening classes and Sunday school. In the factories established at Lowell and Waltham, Massachusetts, by Francis Cabot Lowell and other Boston financiers, boarding houses were built by the company, provision was made for religious worship, and the workers, most of whom were "well-educated and virtuous females," were expected to spend their leisure in libraries and lecture halls. On the Brandywine, the Du Ponts created a model factory town in which the workers, most of whom were Swiss and French, lived in neat company houses, tended their gardens, and sang in the company choir. These arrangements were not quite as idyllic as they were said to be, but the great problem of the welfare of factory workers seemed both far away and susceptible of easy solution.

Urbanization. The beginning of industrialism also brought growing cities, the appearance of intractable urban problems, and the development of American urban life. New York City, America's biggest city, with a large population of French, Dutch, Irish, Jews, Germans, and Negroes, preserved the cosmopolitan character it had possessed since its founding as New Amsterdam by the Dutch. Broadway was the favorite promenade of dandies and fashionable women, yet as late as 1804, a traveler encountered "two Indian young men, with each a bow and arrow in his hand, tripping nimbly along, like two wild animals yet unbroken to the yoke." Wall Street, already the headquarters of banks, money changers, insurance firms, and brokerage houses, was crowded with foot traffic and carriages. Everyone, it was observed, seemed to be in a hurry. Already by early afternoon, many businessmen were slightly under the influence of liquor, a condition described as half and half. It was the climate and the pace of life, they said, that necessitated this frequent recourse to alcoholic refreshment.

Citizens with a fastidious sense of smell were well advised to stay off the streets of American cities. All refuse was thrown into the streets, and pigs and hogs were assigned the work of garbage disposal. Sometimes they tripped up promenaders on Broadway, attacked little children, and contributed to the spread of cholera, but the use of these worthy animals as scavengers and as food outweighed these disadvantages. Pork was the poor man's meat. The problems of pollution, resulting from later advances in technology, had not yet developed.

While the hogs kept the law officers busy, there was comparatively little crime to occupy their attention. Despite the growth of poverty and slums, New York had few robberies or murders, a circumstance attributed to police efficiency, full employment, and the prevalence of republican virtue.

American urban growth in general was unregulated, unplanned, and uncontrolled, a condition which prevailed far into the twentieth century. But the transfer of the seat of government from Philadelphia to Washington, D.C., gave Americans an unparalleled opportunity to engage in city planning on a grand scale. Unlike most American cities, Washington, D.C., did not grow haphazardly; it was the creation of Pierre L'Enfant, one of the greatest of city planners. Although L'Enfant's plan was not followed in its entirety, enough remained to show the imprint of his genius. Washington became a city of magnificent distances and wide-open spaces. In 1800 when Mrs. John Adams came to Washington to become the first First Lady to reside in the President's House—it was not called the White House until it was rebuilt after the British burned it in 1814—she lost her way in the woods which surrounded the capital. The Capitol itself, which was not completed until 1865, was largely the work of William Thornton, Benjamin Henry Latrobe, and Charles Bulfinch.

The Growth of an Interdependent Society

Factories and cities were two of the most conspicuous indications of a basic transformation in society. The world of small farmers, producing food and household supplies for their own use and neither buying nor selling much, was beginning to feel the sharp impact of a new world of commercial producers, producing to sell in order that they might buy. This transformation had already largely occurred in the cultivation of tobacco. The new economic order required the division of labor, a money economy, advanced technology for production, central markets, and a fully developed system for the quick, easy, and cheap transport of goods within the country. Even while the leaders in the

The steam frigate *Fulton the First* was launched in New York in 1814. *Picture: I. N. Phelps Stokes Collection. Prints Division, The New York Public Library*

government were preoccupied with the questions of the freedom of the seas and of access to foreign markets, the Republic was developing an internal economy which would eventually make foreign trade secondary. In this process, the changes in transport and in the technology both of transport and of production were vital.

The Network of Transportation. Thus, by means of the construction of roads, bridges, turnpikes, and canals, and the improvement of navigable rivers, the United States began to become the economic unit envisaged by the founders of the Republic. By 1817 there were 51,600 miles of passable road in the United States, most of it connecting villages and towns with navigable waterways. Pittsburgh and Philadelphia were joined by a highway which traversed the Alleghenies. Thanks to this highway and the other roads that radiated from Philadelphia, more than a thousand covered wagons were regularly engaged in transporting goods to and from the city, creating a serious traffic problem in Market Street.

Steamboats on the Rivers. While these wagons represented an immense growth in the amount of transport, they were hardly an advance in technology. The first major step in the technology of transportation came with the steamboat. In 1787 John Fitch, a Connecticut clockmaker, demonstrated on the Delaware River the first steamboat to operate anywhere in the world. The demonstration was viewed by the members of the Constitutional Convention, which was then in session. At almost the same time, James Ramsey of Maryland patented a steamboat which won the approval of Benjamin Franklin and the American Philosophical Society. But the steamboat had been invented before the public was ready to accept it. Not until 1807 when Robert Fulton's *Clermont* made a successful run between New York and Albany was the steamboat regarded as anything more than an ingenious toy.

PATENTS ISSUED, 1790-1815

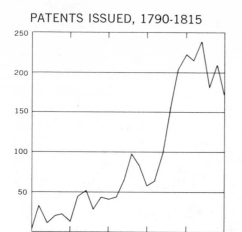

Congress enacted the first patent law on April 10, 1790, and patents were issued for fourteen years on demand of the applicant. No formal investigations for novelty or the other requirements of the law were made until 1836, when the United States Patent Office was created.

Source: Historical Statistics of the United States.

Fulton and his partner, Robert R. Livingston, did not give the steamboat to the country as a free gift. Instead, they tried to make their fortunes by securing monopolies from the states. By 1819 they had been granted monopolies by several states, including New York, and even Russia gave the American entrepreneurs a monopoly of the use of its rivers for fifteen years. Thus the Volga boatmen, as well as the New York–Albany stage drivers, seemed destined to become victims of American technology.

The steamboat was acclaimed the crowning achievement of American inventive genius. Certainly it was the first American invention of world-wide importance that required a new technology and sophisticated engineering. It was deemed appropriate that a democratic country had brought applied science directly to the common man and in a way that affected his everyday life.

The Cotton Gin. Along with improvements in transport, Americans also made significant improvements in the technology of production. One such improvement with fateful results for the American Republic was the cotton gin, perfected by Eli Whitney of Connecticut in 1793. This invention, which made possible the easy separation of cotton fibers from cotton seed, worked a revolution in southern agriculture. Cotton cultivation spread into the interior and superseded tobacco, rice, and indigo as the king of staples. In 1790 a negligible quantity of southern cotton reached Great Britain. By 1812, the South accounted for over half the 63 million pounds of cotton imported by that country. Thus, agricultural production in the South became part of a vast international economic network.

Eli Whitney made a far deeper impress upon the course of American history than did most of the political leaders of his own or succeeding generations. The cotton gin caused the expansion of the plantation system and its concomitant Negro slavery. As a result, slave and free labor came into conflict in the West.

The struggle for control of the territories and new western states proved to be the prelude to civil war.

Machine Tools and Interchangeable Parts. By his inventions, Whitney also aided the North in its crucial struggle with the South. In 1798 Whitney began the use of machine tools in the manufacture of locks of muskets, a method which had already been utilized by a French arms manufacturer. The machines produced parts so exactly similar that they were interchangeable and a musket could be assembled from any set of the parts. Even though Whitney did not perfect this technique, he was one of the important pioneers in the new method of manufacturing which ultimately led to mass production.

Thus the American was beginning to appear upon the stage of history as the man with the machine. "The time is approaching," a Swedish traveler remarked in 1820, "when people will come here from the old continent to learn about invention and perfected methods of production made by this Nation."

American Values

The values and attitudes of Americans were those to be expected of an enterprising people who were stimulated by rapid economic growth and rich economic opportunity and whose equality gave them the fullest access to these economic blessings. They valued material achievement and gave work priority over all other earthly pursuits. Doing a good day's work was the way an American proved that he was a useful citizen. With a continent awaiting development, it was accounted un-American to shirk on the job or, worse still, to live idly on unearned increment. As Michael Chevalier, a French traveler, said: "From the moment he gets up, the American is at his work, and he is absorbed in it till hour of sleep. He never permits pleasure to distract him; public affairs alone have the right to distract him . . . Speculation and business, work and action—these were the preoccupations of Americans." At fifteen, a boy was expected to be engaged in farming or business. By the age of twenty-one, if all went well, he had his farm, workshop, or counting house and was happily married. Chevalier attributed the American males' addiction to business and moneymaking to the fact that they had so little opportunity for sensual gratifications. As a result, he observed, the American "has recourse to business for the strong emotions which he requires to make him feel life. He launches with delight upon the ever-moving sea of speculation. But he always returned to the family fireside, the one fixed point in a world constantly on the move."

For many citizens of the Republic, the American dream was in the process of being converted into a substantial reality. But an ambitious, ever striving people could not find contentment in a country where so much remained to be done and where the prospects opened by hard work and diligence seemed illimitable. Precisely because the future seemed to have so many good things in store, Americans tended to live in the future; like Thomas Jefferson, they "loved to dream." They were eager to hasten the advent of the future because it had never disappointed them. America was a land of rising expectations because expectations were constantly being realized.

The characteristics usually considered distinctively American—restlessness, optimism, rootlessness, preoccupation with moneymaking, willingness to "try anything once" and to take long chances—were the result of the interaction of the enterprising and adventurous kind of people who were drawn to the New World and the unique environment provided by a continent awaiting the vivifying touch of the pioneer, the farmer, and the businessman. In contrast to the relatively immobile European peasantry, Americans readily pulled up stakes and began life anew in some distant locality, usually to the west. The qualities essential to survival in raw frontier communities—resourcefulness, ingenuity, and hardihood—likewise left an imprint upon the American character. It was not only frontiersmen who exhibited these characteristics: Captain Basil Hall observed that American businessmen were "a people of shifts and expedients, always accommodating themselves to circumstances, never losing their confidence, but ever ready to try something else, after a failure in one thing." The American businessman had to learn how to land on his feet: bankruptcy, usually resulting from eagerness to get rich quickly, was a common occurrence. While little social stigma was attached to bankruptcy—it was considered an acceptable way of making a fresh start—it often led to imprisonment for debt. Some of the best-known businessmen of the day, including Robert Morris, spent long terms behind bars. It was not until the enactment of the Bankruptcy Act of 1800 and the gradual easing by the states of the penalties attached to involuntary default that the spectre of imprisonment for debt was finally laid to rest.

Americans were a nation of speculators with a "rage for property." The building of the country was a vast speculation that, like most speculations in America, paid off. Farmers did not prosper merely, or perhaps even principally, by growing crops but by buying land cheap, developing it, and selling it at a higher price. Land was a commodity that was bought and sold with almost as much facility as the crops it produced. An American rarely allowed sentimentality to interfere with a good business deal. Talleyrand conceived a deep contempt for the American character because he encountered only one man in the United States who was not willing to sell anything he possessed for a price. This unique individual refused to part with his dog.

In the early Republic, the principal object of speculation was not government securities or bank stock but land. The most gigantic speculation in American history was the Yazoo scandal. In 1795 by dint of bribing every member save one of the Georgia legislature, four land companies were able to gain possession for $500,000 of 35 million acres, the area comprising almost all of the present states of Alabama and Mississippi. The next year, a newly elected legislature rescinded the contracts on the ground that they had been procured by fraud, but in the meantime the Yazoo companies had begun to sell land to private purchasers. New England, in particular, was swept by a Yazoo craze; land sold in Boston at 12 cents an acre, and hundreds of buyers invested their savings in this dubious real estate.

In 1802 Georgia ceded the territory to the United States for $1,250,000, and in 1814 the holders of Yazoo land warrants were awarded $48 million by the United States government. Everyone profited from the fraud—the speculators, Georgia, and the United States; only the Indians who were forced to cede their lands to the government as part of the settlement came off badly. And in 1810 in the case of *Fletcher* vs. *Peck,* the United States Supreme Court, Chief Justice Marshall presiding, held that the constitutional prohibition against the impairment of the obligation of contracts applied to the Yazoo deal: the state legislature could not invalidate a grant of land made by a previous legislature even though it were obtained by fraud. The doctrine of the sanctity of contracts could hardly have been carried much farther than the Supreme Court took it in this decision. But if the Yazoo story is chiefly remembered today as an episode in constitutional history, it is also illustrative of the economic attitudes and speculative energies of a great many Americans at the beginning of the nineteenth century.

The Balance Sheet in 1815

Such were some of the principal values of the American people, characteristics of American society, and trends of American activity in the first decades of the Republic. By 1815 the idea of an American destiny, wholly independent from that of Europe, had seemingly been brought measurably closer to realization. The United States had demonstrated that it could survive as a republic even though monarchism had triumphed in Europe over the French Revolution and the cause of republicanism. The American Republic had been born in a world dominated by monarchism and absolutism. Nevertheless, since 1783 it had gained in stature, strength, and unity. The power of the people, as the Old World was beginning to realize, was a titan risen in the West, a titan that was to shake the world.

Yet, as John C. Calhoun said in 1817, the rapid growth of the United States was Americans' pride and their danger, their weakness and their strength. For the Union was not necessarily strengthened by growth. In fact, the economic development occurring in the United States during the years 1783–1815 did not augur well for the durability of the Union. Although commerce and manufacturing ultimately proved to be a unifying force in the United States, the growing economic differentiation between the sections portended a sharpening of their long-standing conflict. The question of whether a commercial, industrialized North and an agricultural, staple-producing South could long live together in amity had been raised by 1815. But this issue was just beginning to be perceived by a few far-sighted Americans, and it did not come to the point of crisis for another generation or more. Also just beginning to be perceived was the ominous nature of the division which had occurred during the period 1783–1815 when slavery was eliminated from the northern states and left as the peculiar institution of one section of the American Republic.

SUGGESTED READING

In writing the section dealing with social conditions in the United States, I have drawn extensively upon the accounts of foreign travelers. Among the most important of these books are John Bernard, *Retrospections of America, 1797–1811* (1887); Jacques P. Brissot de Warville, *New Travels in the United States of America*, 2 vols. (1788); John Melish, *Travels in the United States of America* (1812); LaRouchefoucauld-Liancourt, *Travels Through the United States* (1799); Henry Wamsey, *An Excursion in the United States* (1798); Isaac Weld, *Travels Through the United States of North America* (1807); Henry B. Fearon, *Sketches of America* (1818); François Jean, Marquise de Chastellux, *Travels in North America*, 2 vols. (1827); Constantin François Volney, *A View of the Climate and Soil of the United States of America* (1804); Kenneth and Anna M. Roberts, eds., *Moreau de St. Mery's American Journal* (1948); Franklin Scott, ed., *Baron Kickowstrom's America* (1952); Allan Nevins, ed., *American Social History Recorded by British Travelers* (1923); Alfred J. Morrison, trans. and ed., *Travels in the Confederation, 1783–1784,* from the German of Johann David Schoepf, 2 vols. (1911).

The advent of democracy in American politics is the subject matter of Walter R. Fee, *The·Transition from Aristocracy to Democracy in New Jersey* (1933); Dixon Ryan Fox, *The Decline of Aristocracy in the Politics of New York* (1919); David Ludlum, *Social Ferment in Vermont, 1791–1850* (1939).

Cultural nationalism is examined in Charles Carpenter, *The History of American Schoolbooks* (1963); Russel B. Nye, *The Cultural Life of the New Nation, 1776–1830** (1960); David Tyack, "Forming the National Character: Paradox in the Educational Thought of the Revolutionary Generation," *Harvard Educational Review,* Vol. 36 (1966); Noah Webster, *On Being an American: Selected Writings, 1783–1828,* edited by Homer D. Babbidge, Jr. (1963); Harry Warfel, *Noah Webster: Schoolmaster to America* (1936); Dagobert D. Runes, ed., *The Selected Writings of Benjamin Rush* (1947).

The section dealing with American literature during the period 1783–1815 is based upon the following: Vernon L. Parrington, ed., *The Connecticut Wits* (1926); Perry Miller, *The Life of the Mind in America from the Revolution to the Civil War* (1965); Robert E. Spiller, *The Cycle of American Literature** (1956) and *The American Literary Revolution, 1783–1837* (1967); Howard Mumford Jones, *The Theory of American Literature** (1965).

For my discussion of American artists, I have relied upon Neil Harris, *The Artist in American Society, 1790–1860* (1966); Daniel M. Mendelowitz, *A History of American Art* (1960); James T. Flexner, *Gilbert Stuart* (1955).

*Available in a paperback edition

Jefferson's educational ideas are analyzed by James B. Conant, *Thomas Jefferson and the Development of Public Education* (1962).

The suffrage is authoritatively treated by Chilton Williamson, *The American Suffrage from Property to Democracy, 1760–1860** (1960); Richard McCormick, *The History of Voting in New Jersey* (1953); J. R. Pole, *Political Representation in England and the Origins of the American Republic* (1966).

Eli Whitney's contribution to the technology of early America is the subject of Jeannette Mirsky and Allan Nevins, *The World of Eli Whitney** (1952), and C. M. Green, *Eli Whitney and the Birth of American Technology** (1956). Other phases of the industrialization of the United States are treated in C. F. Ware, *The Early New England Cotton Manufacture* (1931); A. B. Hulbert, *Paths of Inland Commerce* (1920); P. D. Jordan, *The National Road* (1948). For the development of steamboats, the student can do no better than to read James J. Flexner, *Steamboats Come True* (1944).

INDEX